ROMAN LYRIC POETRY
Catullus and Horace

ROMAN LYRIC POETRY

CATULLUS AND HORACE

Selected, with Commentary by
A. G. McKAY and D. M. SHEPHERD
McMASTER UNIVERSITY, HAMILTON, CANADA

ST MARTIN'S PRESS
NEW YORK

Selection and editorial matter
© A. G. McKay and D. M. Shepherd 1969 and 1974

First published 1969
Second Edition 1974
Reprinted 1979, 1980, 1982

Published by
MACMILLAN EDUCATION LTD
*Houndmills Basingstoke Hampshire RG21 2XS
and London
Associated companies in Delhi Dublin
Hong Kong Johannesburg Lagos Melbourne
New York Singapore and Tokyo*

Library of Congress catalog card no. 76–83516

ISBN 0 333 06309 0

Printed in Hong Kong

CONTENTS

LIST OF PLATES	6
PREFACE	7
THEMATIC INDEX OF POEMS	9
CONCORDANCE OF NUMBERS	10
INTRODUCTION	13
Catullus	13
Horace	14
Poet and Patron	16
Country Life	18
SELECTED POEMS OF CATULLUS AND HORACE	21
I *Personal Lyric*	21
The Poet and his Craft	21
Love and Friendship	31
II *Reflective and Religious Lyric*	52
Moralizing and Philosophy	52
Hymns – Epithalamia – Prayers	61
III *National and Political Lyric*	69
IV *Humorous and Experimental Lyric*	85
COMMENTARY	95
SELECTED BIBLIOGRAPHY	234
A GLOSSARY OF TECHNICAL AND RHETORICAL TERMS	245
THE METRES OF LYRIC POETRY	249
INDEX NOMINUM	254

LIST OF PLATES

Between pages 48 and 49

A literary triumvirate of Augustan writers: Livy (or Propertius), Vergil, and Horace. (From the Ara Pietatis Augustae, A.D. 43, Villa Medici, Rome)
Deutsches Archäologisches Institut

M. Vipsanius Agrippa, 63 B.C.–A.D. 12, son-in-law of Augustus. (A bust in the Louvre)
Mansell Collection

Maecenas (?), ob. 8 B.C., adviser and diplomatic emissary of Octavian; literary patron of Horace and Vergil. (From the Ara Pacis Augustae, 13–9 B.C., Rome)
Deutsches Archäologisches Institut

The Peninsula of Sirmio (modern Sirmione) on Lake Garda, near Verona.
Fototeca Unione

Horace's estate, looking west to the Sabine Hills, north of Tivoli.
Fototeca Unione

An ancient wall-painting, from Stabiae, of a Campanian seascape, probably Puteoli (modern Pozzuoli). (National Museum, Naples. Height, $11\frac{1}{3}$ inches)
Alinari

A posthumous statue of Augustus found in Livia's villa at Prima Porta near Rome. (Vatican Museum)
Mansell Collection

Part of a reconstruction showing the west end of the Roman Forum. (Reconstruction model, Museo della Civiltà, Rome)
A. G. McKay

PREFACE

Teachers of Latin are sensitive to the importance of the language they teach as an intellectual discipline and adventure, and as a vehicle to the deeper appreciation of Roman culture and of the Greek and Hellenistic legacy to Rome. The Latin texts certainly provide the best insight into the *ethos* of Greco-Roman civilization and society; they are the focal point for discussion and awareness of Roman cultural traits and literary craft.

The general aim of this collection of Horatian and Catullian lyric poetry is to assist the student to a heightened awareness and appreciation of one branch of Latin literature, and to make him a sensitive, critical reader of representative superior works in the field. The exegesis is designed to help him read, with better understanding, larger amounts of Latin than are usually attempted and, as well, to encourage more independent study. Translations, when supplied, favour vigorous, intelligible and idiomatic English.

The poems have been arranged under a series of general headings designed to reveal not only relationships among the poems of the individual poet but also between the two poets. The commentary on the poems is of two kinds: first, essays of a critical, analytical and interpretative nature serve as preface to each section and are designed to provide a guide for the student to the poems of that group; these essays attempt to make the student aware of the poet's use of language and of his employment of imagery as a personal device of communication, and, above all, to instil respect for the organic unity of Roman lyric poetry – its pattern and thought-progression, its variety and levels and extent of meaning. Secondly, assembled after the text proper, short particular notes on each poem draw attention – often by searching questions rather than by flat statements – to crucial aspects of a poem, but avoid, wherever possible, wearisome grammatical exegesis. These notes also provide cross-references to other poems by the same poet or by his partner in this anthology, or to contemporary writing, especially Vergil's. Horace's dependence in various ways on Catullus was unquestionably significant and formative, and Vergil also seems to have provided as much as he derived from his poet-friend Horace who called him his *animae dimidium meae*. Recognition of this cross-fertilization between Horace and Vergil provides the student with a further means of evaluating individual lyrics, and heightens his general awareness of the interdependence of Roman writers. Finally, throughout the text, the editors have provided questions which, they hope, will suggest fresh ways of approaching particular poems.

A fairly extensive bibliography of works mainly in English on Roman poetry, and the lyric in particular, offers additional opportunity for individual work.

The text is not intended to replace the instructor or to reduce that fruitful interplay between teacher and student by which the field of light widens and the work becomes dramatic and exciting. The notes favour a more critical reading of the poems and analysis and evaluation along modern lines, whilst not ignoring the positive merits of grammatical and metrical exegesis. The notes are not intended to impose dogmatic analyses or authoritarian hypotheses; they are designed to encourage debate and thoughtful examination of the poem.

The hope is that this collection of Roman lyric poetry will animate the student's response to imaginative literature and arouse his enthusiasm for further study of Latin; and that it will make available to the student of Latin a text as reflective of modern critical methods as those which the student of the literatures of English and other modern languages have at their disposal.

No vocabulary has been supplied with this text in the belief that the present availability of Latin dictionaries, large-scale and pocket-size, will enable and induce the student to grapple with meaning in a more profitable fashion than is the normal experience with a drastically abbreviated vocabulary in the text.

The text of the poems by Catullus and Horace is that used in the Oxford Classical Texts edition and is reprinted by permission of the Clarendon Press, Oxford.

A. G. McKAY and D. M. SHEPHERD

THEMATIC INDEX OF POEMS

I Personal Lyric
The Poet and His Craft
   Catullus: 1, 50, 65.
   Horace: I 1, 6; II 1, 20; III 30; IV 3.

Love and Friendship
   Catullus: 51, 2, 3, 5, 7, 86, 43, 92, 70, 8, 87, 109, 73, 72, 75, 85, 76, 11 (the Lesbia 'cycle'); 9, 12, 13, 14, 31, 38, 46.
   Horace: I 3, 5, 8, 13, 17, 20, 22, 23, 24, 29; II 7; IV 12.

II Reflective and Religious Lyric
Moralizing and Philosophy
   Catullus: 96, 101.
   Horace: I 4, 9, 11, 34; II 3, 10, 14, 16; IV 7.

Hymns – Epithalamia – Prayers
   Catullus: 34, 62.
   Horace: I 10, 21; III 13, 21, 23; IV 6.

III National and Political Lyric
   Horace: I 2, 7, 14, 37; III 1, 4, 5, 6, 14; IV 5, 15.

IV Humorous and Experimental Lyric
   Catullus: 4, 10, 17, 26, 39, 44, 45, 49, 53, 84, 93.
   Horace: I 16, 30, 38; III 9.

CONCORDANCE OF NUMBERS

CATULLUS (traditional numbers)	RLP*	CATULLUS (traditional numbers)	RLP
1	1	85	25
2	11	86	15
3	12	87	20
4	77	92	17
5	13	93	87
7	14	96	47
8	19	101	48
9	28	109	21
10	78		
11	27	HORACE (traditional numbers)	RLP*
12	29		
13	30		
14	31	I 1	4
17	79	2	66
26	80	3	35
31	32	4	49
34	58	5	36
38	33	6	5
39	81	7	67
43	16	8	37
44	82	9	50
45	83	10	60
46	34	11	51
49	84	13	38
50	2	14	68
51	10	16	88
53	85	17	39
62	59	20	40
65	3	21	61
70	18	22	41
72	23	23	42
73	22	24	43
75	24	29	44
76	26	30	89
84	86	34	52

* RLP = Roman Lyric Poetry

CONCORDANCE OF NUMBERS

HORACE (traditional numbers)	RLP	HORACE (traditional numbers)	RLP
37	69	6	73
38	90	9	91
		13	62
II 1	6	14	74
3	53	21	63
7	45	23	64
10	54	30	8
14	55		
16	56	IV 3	9
20	7	5	75
		6	65
III 1	70	7	57
4	71	12	46
5	72	15	76

INTRODUCTION

Catullus (84–54 B.C.?)

Like so many Roman poets, Catullus came to Rome from distant Cisalpine Gaul. Born in Verona in 84 B.C. and brought up in that provincial setting, he came to the City, in all likelihood, to prepare for a politico-legal career. His manner of life in Rome and his associates suggest that Catullus came from a family of means in Verona.

His period of residence in Rome seems to have coincided with the governorship of Quintus Metellus Celer in Cisalpine Gaul, for it was probably during the latter's term of duty that Catullus was introduced to his wife, Clodia, sister of Publius Clodius Pulcher (died 52 B.C.). Their meeting, and the love affair which followed, inspired love lyrics which helped to revolutionize Roman poetry. Though at least ten years her junior Catullus fell hopelessly in love with her talents and beauty and her emancipated ways. But the happiness and ecstasy were shortlived, particularly after the death of Metellus soon after his consulship of 60 B.C. Inconstant and deceitful, Clodia's actions excited Catullus to accusation and scurrilous invective, to protestations of love and hate alike. His brother's death in the Troad in Asia Minor in 59 B.C. added to his depression. During an absence from Rome, probably at the family estate on Lake Garda, his closest friend, Marcus Caelius Rufus, supplanted him in Clodia's favour. The poet's return to Rome was the occasion for further efforts on his part to regain Clodia's physical love, now that the matter of fidelity and the spiritual and intellectual aspects of their earlier love were no longer in question. Exasperated and embittered, and disenchanted with love, Catullus left Italy as a member of the *cohors* of Gaius Memmius, pro-praetor of Bithynia-Pontus during 57–56 B.C. Such an appointment was a regular stage for anyone with designs on a public career, and Catullus may have decided to try his fortunes in the political arena after his disastrous love-affair. Memmius proved to be a hard-fisted administrator, not inclined to reward his staff members with opportunities for lucrative, often dishonest, activities. After paying his respects at his brother's tomb Catullus returned to Italy by yacht in the spring of 56 B.C. His last two years were spent in Lombardy and Rome, perhaps with periodic forays to the pleasure grounds of Baiae, near Naples, where Clodia had displayed herself earlier.

Contact with the celebrities of his day seems limited. Cicero he knew and respected as an advocate; Caesar he disliked personally, although he was ultimately reconciled with him (Suetonius, *Julius Caesar* 73). For Mamurra, Caesar's engineer from Formiae, he had only contempt [Catullus 29, 57, 93, 87].*

Horace (65–8 B.C.)

The circumstances of Horace's birth and upbringing offer a complete contrast to those surrounding Catullus. While the latter's family seems to have been in a position to offer him every advantage of wealth and opportunity to political advancement, if he wished to grasp it, Horace was born the son of a former slave, who obtained his freedom by his own efforts. Catullus makes no reference to his family in his surviving verse; Horace's earlier poetry, especially the *Satires*, is full of expressions of gratitude to his father's protective care and paternal devotion. Not content to allow his promising son to waste his talents in his native Venusia (in Apulia), he took his son to Rome to continue his schooling, and personally acted as his *paedagogus*, escorting the boy to his teacher's school and home again. His father's reflections to the young Horace on the passing scene in Rome laid the foundations of the boy's moral education.

His father had become wealthy enough from his profession of *coactor* (an agent in auction transactions between seller and buyer) to give his son a further period of education, and probably in 46 B.C. sent him to Athens to study philosophy and extend his knowledge of Greek literature. In the autumn of 44, Roman circles in Athens were stirred by the arrival of M. Brutus, one of the leaders of the conspiracy which plotted the events of the Ides of March. Although Brutus posed as a student of philosophy, his real intentions soon became clear: to raise a force in the eastern provinces which could counter the growing power of the Second Triumvirate of Octavian, M. Antony and Lepidus, which would hold the eastern empire for the Republic and the Senate, and eventually recover Italy and the East. With the thoughtless enthusiasm of an undergraduate, Horace cast his lot with Brutus. He probably travelled with him in Macedonia and Asia Minor during 43 and 42, and was posted as a *tribunus militum* in Brutus' growing army. He took part – ingloriously, he says – in the crucial battle of Philippi, and when the forces of the Liberators were decisively defeated, he decided, like Cicero after

---

* All references to the poems of Catullus and to the *Odes* of Horace in the commentary are to the traditional numbers; when the poem also occurs in this collection, its number in this collection appears in brackets: e.g. Cat. 1 (1); Horace, *Odes* I 1 (4).

Pharsalus, to make that the end of the war, instead of continuing the resistance with the forces of Sextus Pompey.

Horace returned to Rome, faced with the prospect of suing for pardon and of making a living. His father seems to have died during his absence in Greece, and the family property was confiscated by the ruling *junta*, like Vergil's paternal inheritance near Mantua, to provide rewards of land for the victorious troops of the Triumvirs. Yet Horace could not have been completely destitute; once he received his pardon in the general amnesty of 39, he was able to purchase a post in the civil service as one of the *scribae quaestorii*, the clerks in the Treasury whose duty was to supervise the slaves who kept the public accounts and to serve as secretaries of the college of quaestors. About the same time he began to devote himself seriously to poetry, experimenting with epodes in the manner of Archilochus, and with satire, following the example of the great second-century satirist Lucilius. His circle of acquaintances among the young men with literary interests in Rome began to grow; the young Vergil, whose *Bucolics* were published in 37, and Varius Rufus soon became his friends. Almost certainly his earliest poetic efforts were read aloud or circulated in manuscript among such friends as these. Through the friendship of Vergil and Varius, in the spring of 38, he was introduced to the great and influential adviser of Octavian, C. Maecenas, and nine months later was invited to join the great man's intimate circle.

From this point, all barriers fall away for Horace; the rest of his life is devoted to literature, friendship, and, once Octavian established his unchallenged claim to power, warm support for the Augustan regime; however, he declined Augustus' invitation to join his official family as private secretary.

In 35 he assembled ten satires for publication; in 30 a further collection of eight satires was issued, as well as seventeen epodes. The first three books of *Carmina* (*Odes*) appeared in 23, to lukewarm public response. They were followed by *Epistles I*, *Epistles II*, *Odes IV* and the *Carmen Saeculare*, composed by imperial command in 17 for the Secular Games. His life would seem to have been rich and satisfying, passed amid the peace which had at long last come to Rome and her empire, amid scenes and with friends he loved. His end came quietly on 27 November 8 B.C., only a few weeks after the death of his friend and patron Maecenas. He was buried on the Esquiline, near the tomb of Maecenas.

Poet and Patron

Patronage may exert itself in different ways. It may stipulate what the artist shall produce and may specify or require certain subjects or insist on a general style as well as specific traits. Ancient Egypt, Nazi Germany and the Soviet Union have laid down such requirements for their artists. Our own society displays such patronage mainly in commercial art, the medium of advertising. Rome rarely imposed such direction or limitation on its artists, least of all on such independent spirits as Catullus and Horace.

Patronage may also work by attraction. Poets, musicians and the like may be attracted to a particular social or political circle by reason of its special point of view, a sympathetic moral or intellectual climate, as well as by the prospect of financial support. This sort of patronage operates most notably during periods of social change or revolution, it certainly did so during revolutionary times in Republican Rome, and again in the eighteenth and nineteenth centuries in Europe. French artists like David were caught up in the aims and ideals of the revolutionary group, and in the ensuing enthusiasm for Napoleon and the Empire.

So Vergil and Horace extolled, in their different ways, the greatness of Octavian-Augustus, not without criticism and protest, but with a general sense of gratitude for the peace which his régime produced and guaranteed. Horace certainly did not write to sanction the Principate, but his verse was neatly integrated with his environment.

Poets in Rome required either independent means or a patron if they were to pursue their calling. There was no system of royalties in existence, no chance to sell a manuscript to a publisher, and no copyright. Patronage, with its promise of financial independence, was a necessity for poets. Martial remarked to his contemporaries that if there were more patrons like Maecenas there would be more poets like Vergil, which is both a compliment to the man whose name has become a byword for enlightened patronage, and an indication that patronage was a vital necessity for artists and writers in Rome. Catullus may have enjoyed a double patronage during his short career. Gaius Memmius, whom he accompanied to Bithynia in 57–56 B.C. as a member of his *cohors*, possessed literary leanings. Lucretius dedicated his *De Rerum Natura* to him. But Catullus certainly never speaks enthusiastically of Memmius' support or his intellectual leanings. Cornelius Nepos to whom the collection (*libellus*, perhaps poems 1–60) is dedicated was a notable writer and also a native of Cisalpine Gaul. Nepos may very well have assisted Catullus with introductions when he arrived in Rome about 62 B.C., and Catullus thanks him for his support against adverse critics before his reputation as a poet was established.

Horace was introduced to Maecenas by Vergil and Varius and received into the circle (cf *Sat.* II 6, lines 41–2: *suorum in numero*; and *Sat.* I 6, lines 45–64). Maecenas was immensely wealthy, notorious for his ostentatious living and often ridiculed for his eccentricities and sybaritic way of life; but as an administrator and diplomat he earned the respect of Octavian and the populace. On two occasions which Horace has recorded, Maecenas was accorded a popular ovation in the theatre after his recovery from a serious illness (*Odes* I 20 (40), lines 3–8; II 17, lines 25–6). His gift of an estate at Licenza came to Horace in 33 B.C., shortly after the appearance of the first book of *Satires*. The *Odes*, Books I–III, were dedicated to Maecenas with respect and affection [*Odes* I 1 (4)]. The circle of Maecenas was a loosely organized company of congenial companions, free to express themselves on any topic and never forced to subscribe to any official policy. The notion that Maecenas was some sort of Minister of Propaganda or head of an official Press Bureau is probably false. Maecenas was himself an experimenter in prose and verse, capable of writing hendecasyllables on personal themes, including a poem addressed to Horace. Others who benefited from the disinterested generosity of Maecenas were Vergil, Varius Rufus, Plotius Tucca and Quintilius Varus.

During the several absences of Octavian-Augustus from Rome Maecenas assumed the direction of the caretaker government and evidently proved an effective agent. But his tenure of authority terminated somewhat abruptly in 23 B.C. Some have thought that Maecenas was the loser in a secret power struggle with Agrippa. But he may also have been guilty of an indiscretion in connection with the plot of his brother-in-law, Varro Murena, against the Emperor's life. Thereafter Maecenas seems to have entered into voluntary semi-retirement, living an Epicurean existence, content in the company of his poet friends. The offer of a post as private secretary to Augustus was, as we have seen, politely but firmly turned down by Horace. But when the assignment to compose the *Carmen Saeculare* came in 17 B.C., Horace could not refuse the imperial commission; again, in 13 B.C. or later, a fourth book of the *Odes* followed its predecessors, celebrating *inter alia* the victories of Augustus' stepsons Drusus and Tiberius, and accepting the present divinity of the Emperor.

Country Life

After his return from Bithynia in 56 B.C., Catullus extolled the loveliness of his country place on the peninsula of Sirmio [31 (32)]. The site today is covered with olive trees and gardens and projects narrowly into Lake Garda, largest of the Lombard lakes and largest in Italy. At the extreme northern tip of the peninsula, Catullus' 'gem of islands and almost islands', the substructures of a handsome villa come into view, a great building of early Imperial date, facing the lake and the mountains. Alfred Lord Tennyson visited Sirmio in 1880 and enthused rhapsodically over the 'home' of Catullus which he had reached by rowboat from the village of Desenzano where the peninsula joins the mainland:

> Row us out from Desenzano, to your Sirmione row!
> So they row'd, and there we landed – 'O venusta Sirmio'!
> There to me thro' all the groves of olive in the summer glow,
> There beneath the Roman ruin where the purple flowers grow,
> Came that 'Ave atque Vale' of the Poet's hopeless woe,
> Tenderest of Roman poets nineteen-hundred years ago,
> 'Frater Ave atque Vale' – as we wander'd to and fro
> Gazing at the Lydian laughter of the Garda Lake below
> Sweet Catullus's all-but-island, olive-silvery Sirmio!

Catullus' home was probably much more modest [cf Cat. 13 (30); 26 (80)], but it was nicely situated on the lakeshore, with a small garden, some olive trees, and modest appointments. Gilbert Highet has assessed the landscape with sensitivity:

> 'The air is clear and cool there. It moves constantly; the lake water is seldom still; marching clouds move over the distant mountains; contours and lights change and develop. This was not a soft and sleepy landscape. Wherever the eye falls, there are strong-boned hills, and ridges, climbing higher and higher to the Alps. We come closer to his soul when, with his single small volume of poems (a promise of far richer possibilities unfulfilled) in our hand, we stand above the endlessly rolling waves that beat on Sirmio, and watch the olive-trees, twisted into shapes like those of tormented prisoners, tossing their arms wildly in the air, and feel upon our faces the tearful violence of the restless and passionate wind.'*

* G. Highet, *Poets in a Landscape* (1957) pp. 45–6.

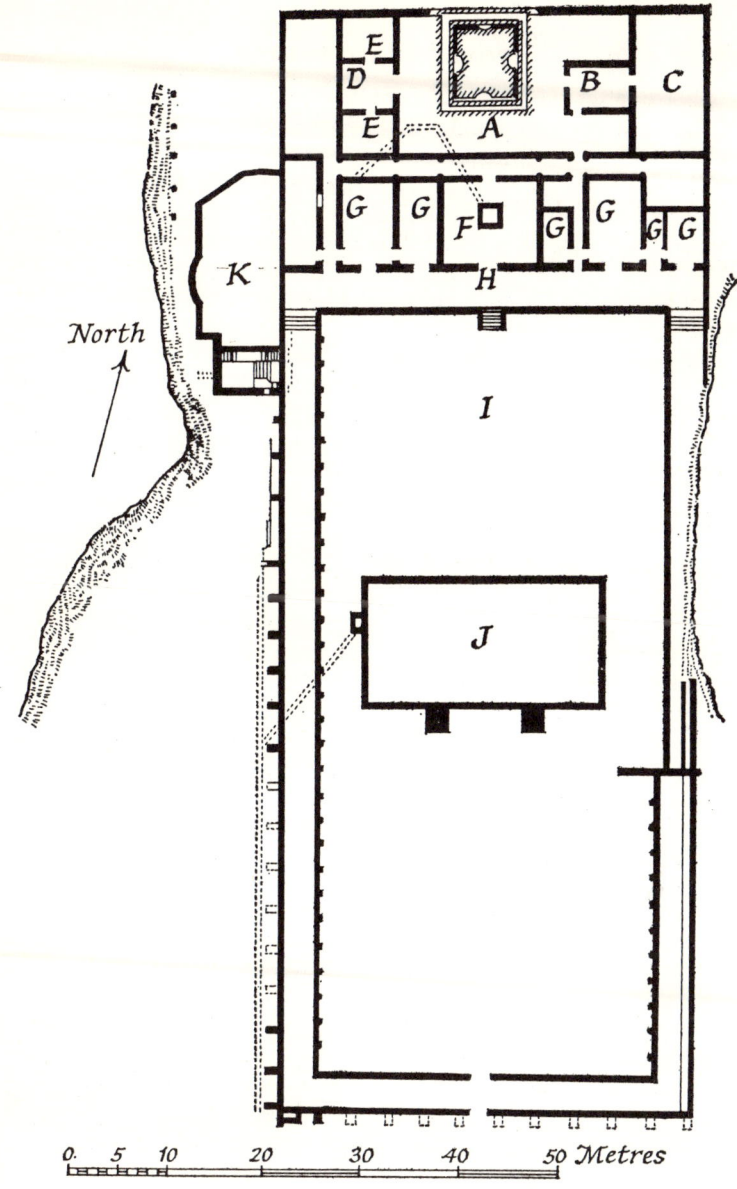

Plan of Horace's country estate

The single-storied villa contained approximately twelve rooms, two atrium courts (*A* and *F*), a summer triclinium (*B*) and a winter triclinium (*C*), a tablinum (*D*), and two alae (*E*), numerous bedrooms and oeci (*G*), a covered portico, *cryptoporticus*, with windows opening on to the landscaped garden, *hortus* (*I*), a water tank, *piscina* (*J*), and a bathing facility (*K*).

The slopes of Lucretilis to the west of the villa supported a forest of elms and oaks; a spring, Fons Bandusiae, watered the estate and its flocks. Five peasant families lived on the property and eight slaves worked the cultivated areas (G. Lugli, *Horace's Sabine Farm*, Rome, 1930).

Shortly after the publication of his first book of *Satires* in 35 B.C., Horace became a landholder in the Sabine Hills, thanks to the benevolent patronage of Maecenas.

The site of the Sabine Farm has been much debated, but literary, topographical and archaeological evidence combine to favour a location near modern Licenza (ancient Ustica) where the extant villa is almost certainly Horace's. The view that Horace had a second country home at Tibur (*mod.* Tivoli), on the site of S. Antonio, has been successfully refuted.

Horace expresses gratitude to his patron for the gift of this house and property on many occasions, for the poet grew to love the villa and its quiet unspoilt situation. Although he regularly uses such modest expressions as 'modus non ita magnus', 'villula', 'agellus', 'angulus ille', the existing remains suggest that Horace lived in a spacious mansion, with a superb setting and fertile and extensive lands. The villa was confined to a single storey, but contained about twelve rooms, grouped about two courts with central fountains. A bathing establishment adjoined the western side of the villa, while on the southern side there was a large walled garden with a central pool (*piscina*), and on the west, on the slopes of Lucretilis (*mod.* Monte Gennaro), a woodland of elms and oaks. A spring, probably the poet's *Fons Bandusiae*, burst from the same slopes and was a tributary of the Digentia (Licenza). The acreage near the stream was well-watered and produced cereal crops. An orchard lay towards Roccagiovane, on the drive which led from the Via Valeria to the poet's residence. In this same area was a vineyard which used elms and olive trees to support the vines. An olive grove probably lay on the hillock between the villa and the Digentia river, and there were additional fields and slopes for the pasturage of goats, sheep, and oxen. Five families of free peasants (*coloni*) were tenants on Horace's property, and eight slaves ministered to his needs.

Horace bequeathed all his property to Augustus in 8 B.C., and the Emperor, perhaps adhering to Maecenas' dying request: *Horati Flacci ut mei esto memor*, probably maintained the Sabine Farm carefully during his lifetime. Thereafter the property fell into disuse and decay until, during the second century A.D. it revived under a private owner once again, a successful fish-breeder.*

---

* For additional details and illustrations, consult G. Lugli, *Horace's Sabine Farm*, translated by G. Bagnani (Rome, 1930); Thomas D. Price, 'A Restoration of Horace's Sabine Villa', in *Memoirs of the American Academy at Rome*, x (1932) pp. 135–42 (plates 34–42).

SELECTED POEMS OF CATULLUS AND HORACE

I Personal Lyric

THE POET AND HIS CRAFT

Catullus' poetic output was small: sixty poems in a variety of metres (1–60), a collection of epithalamia, an epyllion, and longer lyrics (61–8), and a collection of elegiacs (69–116). The subject matter of the first and last groups is virtually the same, although the polymetric poems tend to be more emotional, perhaps because they were less constrained by the dictates of the elegiac couplet.

Catullus did not compose his lyrics in a vacuum, without guidance from his predecessors and contemporaries. Scholars have found traces of Homer, Hesiod and Greek tragedy in his lines. He actually translates Sappho on one occasion [51: (10)], and shared the intelligentsia's admiration for the writers of Hellenistic Alexandria, perhaps because they were more contemporary and less classical. But he also owes much to his Roman heritage. Roman poetry before Catullus was firmly grounded in epic, tragedy and comedy, satire and, more recently, epigram. Poets like Naevius and Ennius, patronised by wealthy men of prominence and encouraged to express the values of the society which tolerated and supported them, produced poetry marked by an air of seriousness, dignity and occasional pomposity. Comedy, of course, in the hands of Plautus and Terence, and satire, in the output of Lucilius, provided livelier colloquial material which was metrically varied and inclined to treat more personal topics, friendship, family relations, and sentimental love. But no matter how large the indebtedness, Catullus is never a plagiarist, for, although he was influenced by other artists, his poetry is conditioned by his own life, by his emotions and unique psychological reactions. The epigram was more of a contemporary experiment. Although traditional and formal, and a heritage from Greece, these abbreviated verse-forms were apt to treat a wide variety of topics, including love, literature and mankind. Poetry of instruction and entertainment for the community, which had been the normal rule, yielded to poetry of self-expression within a carefully designed formal compass. The men who wrote epigrams tended to come from a fashionable, urbane society, free from patronage and its limitation, often youthful, often rebellious – men such as Lutatius Catulus, Valerius Aedituus and Porcius Licinius. Valerius Aedituus has left behind an epigram which is strongly suggestive of Catullus 51 (10) and Horace, *Odes* I 13 (38):

> Dicere cum conor curam tibi, Pamphila, cordis,
> quid mi abs te quaeram, verba labris abeunt,
> per pectus manat subito subido mihi sudor:
> sic tacitus, subidus, dum pudeo, pereo.
>
> (subidus – *confused*)

Though today these men are little more than names in text books, they played an important and guiding role in the evolution of the New Poetry, new both in its subject matter and in its modes of expression. Poetry entered upon a time of decisive change; poets no longer saw themselves as 'servants of society'; they chose to give expression to their private emotions, their feelings about one another, about their poetic experiments and the society in which they lived. The unit of their expression became the short poem, intensely personal and structurally complex.

Catullus shared the ideals of the Poetae Novi, or Neoterics as they were sometimes called – less a school or a movement than a group of poets of like mind, some of them political as well as literary firebrands who sought to escape from the tyranny of the older verse-forms and subject matter. Hellenistic poetry, some of it contemporary, undoubtedly inspired certain of their writings – works like Helvius Cinna's *Zmyrna* (Catullus 95), intellectual poetry charged with learned allusions, mythology, and references to far-away places which would lend enchantment and romantic distance, allusions which were sometimes deliberately novel and *recherché*. Their poetry was open to criticism on the grounds of its obscurity, its facile nature, its parade of learning, and its rich and troublesome allusiveness.

Horace is markedly different in his approach to composition. His formal odes, notably the Roman Odes [III 1–6] and the so-called Parade Odes (I 1–9), are constructed along an architectural, almost monumental plan (cf *Odes* III 30 (8): *exegi monumentum*). But the danger that the blocks of stanzaic expression might appear disjointed or isolated was avoided by the adroit use of *link-words*, predominant *metaphors*, and the like. In fact, all the trappings of Roman rhetorical practice and poetical expertise are to be found in his lines: *rhetorical questions, imperatives, apostrophe, personification*, and *repartee*: intentional *understatement* (litotes) and *paradox* occur frequently; *transferred epithets, repetition*, and *asyndeton* combine to ensure unity and progression within the poems. Analysis along the lines suggested throughout the notes will provide considerable insight into Horace's mastery of structure, design and thought-sequence in the *Odes*. Almost every line is intimately and consecutively united with its neighbours and with other passages within the same ode.

Structural Study of the poems, as urged in this volume, requires the student to engage with several important questions almost from the outset. What is the *subject* of the Ode – Are their *several subjects*? How does Horace develop his subject *matter*? What *means of transition* between the several sections of the ode can be detected? How are the *parts related to the whole*? How does Horace obtain *unity*? An analysis of the ode to discover its *organization* and its *message* is essential to the proper interpretation of the lyrics contained in this collection.

Several *patterns* have been detected and provide useful guides to the explication of the poems.

1 a *formal pattern*, usually intricate and sometimes cyclical (e.g. *Odes* I 1 (4); II 1 (6)
2 odes with *several closely connected themes*, less formally constructed than those of Group (1) [e.g. *Odes* I 14 (68)]
3 *crescendo* and *diminuendo* types of pattern, whereby reflection expands to generalization or a larger view, or generalization contracts to a personal application [e.g. *crescendo*-type, *Odes* I 3 (35); *diminuendo* type, *Odes* I 4 (49); I 5 (36); I 9 (50); III 5 (72)]
4 *a surprise ending*, almost epigrammatic in its suddenness and its sharp incisive manner, often resorted to by Horace, at the close of odes of the *diminuendo*-type [e.g. *Odes* I 22 (41); II 14 (55); III 29]
5 *linear* structure implying a relaxed, almost meditative progression, inconspicuously artful and reflective [e.g. *Odes* I 29 (44); I 37 (69)]

Unity, or *natural continuity*, is integral to Horace's poetry (*simplex et unum*); *imagery* and *symbolism* are the basic stuff of his verse and the area within which he particularly displays his genius and his ability to charm and convince (*dulce*); and there are the equally practical considerations of *relevance* (*ad eventum*) and *adaptability* or *usefulness* (*utile*) for the reader or addressee.

Horace works within a Greek and Roman lyrical tradition. There is an impression of almost casual progression and natural design in the odes which are, however, upon closer examination, as logical in structure and argument as Lucretius' *De Rerum Natura*. The discovery of this remarkable element, the *marriage of formal and informal elements*, in his poetry is to begin to appreciate Horace's distinctive talent. Proportion and pattern, symmetry and structure, and care (*labor*) in their discovery and making, are the hallmarks of Horatian poetry.

Both poets, Catullus and Horace, shared a preference for concrete and pictorial imagery, a feature which often imparts a sense of informality to poems or situations of a serious or formal importance. But Horace advances far beyond the somewhat limited repertoire of image and metaphor of his predecessor in lyric. Catullus finds the sources of his mostly static imagery in external nature, in agriculture, in the elements of fire and water, in mercantilism and in mythology. Horace finds a more varied and dynamic imagery in sea and sky, land and seascape, commerce, politics, law, architecture, mythology and legend; allegory is a device which he employs repeatedly in such instances as the ship of state [*Odes* I 14 (68)] and the voyage of life [*Odes* II 10 (54), lines 1–4]. *Metaphor* and *personification* are also a vital part of his poetic vision, which customarily sees things double and detects an *ambiguity* which is of the essence of poetry. *Contrast* and *antithesis* are equally basic to his verse, and almost everything which he treats presents itself in a double aspect: the past suggests the present, the mythical invades the actual, the abstract evokes the concrete, and pleasure suggests sadness; life is never far removed from the vision of death. An alertness to this principle of contrast or bipolarity is basic to an understanding and proper appreciation of Horatian lyric.

1

Cui dono lepidum novum libellum
arida modo pumice expolitum?
Corneli, tibi: namque tu solebas
meas esse aliquid putare nugas
iam tum, cum ausus es unus Italorum   5
omne aevum tribus explicare cartis
doctis, Iuppiter, et laboriosis.
quare habe tibi quidquid hoc libelli
qualecumque; quod, o patrona virgo,
plus uno maneat perenne saeclo.   10
               (*Catullus 1*)

2

Hesterno, Licini, die otiosi
multum lusimus in meis tabellis,

ut convenerat esse delicatos:
scribens versiculos uterque nostrum
ludebat numero modo hoc modo illoc,
reddens mutua per iocum atque vinum.
atque illinc abii tuo lepore
incensus, Licini, facetiisque,
ut nec me miserum cibus iuvaret
nec somnus tegeret quiete ocellos,
sed toto indomitus furore lecto
versarer, cupiens videre lucem,
ut tecum loquerer simulque ut essem.
at defessa labore membra postquam
semimortua lectulo iacebant,
hoc, iucunde, tibi poema feci,
ex quo perspiceres meum dolorem.
nunc audax cave sis, precesque nostras,
oramus, cave despuas, ocelle,
ne poenas Nemesis reposcat a te.
est vemens dea: laedere hanc caveto.
(Catullus 50)

3

Etsi me assiduo confectum cura dolore
   sevocat a doctis, Ortale, virginibus,
nec potis est dulcis Musarum expromere fetus
   mens animi, tantis fluctuat ipsa malis –
namque mei nuper Lethaeo gurgite fratris
   pallidulum manans alluit unda pedem,
Troia Rhoeteo quem subter litore tellus
   ereptum nostris obterit ex oculis.

    . . .

   numquam ego te, vita frater amabilior,
aspiciam posthac? at certe semper amabo,
   semper maesta tua carmina morte canam,
qualia sub densis ramorum concinit umbris
   Daulias, absumpti fata gemens Ityli. –
sed tamen in tantis maeroribus, Ortale, mitto
   haec expressa tibi carmina Battiadae,
ne tua dicta vagis nequiquam credita ventis
   effluxisse meo forte putes animo,

ut missum sponsi furtivo munere malum
    procurrit casto virginis e gremio,
quod miserae oblitae molli sub veste locatum,
    dum adventu matris prosilit, excutitur,
atque illud prono praeceps agitur decursu,
    huic manat tristi conscius ore rubor.

(Catullus 65)

4

Maecenas atavis edite regibus,
o et praesidium et dulce decus meum,
sunt quos curriculo pulverem Olympicum
collegisse iuvat, metaque fervidis
evitata rotis palmaque nobilis
terrarum dominos evehit ad deos;
hunc, si mobilium turba Quiritium
certat tergeminis tollere honoribus;
illum, si proprio condidit horreo
quidquid de Libycis verritur areis.
gaudentem patrios findere sarculo
agros Attalicis condicionibus
numquam dimoveas ut trabe Cypria
Myrtoum pavidus nauta secet mare.
luctantem Icariis fluctibus Africum
mercator metuens otium et oppidi
laudat rura sui; mox reficit ratis
quassas, indocilis pauperiem pati.
est qui nec veteris pocula Massici
nec partem solido demere de die
spernit, nunc viridi membra sub arbuto
stratus, nunc ad aquae lene caput sacrae.
multos castra iuvant et lituo tubae
permixtus sonitus bellaque matribus
detestata. manet sub Iove frigido
venator tenerae coniugis immemor,
seu visa est catulis cerva fidelibus,
seu rupit teretes Marsus aper plagas.
me doctarum hederae praemia frontium
dis miscent superis, me gelidum nemus
nympharumque leves cum Satyris chori
secernunt populo, si neque tibias

Euterpe cohibet nec Polyhymnia
Lesboum refugit tendere barbiton.
quodsi me lyricis vatibus inseres, 35
sublimi feriam sidera vertice.
    (*Horace*, Odes *I 1*)

5

Scriberis Vario fortis et hostium
victor Maeonii carminis alite,
quam rem cumque ferox navibus aut equis
 miles te duce gesserit:

nos, Agrippa, neque haec dicere nec gravem 5
Pelidae stomachum cedere nescii
nec cursus duplicis per mare Ulixei
 nec saevam Pelopis domum

conamur, tenues grandia, dum pudor
imbellisque lyrae Musa potens vetat 10
laudes egregii Caesaris et tuas
 culpa deterere ingeni.

quis Martem tunica tectum adamantina
digne scripserit aut pulvere Troico
nigrum Merionen aut ope Palladis 15
 Tydiden superis parem?

nos convivia, nos proelia virginum
sectis in iuvenes unguibus acrium
cantamus vacui, sive quid urimur
 non praeter solitum leves. 20
    (*Horace*, Odes *I 6*)

6

Motum ex Metello consule civicum
bellique causas et vitia et modos
 ludumque Fortunae gravisque
  principum amicitias et arma

nondum expiatis uncta cruoribus, 5
periculosae plenum opus aleae,
   tractas, et incedis per ignis
      suppositos cineri doloso.

paulum severae Musa tragoediae
desit theatris: mox ubi publicas 10
   res ordinaris, grande munus
      Cecropio repetes cothurno,

insigne maestis praesidium reis
et consulenti, Pollio, curiae,
   cui laurus aeternos honores 15
      Delmatico peperit triumpho.

iam nunc minaci murmure cornuum
perstringis auris, iam litui strepunt,
   iam fulgor armorum fugaces
      terret equos equitumque vultus. 20

audire magnos iam videor duces
non indecoro pulvere sordidos,
   et cuncta terrarum subacta
      praeter atrocem animum Catonis.

Iuno et deorum quisquis amicior 25
Afris inulta cesserat impotens
   tellure victorum nepotes
      rettulit inferias Iugurthae.

quis non Latino sanguine pinguior
campus sepulcris impia proelia 30
   testatur auditumque Medis
      Hesperiae sonitum ruinae?

qui gurges aut quae flumina lugubris
ignara belli? quod mare Dauniae
   non decoloravere caedes? 35
      quae caret ora cruore nostro?

sed ne relictis, Musa procax, iocis
Ceae retractes munera neniae,
   mecum Dionaeo sub antro
      quaere modos leviore plectro. 40
          (*Horace*, Odes *II 1*)

7

Non usitata nec tenui ferar
penna biformis per liquidum aethera
   vates, neque in terris morabor
      longius, invidiaque maior

urbis relinquam. non ego pauperum 5
sanguis parentum, non ego quem vocas,
   dilecte Maecenas, obibo
      nec Stygia cohibebor unda.

iam iam residunt cruribus asperae
pelles, et album mutor in alitem 10
   superne, nascunturque leves
      per digitos umerosque plumae.

iam Daedaleo notior Icaro
visam gementis litora Bosphori
   Syrtisque Gaetulas canorus 15
      ales Hyperboreosque campos.

me Colchus et qui dissimulat metum
Marsae cohortis Dacus et ultimi
   noscent Geloni, me peritus
      discet Hiber Rhodanique potor. 20

absint inani funere neniae
luctusque turpes et querimoniae;
   compesce clamorem ac sepulcri
      mitte supervacuos honores.
           (*Horace*, Odes *II 20*)

8

Exegi monumentum aere perennius
regalique situ pyramidum altius,
quod non imber edax, non Aquilo impotens
possit diruere aut innumerabilis
annorum series et fuga temporum. 5
non omnis moriar, multaque pars mei

vitabit Libitinam: usque ego postera
crescam laude recens, dum Capitolium
scandet cum tacita virgine pontifex.
dicar, qua violens obstrepit Aufidus 10
et qua pauper aquae Daunus agrestium
regnavit populorum, ex humili potens
princeps Aeolium carmen ad Italos
deduxisse modos. sume superbiam
quaesitam meritis et mihi Delphica 15
lauro cinge volens, Melpomene, comam.
(*Horace*, Odes *III 30*)

9

Quem tu, Melpomene, semel
nascentem placido lumine videris,
 illum non labor Isthmius
clarabit pugilem, non equus impiger
 curru ducet Achaico 5
victorem, neque res bellica Deliis
 ornatum foliis ducem,
quod regum tumidas contuderit minas,
 ostendet Capitolio:
sed quae Tibur aquae fertile praefluunt 10
 et spissae nemorum comae
fingent Aeolio carmine nobilem.
 Romae principis urbium
dignatur suboles inter amabilis
 vatum ponere me choros, 15
et iam dente minus mordeor invido.
 o, testudinis aureae
dulcem quae strepitum, Pieri, temperas,
 o mutis quoque piscibus
donatura cycni, si libeat, sonum, 20
 totum muneris hoc tui est,
quod monstror digito praetereuntium
 Romanae fidicen lyrae:
quod spiro et placeo, si placeo, tuum est.
 (*Horace*, Odes *IV 3*)

LOVE AND FRIENDSHIP

The intensity of Catullus' love for Lesbia almost foredoomed him to disappointment and disenchantment. His youthful ardour for an older woman was vastly different from the normal transitory affairs and infatuations of men of his age in Rome. Though initially the product of *otium* [51 (10), lines 13-16], the adulterous relationship was soon transformed by his emotions and heart-searchings into something wonderful and unique. Perhaps because he was aware of the sordid nature of their love Catullus felt impelled to idealize and ennoble the relationship. So Clodia was cast as Lesbia, with intimations of Sapphic intensity and poetic creativity, and with antique romantic associations. Catullus sought to define the nature of his love for Clodia in terms of the beloved as partner in mind and body and soul. For him, perfect love was comparable to the affection felt within a family, a mixture of respectful fondness, of sacrificial dedication and fidelity. No one before Catullus had tried so desperately to give expression to the meaning and nature of love. In his attempt to sublimate his passion for Clodia, Catullus turned men's minds into new channels of thought about love and its proper expression. The unique character of his love emerges sharply and instructively from comparison with love affairs in Roman Comedy and with other love poems which he composed recording his own and others' casual involvements with different women.

The qualities which inspired his love for Lesbia at the outset were equally essential to his friendships for men who were characterized frequently as *venustus*, *lepidus*, *urbanus* and *facetus*. Taste and elegance, sophistication, urbanity and wit, creativity and fidelity ranked high in his requirements of his friends; disillusionment led regularly to fierce reaction, to scathing poetical indictments. The *Poetae Novi* were his closest friends, young men with whom he could exchange his views freely on poetry and its criticism, men of good taste (*docti*) with whom he could converse on matters of life and death, and love. Among his closest friends were Licinius Calvus, the orator [Cat. 14 (31); 53 (85)], Helvius Cinna, the politician [Cat. 10 (78)], Cornificius, the scholar-poet [38 (33)], Hortensius, Cicero's rival in the courts [65 (3)], Cornelius Nepos, historian and poet [1 (1)] and probably Quintilius Varus [10 (78)] and Furius Bibaculus [11 (27); 26 (80)].

For Horace, love is the prerogative of youth [Odes I 30 (89), line 7], and his somewhat cynical poems were the product of his middle-age. Composed carefully and reflectively, usually urbane and somewhat detached, his love lyrics lack the urgency and the sincerity of the Catullian lyrics. Both share the same colloquial vocabulary of love, but the address is entirely different. The conflict of love and its definition never disrupted or controlled Horace's life as it did Catullus'. Horace's poetry remained tidy and restrained; Catullus' emotions were deeper and the inspiration of love was obviously greater. Horace's women in love all bear Greek names, indicating that they were either freedwomen or courtesans. Because it was the usual practice of Roman young men to prefer transitory attachments to matrimony in their earlier years, Horace simply adhered to the normal poetic practice which Catullus had unsettled by his love lyrics to Clodia.

Both poets have their ideal definition of love. Catullus exalts his relationship with his beloved into a non-physical, intellectual, almost spiritual sphere where the traditional language of love's affirmation gives way to new concepts of constancy (*fides*) and fidelity (*pietas*), and where the relationship is defined as *aeternum sanctae foedus amicitiae*. His poems addressed to Lesbia are intimate reveries, compressed, deft, and subtle; they are far removed from love songs of careless rapture or infatuation. Horace, on the other hand, who is habitually inclined to moralize, favours marital harmony as the ideal norm in love [*Odes* I 13 (38), 17–29]. He is less concerned with the Catullian ideal of love as 'a contract and eternal bond of love', and more with the ideal love as tranquillity, an almost bucolic ideal of peace and quietude. Instead of straining, like Catullus, with definitions and new patterns of love and purity, Horace tends to provide genial, urbane essays *about* love, lacking in warmth and passion, but nonetheless sophisticated and exquisite.

In early life, debating how best to improve himself, Horace resolved to become a better friend:

hoc faciens vivam melius. Sic dulcis amicis
occurram.

(*Sat.* I 4, lines 135–6)

In the satire describing his journey to Brundisium with Maecenas and other friends, he gives way to sheer delight on the arrival of Vergil, Plotius and Varius to join the party:

nil ego contulerim iucundo sanus amico.

(*Sat.* I 5, line 44)

When Horace entertained at his Sabine Farm, one of the favourite topics of discussion after dinner was the origin of friendship:

quidve ad amicitias, usus rectumne, trahat nos.

(*Sat.* II 6, line 75)

PERSONAL LYRIC

Friendship has been termed the one redeeming feature of Epicureanism, and many scholars are inclined to assign Horace to the ranks of this group on this ground alone. But convictions and behaviour in this one area of life are hardly enough to account him a follower of Epicurus. Indeed Horace himself categorically stated:

> nullius addictus iurare in verba magistri,
> quo me cumque rapit tempestas deferor hospes.
> *(Epist.* I 1, lines 14-15)

The poet is outspoken against those who betray friendship, and so, in a negative way, he indicates his own tenets and values in the matter of *amicitia*:

> absentem qui rodit amicum,
> qui non defendit alio culpante, solutos
> qui captat risus hominum famamque dicacis,
> fingere qui non visa potest, commissa tacere
> qui nequit. . .
> *(Sat.* I 4, lines 81-5)

Horace knew the company and intimacy of some great men of his time – Maecenas and Pollio and Augustus. Agrippa seems to have been somewhat less of a friend. On occasion Horace must have prided himself on these relationships, although he was not ready to accept their largesse on a grand scale, and professed to be satisfied with his modest estate:

> nihil supra
> deos lacesso, nec potentem amicum
> largiora flagito,
> satis beatus unicis Sabinis.
> *(Odes* II 18, lines 11-14)

As a result of his own cruel experiences with Civil War at home and in the field Horace became a non-partisan foe of internecine strife. Many of his friends had once shared his Republican sentiments, but had found it possible to compromise with the New Society: Dellius: *Odes* III 3, Messalla Corvinus: *Odes* III 21 (63), Sestius: *Odes* I 4 (49), Munatius Plancus: *Odes* I 7 (67), Asinius Pollio: *Odes* II 1 (6), Pompeius: *Odes* II 7 (45), and Murena: *Odes* II 10 (54). Horace was never disloyal to his old comrades in arms and remained respectful to the defeated cause.

His affection for Vergil was genuine and enthusiastic. As a token of his complete unanimity he calls Vergil 'animae dimidium meae' (*Odes* I 3 (35), line 8). Cicero's essay *De Amicitia* (21, 80–2) provides an instructive parallel to Horace's phrases:

> alterum anquirit cuius animum ita cum suo misceat, ut efficiat paene unum ex duobus.

For Maecenas Horace expresses his devotion and affection repeatedly. Twice he invites the great statesman to share his festive board and find relaxation from his political anxieties [*Odes* III 8; III 29]. The twenty-ninth ode of Book III, immediately preceding the Epilogue which finishes the collection (and to which he probably had no intention of adding a supplement), is a lyrical adieu to his patron-friend, a summing-up of their relationship. And Maecenas seems to have responded in kind, for his deathbed wish reported to Augustus was

> Horati Flacci ut mei esto memor.

Maecenas is frequently called Horace's patron. Though true enough in the modern interpretation of their relationship as poet and benefactor, Horace never, in fact, defines the relationship as one of *patronus* and *cliens*. He calls Maecenas his 'praesidium et dulce decus meum', 'mearum grande decus columenque rerum', and 'meae partem animae'. Each helped the other and they shared their pleasures mutually. The Sabine Farm was an agreeable site for happy reunions, where liberty of action was the code, but where moderation reigned.

Horace is inclined, now and again, to use lyric for sermonizing, to instruct his friends in his favourite precepts, but he was never possessive of his friends, or petulant over their failings; he showed remarkable tact and understanding of other men's foibles. And he was ready to sympathize and commiserate when the need arose. He could rid Maecenas of his morbid fears of premature death; he could equally well console persons who had lost loved ones, particularly Vergil on the loss of their dear and mutual friend Quintilius Varus whose frank and disinterested critiques of their work won their love and respect. Candor in a poet-friend and a literary critic was Horace's ideal – and when Maecenas criticized Horace for a dilatory attitude towards writing, the poet replied, addressing him as 'candide Maecenas' [*Epode* 14, line 5]. Plotius, Varius and Vergil are included among the poet's favourites –

animae quales neque candidiores
terra tulit, neque quis me sit devinctior alter.
(Sat. I 5, lines 41–2)

10

Ille mi par esse deo videtur,
ille, si fas est, superare divos,
qui sedens adversus identidem te
    spectat et audit

dulce ridentem, misero quod omnis   5
eripit sensus mihi: nam simul te,
Lesbia, aspexi, nihil est super mi
. . .
lingua sed torpet, tenuis sub artus
flamma demanat, sonitu suopte   10
tintinant aures, gemina teguntur
    lumina nocte.

otium, Catulle, tibi molestum est:
otio exsultas nimiumque gestis:
otium et reges prius et beatas   15
    perdidit urbes.
(Catullus 51)

11

Passer, deliciae meae puellae,
quicum ludere, quem in sinu tenere,
cui primum digitum dare appetenti
et acris solet incitare morsus,
cum desiderio meo nitenti   5
carum nescio quid lubet iocari,
et solaciolum sui doloris,
credo, ut tum gravis acquiescat ardor:
tecum ludere sicut ipsa possem
et tristis animi levare curas!   10
(Catullus 2)

12

Lugete, o Veneres Cupidinesque,
et quantum est hominum venustiorum:

passer mortuus est meae puellae,
passer, deliciae meae puellae,
quem plus illa oculis suis amabat.
nam mellitus erat suamque norat
ipsam tam bene quam puella matrem,
nec sese a gremio illius movebat,
sed circumsiliens modo huc modo illuc
ad solam dominam usque pipiabat;
qui nunc it per iter tenebricosum
illud, unde negant redire quemquam.
at vobis male sit, malae tenebrae
Orci, quae omnia bella devoratis:
tam bellum mihi passerem abstulistis.
o factum male! o miselle passer!
tua nunc opera meae puellae
flendo turgiduli rubent ocelli.
(Catullus 3)

13

Vivamus, mea Lesbia, atque amemus,
rumoresque senum severiorum
omnes unius aestimemus assis!
soles occidere et redire possunt:
nobis cum semel occidit brevis lux,
nox est perpetua una dormienda.
da mi basia mille, deinde centum,
dein mille altera, dein secunda centum,
deinde usque altera mille, deinde centum.
dein, cum milia multa fecerimus,
conturbabimus illa, ne sciamus,
aut ne quis malus invidere possit,
cum tantum sciat esse basiorum.
(Catullus 5)

14

Quaeris, quot mihi basiationes
tuae, Lesbia, sint satis superque.
quam magnus numerus Libyssae harenae
lasarpiciferis iacet Cyrenis

  oraclum Iovis inter aestuosi 5
  et Batti veteris sacrum sepulcrum;
  aut quam sidera multa, cum tacet nox,
  furtivos hominum vident amores:
  tam te basia multa basiare
  vesano satis et super Catullo est, 10
  quae nec pernumerare curiosi
  possint nec mala fascinare lingua.
       (Catullus 7)

15

Quintia formosa est multis. mihi candida, longa,
 recta est: haec ego sic singula confiteor.
totum illud formosa nego: nam nulla venustas,
 nulla in tam magno est corpore mica salis.
Lesbia formosa est, quae cum pulcerrima tota est, 5
 tum omnibus una omnis surripuit Veneres.
      (Catullus 86)

16

  Salve, nec minimo puella naso
  nec bello pede nec nigris ocellis
  nec longis digitis nec ore sicco
  nec sane nimis elegante lingua,
  decoctoris amica Formiani. 5
  ten provincia narrat esse bellam?
  tecum Lesbia nostra comparatur?
  o saeclum insapiens et infacetum!
      (Catullus 43)

17

Lesbia mi dicit semper male nec tacet umquam
 de me: Lesbia me dispeream nisi amat.
quo signo? quia sunt totidem mea: deprecor illam
 assidue, verum dispeream nisi amo.
      (Catullus 92)

18

Nulli se dicit mulier mea nubere malle
   quam mihi, non si se Iuppiter ipse petat.
dicit: sed mulier cupido quod dicit amanti,
   in vento et rapida scribere oportet aqua.
(Catullus 70)

19

Miser Catulle, desinas ineptire,
et quod vides perisse perditum ducas.
fulsere quondam candidi tibi soles,
cum ventitabas quo puella ducebat
amata nobis quantum amabitur nulla.   5
ibi illa multa cum iocosa fiebant,
quae tu volebas nec puella nolebat,
fulsere vere candidi tibi soles.
nunc iam illa non volt: tu quoque inpotens noli,
nec quae fugit sectare, nec miser vive,   10
sed obstinata mente perfer, obdura.
vale, puella. iam Catullus obdurat,
nec te requiret nec rogabit invitam.
at tu dolebis, cum rogaberis nulla.
scelesta, vae te, quae tibi manet vita?   15
quis nunc te adibit? cui videberis bella?
quem nunc amabis? cuius esse diceris?
quem basiabis? cui labella mordebis?
at tu, Catulle, destinatus obdura.
(Catullus 8)

20

Nulla potest mulier tantum se dicere amatam
   vere, quantum a me Lesbia amata mea est.
nulla fides ullo fuit umquam foedere tanta,
   quanta in amore tuo ex parte reperta mea est.
(Catullus 87)

21

Iucundum, mea vita, mihi proponis amorem
    hunc nostrum inter nos perpetuumque fore.
di magni, facite ut vere promittere possit,
    atque id sincere dicat et ex animo,
ut liceat nobis tota perducere vita   5
    aeternum hoc sanctae foedus amicitiae.
                                     (*Catullus 109*)

22

Desine de quoquam quicquam bene velle mereri
    aut aliquem fieri posse putare pium.
omnia sunt ingrata, nihil fecisse benigne
    [prodest,] immo etiam taedet obestque magis;
ut mihi, quem nemo gravius nec acerbius urget,   5
    quam modo qui me unum atque unicum amicum habuit.
                                     (*Catullus 73*)

23

Dicebas quondam solum te nosse Catullum,
    Lesbia, nec prae me velle tenere Iovem.
dilexi tum te non tantum ut vulgus amicam,
    sed pater ut gnatos diligit et generos.
nunc te cognovi: quare etsi impensius uror,   5
    multo mi tamen es vilior et levior.
qui potis est, inquis? quod amantem iniuria talis
    cogit amare magis, sed bene velle minus.
                                     (*Catullus 72*)

24

Huc est mens deducta tua mea, Lesbia, culpa
    atque ita se officio perdidit ipsa suo,
ut iam nec bene velle queat tibi, si optima fias,
    nec desistere amare, omnia si facias.
                                     (*Catullus 75*)

25

Odi et amo. quare id faciam, fortasse requiris?
   nescio, sed fieri sentio et excrucior.
                                            (Catullus 85)

26

Siqua recordanti benefacta priora voluptas
   est homini, cum se cogitat esse pium,
nec sanctam violasse fidem, nec foedere nullo
   divum ad fallendos numine abusum homines,
multa parata manent in longa aetate, Catulle,   5
   ex hoc ingrato gaudia amore tibi.
nam quaecumque homines bene cuiquam aut dicere possunt
   aut facere, haec a te dictaque factaque sunt.
omnia quae ingratae perierunt credita menti.
   quare iam te cur amplius excrucies?   10
quin tu animo offirmas atque istinc teque reducis,
   et dis invitis desinis esse miser?
difficile est longum subito deponere amorem,
   difficile est, verum hoc qua lubet efficias:
una salus haec est, hoc est tibi pervincendum,   15
   hoc facias, sive id non pote sive pote.
o di, si vestrum est misereri, aut si quibus umquam
   extremam iam ipsa in morte tulistis opem,
me miserum aspicite et, si vitam puriter egi,
   eripite hanc pestem perniciemque mihi,   20
quae mihi subrepens imos ut torpor in artus
   expulit ex omni pectore laetitias.
non iam illud quaero, contra me ut diligat illa,
   aut, quod non potis est, esse pudica velit:
ipse valere opto et taetrum hunc deponere morbum.   25
   o di, reddite mi hoc pro pietate mea.
                                            (Catullus 76)

27

Furi et Aureli, comites Catulli,
sive in extremos penetrabit Indos,
litus ut longe resonante Eoa
          tunditur unda,

sive in Hyrcanos Arabasve molles, 5
seu Sagas sagittiferosve Parthos,
sive quae septemgeminus colorat
    aequora Nilus,

sive trans altas gradietur Alpes,
Caesaris visens monimenta magni, 10
Gallicum Rhenum horribile aequor ulti-
    mosque Britannos,

omnia haec, quaecumque feret voluntas
caelitum, temptare simul parati,
pauca nuntiate meae puellae 15
    non bona dicta.

cum suis vivat valeatque moechis,
quos simul complexa tenet trecentos,
nullum amans vere, sed identidem omnium
    ilia rumpens; 20

nec meum respectet, ut ante, amorem,
qui illius culpa cecidit velut prati
ultimi flos, praetereunte postquam
    tactus aratro est.
                (*Catullus 11*)

28

Verani, omnibus e meis amicis
antistans mihi milibus trecentis,
venistine domum ad tuos penates
fratresque unanimos anumque matrem?
venisti. o mihi nuntii beati! 5
visam te incolumem audiamque Hiberum
narrantem loca, facta, nationes,
ut mos est tuus, applicansque collum
iucundum os oculosque suaviabor.
o quantum est hominum beatiorum, 10
quid me laetius est beatiusve?
              (*Catullus 9*)

29

Marrucine Asini, manu sinistra
non belle uteris: in ioco atque vino
tollis lintea neglegentiorum.

hoc salsum esse putas? fugit te, inepte:
quamvis sordida res et invenusta est.
non credis mihi? crede Pollioni
fratri, qui tua furta vel talento
mutari velit: est enim leporum
differtus puer ac facetiarum.
quare aut hendecasyllabos trecentos
exspecta, aut mihi linteum remitte,
quod me non movet aestimatione,
verum est mnemosynum mei sodalis.
nam sudaria Saetaba ex Hiberis
miserunt mihi muneri Fabullus
et Veranius: haec amem necesse est
ut Veraniolum meum et Fabullum.
                        (*Catullus 12*)

30

Cenabis bene, mi Fabulle, apud me
paucis, si tibi di favent, diebus,
si tecum attuleris bonam atque magnam
cenam, non sine candida puella
et vino et sale et omnibus cachinnis.
haec si, inquam, attuleris, venuste noster,
cenabis bene; nam tui Catulli
plenus sacculus est aranearum.
sed contra accipies meros amores
seu quid suavius elegantiusve est:
nam unguentum dabo, quod meae puellae
donarunt Veneres Cupidinesque,
quod tu cum olfacies, deos rogabis,
totum ut te faciant, Fabulle, nasum.
                        (*Catullus 13*)

31

Ni te plus oculis meis amarem,
iucundissime Calve, munere isto
odissem te odio Vatiniano:
nam quid feci ego quidve sum locutus,
cur me tot male perderes poetis?
isti di mala multa dent clienti,
qui tantum tibi misit impiorum.

quod si, ut suspicor, hoc novum ac repertum
munus dat tibi Sulla litterator,
non est mi male, sed bene ac beate,   10
quod non dispereunt tui labores.
di magni, horribilem et sacrum libellum!
quem tu scilicet ad tuum Catullum
misti, continuo ut die periret,
Saturnalibus, optimo dierum!   15
non non hoc tibi, false, sic abibit.
nam, si luxerit, ad librariorum
curram scrinia, Caesios, Aquinos,
Suffenum, omnia colligam venena,
ac te his suppliciis remunerabor.   20
vos hinc interea valete abite
illuc, unde malum pedem attulistis,
saecli incommoda, pessimi poetae.
                    (*Catullus 14*)

32

Paene insularum, Sirmio, insularumque
ocelle, quascumque in liquentibus stagnis
marique vasto fert uterque Neptunus,
quam te libenter quamque laetus inviso,
vix mi ipse credens Thuniam atque Bithunos   5
liquisse campos et videre te in tuto.
o quid solutis est beatius curis,
cum mens onus reponit, ac peregrino
labore fessi venimus larem ad nostrum,
desideratoque acquiescimus lecto?   10
hoc est quod unum est pro laboribus tantis.
salve, o venusta Sirmio, atque ero gaude
gaudente, vosque, o Lydiae lacus undae,
ridete quidquid est domi cachinnorum.
                    (*Catullus 31*)

33

Malest, Cornifici, tuo Catullo,
malest, me hercule, et laboriose,
et magis magis in dies et horas.
quem tu, quod minimum facillimumque est,
qua solatus es allocutione?   5

irascor tibi. sic meos amores?
paulum quid lubet allocutionis,
maestius lacrimis Simonideis.

(*Catullus 38*)

34

Iam ver egelidos refert tepores,
iam caeli furor aequinoctialis
iucundis Zephyri silescit auris.
linquantur Phrygii, Catulle, campi
Nicaeaeque ager uber aestuosae: 5
ad claras Asiae volemus urbes.
iam mens praetrepidans avet vagari,
iam laeti studio pedes vigescunt.
o dulces comitum valete coetus,
longe quos simul a domo profectos 10
diversae variae viae reportant.

(*Catullus 46*)

35

Sic te diva potens Cypri,
sic fratres Helenae, lucida sidera,
ventorumque regat pater
obstrictis aliis praeter Iapyga,
navis, quae tibi creditum 5
debes Vergilium, finibus Atticis
reddas incolumem precor,
et serves animae dimidium meae.
illi robur et aes triplex
circa pectus erat, qui fragilem truci 10
commisit pelago ratem
primus, nec timuit praecipitem Africum
decertantem Aquilonibus
nec tristis Hyadas nec rabiem Noti,
quo non arbiter Hadriae 15
maior, tollere seu ponere vult freta.
quem mortis timuit gradum,
qui siccis oculis monstra natantia,
qui vidit mare turbidum et
infamis scopulos Acroceraunia? 20
nequiquam deus abscidit

  prudens Oceano dissociabili
   terras, si tamen impiae
non tangenda rates transiliunt vada.
   audax omnia perpeti
gens humana ruit per vetitum nefas.
   audax Iapeti genus
ignem fraude mala gentibus intulit.
   post ignem aetheria domo
subductum macies et nova febrium
   terris incubuit cohors,
semotique prius tarda necessitas
   leti corripuit gradum.
expertus vacuum Daedalus aera
   pennis non homini datis:
perrupit Acheronta Herculeus labor.
   nil mortalibus ardui est:
caelum ipsum petimus stultitia neque
   per nostrum patimur scelus
iracunda Iovem ponere fulmina.
     (*Horace*, Odes *I 3*)

36

Quis multa gracilis te puer in rosa
perfusus liquidis urget odoribus
   grato, Pyrrha, sub antro?
    cui flavam religas comam,

simplex munditiis? heu quotiens fidem
mutatosque deos flebit et aspera
   nigris aequora ventis
    emirabitur insolens,

qui nunc te fruitur credulus aurea,
qui semper vacuam, semper amabilem
   sperat, nescius aurae
    fallacis! miseri, quibus

intemptata nites. me tabula sacer
votiva paries indicat uvida
   suspendisse potenti
    vestimenta maris deo.
     (*Horace*, Odes *I 5*)

37

    Lydia, dic, per omnis
hoc deos vere, Sybarin cur properes amando
    perdere, cur apricum
oderit campum, patiens pulveris atque solis,
    cur neque militaris 5
inter aequalis equitet, Gallica nec lupatis
    temperet ora frenis?
cur timet flavum Tiberim tangere? cur olivum
    sanguine viperino
cautius vitat neque iam livida gestat armis 10
    bracchia, saepe disco,
saepe trans finem iaculo nobilis expedito?
    quid latet, ut marinae
filium dicunt Thetidis sub lacrimosa Troiae
    funera, ne virilis 15
cultus in caedem et Lycias proriperet catervas?
            (*Horace*, Odes *I 8*)

38

    Cum tu, Lydia, Telephi
cervicem roseam, cerea Telephi
    laudas bracchia, vae meum
fervens difficili bile tumet iecur.
    tum nec mens mihi nec color 5
certa sede manent, umor et in genas
    furtim labitur, arguens
quam lentis penitus macerer ignibus.
    uror, seu tibi candidos
turparunt umeros immodicae mero 10
    rixae, sive puer furens
impressit memorem dente labris notam.
    non, si me satis audias,
speres perpetuum dulcia barbare
    laedentem oscula quae Venus 15
quinta parte sui nectaris imbuit.
    felices ter et amplius
quos irrupta tenet copula nec malis

    divulsus querimoniis
suprema citius solvet amor die.   20
        (*Horace*, Odes *I 13*)

39

Velox amoenum saepe Lucretilem
mutat Lycaeo Faunus et igneam
    defendit aestatem capellis
        usque meis pluviosque ventos.

impune tutum per nemus arbutos   5
quaerunt latentis et thyma deviae
    olentis uxores mariti,
        nec viridis metuunt colubras

nec Martialis Haediliae lupos,
utcumque dulci, Tyndari, fistula   10
    valles et Usticae cubantis
        levia personuere saxa.

di me tuentur, dis pietas mea
et musa cordi est. hic tibi copia
    manabit ad plenum benigno   15
        ruris honorum opulenta cornu:

hic in reducta valle Caniculae
vitabis aestus et fide Teia
    dices laborantis in uno
        Penelopen vitreamque Circen: 20

hic innocentis pocula Lesbii
duces sub umbra, nec Semeleius
    cum Marte confundet Thyoneus
        proelia, nec metues protervum

suspecta Cyrum, ne male dispari   25
incontinentis iniciat manus
    et scindat haerentem coronam
        crinibus immeritamque vestem.
        (*Horace*, Odes *I 17*)

40

Vile potabis modicis Sabinum
cantharis, Graeca quod ego ipse testa

conditum levi, datus in theatro
 cum tibi plausus,

care Maecenas eques, ut paterni
fluminis ripae simul et iocosa
redderet laudes tibi Vaticani
 montis imago.

Caecubum et prelo domitam Caleno
tu bibes uvam: mea nec Falernae
temperant vites neque Formiani
 pocula colles.
 (*Horace*, Odes *I 20*)

41

Integer vitae scelerisque purus
non eget Mauris iaculis neque arcu
nec venenatis gravida sagittis,
 Fusce, pharetra,

sive per Syrtis iter aestuosas
sive facturus per inhospitalem
Caucasum vel quae loca fabulosus
 lambit Hydaspes.

namque me silva lupus in Sabina,
dum meam canto Lalagen et ultra
terminum curis vagor expeditis,
 fugit inermem,

quale portentum neque militaris
Daunias latis alit aesculetis
nec Iubae tellus generat, leonum
 arida nutrix.

pone me pigris ubi nulla campis
arbor aestiva recreatur aura,
quod latus mundi nebulae malusque
 Iuppiter urget;

pone sub curru nimium propinqui
solis in terra domibus negata:
dulce ridentem Lalagen amabo,
 dulce loquentem.
 (*Horace*, Odes *I 22*)

A literary triumvirate of Augustan writers
From left to right, Livy (or Propertius), Vergil, and Horace; in the foreground, an acolyte. Horace's known characteristics – 'short, prematurely grey, fond of the sunshine, irascible but easily appeased' are perhaps discernible in this portrait relief. (From the Ara Pietatis Augustae, 43 A.D., Villa Medici, Rome)

M. Vipsanius Agrippa, 63 B.C.–A.D. 12
Son-in-law of Augustus, distinguished by his deep-set eyes and scowling countenance, the military and naval genius of Octavian at Mylae, 36 B.C., and at Actium, 31 B.C. (A bust in the Louvre)

Maecenas (?) ob. 8 B.C.
Intimate friend, advisor, and diplomatic emissary of Octavian; literary patron, friend, and benefactor of Horace and Vergil. (From the Ara Pacis Augustae, 13–9 B.C., Rome)

The Peninsula of Sirmio (modern Sirmione) on Lake Garda, near Verona
The remains belong not to Catullus' country-place but to a palatial villa of Imperial date.

Horace's estate
Looking west to the Sabine Hills near modern Licenza in the valley of the Digentia, north of Tivoli. Once the property of Maecenas, it became Horace's favourite retreat in summer and autumn, vying with Baiae, Velia and Rome for his presence.

An ancient wall-painting from Stabiae

A Campanian seascape, probably Puteoli (modern Pozzuoli), the major port of Republican Rome before the development of Ostia. The piers and waterfront constructions and the general activity in the harbour recall the extravagant buildings and general liveliness of nearby ancient Baiae. The terraced villa on the left with the oscilla suspended between the columns is typical of the palatial villas set amidst the pleasure domes of the Campanian shoreline. (National Museum, Naples. Height, 11⅓ inches)

Augustus of Prima Porta

A posthumous statue of the emperor found in Livia's villa at Prima Porta near Rome. Depicted as Imperator, Augustus addresses his troops and wears a military cloak, *paludamentum*, and decorative breastplate, *lorica*, which elaborates the cosmic setting of his rule and his accomplishments – the subjection of Spain and Gaul, and the recovery of the Parthian standards in 20 B.C. The dolphin recalls his ties with Venus Marina, and the child Amor, possibly one of his grandsons, is token of his dynastic designs and hopes for the future. (Vatican Museum)

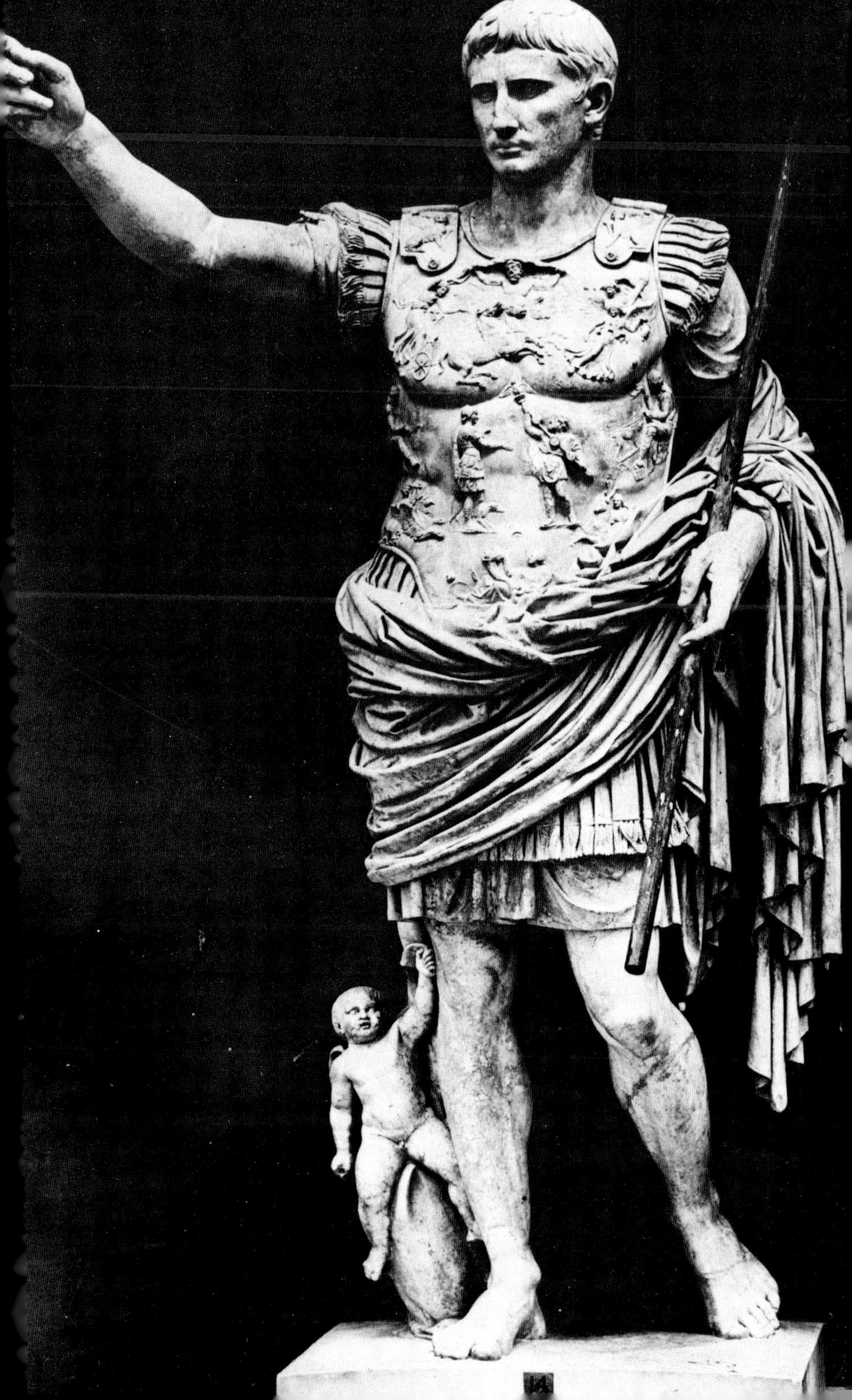

A reconstruction of the west end of the Roman Forum
On the left, in the foreground, the House of the Vestals (partial), the circular Temple of Vesta, the temple of Castor, and triple arch of Augustus; the temple of the Deified Julius (centre), the Basilica Julia, the Temple of Saturn (where Horace worked as Treasury clerk), and the Rostra.

On the right, in the foreground, the Basilica Nova (partial), the Temple of Antoninus and Faustina, the Basilica Aemilia, and the Senate House.

Behind the arch of Septimus Severus rise the Temple of Concord, the Temple of the Deified Vespasian (left), the Tabularium (Records Office), and the Capitoline Hill with the Temple of Jupiter Capitolinus (left) and the Temple of Juno Moneta on the Arx (right). (Reconstruction model, Museo della Civiltà, Rome)

42

Vitas inuleo me similis, Chloe,
quaerenti pavidam montibus aviis
    matrem non sine vano
        aurarum et silvae metu.

nam seu mobilibus veris inhorruit
adventus foliis seu virides rubum
    dimovere lacertae,
        et corde et genibus tremit.

atqui non ego te tigris ut aspera
Gaetulusve leo frangere persequor:
    tandem desine matrem
        tempestiva sequi viro.
        (*Horace*, Odes *I 23*)

43

Quis desiderio sit pudor aut modus
tam cari capitis? praecipe lugubris
cantus, Melpomene, cui liquidam pater
    vocem cum cithara dedit.

ergo Quintilium perpetuus sopor
urget! cui Pudor et Iustitiae soror,
incorrupta Fides, nudaque Veritas
    quando ullum inveniet parem?

multis ille bonis flebilis occidit,
nulli flebilior quam tibi, Vergili.
tu frustra pius heu non ita creditum
    poscis Quintilium deos.

quid si Threicio blandius Orpheo
auditam moderere arboribus fidem,
num vanae redeat sanguis imagini,
    quam virga semel horrida,

non lenis precibus fata recludere,
nigro compulerit Mercurius gregi?
durum: sed levius fit patientia
    quidquid corrigere est nefas.
        (*Horace*, Odes *I 24*)

44

Icci, beatis nunc Arabum invides
gazis, et acrem militiam paras
    non ante devictis Sabaeae
        regibus, horribilique Medo

nectis catenas? quae tibi virginum 5
sponso necato barbara serviet?
    puer quis ex aula capillis
        ad cyathum statuetur unctis,

doctus sagittas tendere Sericas
arcu paterno? quis neget arduis 10
    pronos relabi posse rivos
        montibus et Tiberim reverti,

cum tu coemptos undique nobilis
libros Panaeti Socraticam et domum
    mutare loricis Hiberis, 15
        pollicitus meliora, tendis?
                (*Horace*, Odes *I 29*)

45

O saepe mecum tempus in ultimum
deducte Bruto militiae duce,
    quis te redonavit Quiritem
        dis patriis Italoque caelo,

Pompei, meorum prime sodalium? 5
cum quo morantem saepe diem mero
    fregi coronatus nitentis
        malobathro Syrio capillos.

tecum Philippos et celerem fugam
sensi relicta non bene parmula, 10
    cum fracta virtus, et minaces
        turpe solum tetigere mento.

sed me per hostis Mercurius celer
denso paventem sustulit aere;
    te rursus in bellum resorbens 15
        unda fretis tulit aestuosis.

ergo obligatam redde Iovi dapem
longaque fessum militia latus
    depone sub lauru mea, nec
        parce cadis tibi destinatis.   20

oblivioso levia Massico
ciboria exple; funde capacibus
    unguenta de conchis. quis udo
        deproperare apio coronas

curatve myrto? quem Venus arbitrum   25
dicet bibendi? non ego sanius
    bacchabor Edonis: recepto
        dulce mihi furere est amico.
                (*Horace*, Odes *II* 7)

46

Iam veris comites, quae mare temperant,
impellunt animae lintea Thraciae;
iam nec prata rigent nec fluvii strepunt
    hiberna nive turgidi.

nidum ponit Ityn flebiliter gemens   5
infelix avis et Cecropiae domus
aeternum opprobrium, quod male barbaras
    regum est ulta libidines.

dicunt in tenero gramine pinguium
custodes ovium carmina fistula   10
delectantque deum cui pecus et nigri
    colles Arcadiae placent.

adduxere sitim tempora, Vergili;
sed pressum Calibus ducere Liberum
si gestis, iuvenum nobilium cliens,   15
    nardo vina merebere.

nardi parvus onyx eliciet cadum,
qui nunc Sulpiciis accubat horreis,
spes donare novas largus amaraque
    curarum eluere efficax.   20

ad quae si properas gaudia, cum tua
velox merce veni: non ego te meis
immunem meditor tingere poculis,
    plena dives ut in domo.

> verum pone moras et studium lucri, 25
> nigrorumque memor, dum licet, ignium
> misce stultitiam consiliis brevem:
> dulce est desipere in loco.
>
> (*Horace*, Odes *IV 12*)

II Reflective and Religious Lyric

MORALIZING AND PHILOSOPHY

There are features of Horace's philosophical or moralizing poems which seem, on the surface, to be outright Epicurean sentiments: a materialistic view of life, tinged with pessimism, and a concern with the brevity and uncertainty of life and happiness. The 'carpe diem' ethic, popularly ascribed to Horace, is by no means his own formulation. It represents an age-old reaction to the vicissitudes of life, and is nothing but a simple, unsophisticated response to the wear and tear of earthly existence. Horace, like most Romans, was concerned with the practical problems of daily life, and he sought and periodically formulated what he regarded as an adequate response to the challenge of living.

Although Horace was prone to indulge in philosophical discussion with his friends

> utrumne
> divitiis homines an sint virtute beati,
> quidve ad amicitias, usus rectumne, trahat nos,
> et quae sit natura boni summumque quid eius.
>
> (*Sat.* II 6, lines 73–6)

one cannot be certain what tenets he would have advanced in the discussion. In *Epist.* I 1, lines 13–19 he asserts that he has abandoned poetry (i.e. lyric) to find a system or code of life:

> ac ne forte roges, quo me duce, quo lare tuter:
> nullius addictus iurare in verba magistri,
> quo me cumque rapit tempestas, deferor hospes.
> nunc agilis fio et mersor civilibus undis,
> virtutis verae custos rigidusque satelles;
> nunc in Aristippi furtim praecepta relabor,
> et mihi res, non me rebus subiungere conor.

Stoic duty (*officium*) and self-discipline are countered not so much by Epicurean ataraxy (imperturbability) or apathy as by the lively ethic of the hedonistic Aristippus, for whom Horace expresses outright admiration (*Epist.* I 17, lines 13–22).

It is absurd to take the witty allusion to himself as 'Epicuri de grege porcum' (*Epist.* I 4, line 16) as a serious declaration of his fidelity to Epicurean principles. Undoubtedly certain features of the Epicurean ethic appealed to Horace: the doctrine of happiness as the *summum bonum* of existence, and the non-intervention of the gods in human life. But the disbelief in divine interference and in the powers of the gods is apparently shattered and reversed in *Odes* I 34 (52): thunder rumbles in a clear sky, and the Lucretian argument that such a phenomenon was impossible and therefore testimony against divine intrusion into the natural realm is dissolved. Or so the poet alleges. Some have connected the change of view to Augustus' new emphasis on religion, or to Vergil's religious example. But Horace never renounced Epicureanism completely.

Horace sought what was practical in the various systems: Stoicism, Cynicism, Epicureanism and the Peripatetics. He favoured a code of simplicity and, in his own phrase, *aurea mediocritas* 'the golden mean' [*Odes* II 10 (54), line 5]. Cicero, in examining the proper conduct of life, had recommended keeping to 'the mean, which lies between the too much and the too little' (*mediocritatem illam tenere, quae est inter nimium et parum*: *De Officiis* I 25, 89). But Horace's 'golden' rule was less stringent than Cicero's 'mean' and less technical than the Aristotelian formal doctrine of virtuous conduct. For Stoic rigidity and asceticism he had no fondness. Perfection was probably, in his view, unattainable. But he shares the Stoic – which was basically the Roman – attitude towards man's duties to the state, the gods (and particularly the rustic divinities) and to the family. The Roman Odes are strongly infused with Stoic values: endurance, and courage, and patriotism, unimpeachable moral behaviour, and selfless service. Avarice, conspicuous extravagance, ambition, and fickle behaviour were anathema to Horace, but such an attitude may stem as much from the strict training he received from his father as from his Roman character and theoretical beliefs. In the Roman Odes Horace presents himself as *sacerdos Musarum* ('mouthpiece of the Muses'), the inspired agent of truth. And in this conception of himself he assumes the guise of a didactic poet, and teaches by his own example and those of others, notably in the *Epistles* and *Satires*, but in the lyrics as well. Homer (*Epist.* I, 2, lines 3–4) was the prime teacher in verse, mixing the *utile* and *dulce* (expedient and appealing) in his epic lines, debating the great questions of philosophy:

quid sit pulchrum, quid turpe, quid utile, quid non.

In the last analysis, Horace appears to be an earnest and thoughtful man, intent on enjoying life moderately, and living according to a code which suited the main elements of the Roman character. But the best definition of his beliefs is to call them eclectic, neither Stoic nor Epicurean. He certainly took this selective and adaptive attitude towards his poetic craft, adapting his Greek models to his own needs and those of his age. So too in his daily life he lived carefully but with evident pleasure in the midst of an age when morals were noticeably wanting; he renounced ambition, even though his probable equestrian status would have helped him to office, so as to enjoy the company of the Emperor and his counsellors, and of poets of a like mind; he enjoyed the favour of Maecenas and kept his integrity as an outspoken and devoted friend rather than an obsequious client; and he was able to refuse a post as Augustus' private secretary without antagonizing the Emperor.

To the end he retained his 'unconquerable soul' and owed allegiance to no man or system.

47

Si quicquam mutis gratum acceptumve sepulcris
  accidere a nostro, Calve, dolore potest,
quo desiderio veteres renovamus amores
  atque olim missas flemus amicitias,
certe non tanto mors immatura dolori est 5
  Quintiliae, quantum gaudet amore tuo.

(*Catullus 96*)

48

Multas per gentes et multa per aequora vectus
  advenio has miseras, frater, ad inferias,
ut te postremo donarem munere mortis
  et mutam nequiquam alloquerer cinerem.
quandoquidem fortuna mihi tete abstulit ipsum, 5
  heu miser indigne frater adempte mihi,
nunc tamen interea haec, prisco quae more parentum
  tradita sunt tristi munere ad inferias,

accipe fraterno multum manantia fletu,
    atque in perpetuum, frater, ave atque vale.   10
                    (*Catullus 101*)

49

Solvitur acris hiems grata vice veris et Favoni,
    trahuntque siccas machinae carinas,
ac neque iam stabulis gaudet pecus aut arator igni,
    nec prata canis albicant pruinis.
iam Cytherea choros ducit Venus imminente Luna,   5
    iunctaeque Nymphis Gratiae decentes
alterno terram quatiunt pede, dum gravis Cyclopum
    Vulcanus ardens visit officinas.
nunc decet aut viridi nitidum caput impedire myrto
    aut flore terrae quem ferunt solutae;   10
nunc et in umbrosis Fauno decet immolare lucis,
    seu poscat agna sive malit haedo.
pallida Mors aequo pulsat pede pauperum tabernas
    regumque turris. o beate Sesti,
vitae summa brevis spem nos vetat incohare longam.   15
    iam te premet nox fabulaeque Manes
et domus exilis Plutonia; quo simul mearis,
    nec regna vini sortiere talis,
nec tenerum Lycidan mirabere, quo calet iuventus
    nunc omnis et mox virgines tepebunt.   20
                    (*Horace,* Odes *I 4*)

50

    Vides ut alta stet nive candidum
    Soracte, nec iam sustineant onus
        silvae laborantes, geluque
        flumina constiterint acuto.

    dissolve frigus ligna super foco   5
    large reponens atque benignius
        deprome quadrimum Sabina,
        o Thaliarche, merum diota:

    permitte divis cetera, qui simul
    stravere ventos aequore fervido   10

deproeliantis, nec cupressi
nec veteres agitantur orni.

quid sit futurum cras fuge quaerere et
quem Fors dierum cumque dabit lucro
appone, nec dulcis amores 15
sperne puer neque tu choreas,

donec virenti canities abest
morosa. nunc et campus et areae
lenesque sub noctem susurri
composita repetantur hora, 20

nunc et latentis proditor intimo
gratus puellae risus ab angulo
pignusque dereptum lacertis
aut digito male pertinaci.
(*Horace*, Odes *I 9*)

51

Tu ne quaesieris, scire nefas, quem mihi, quem tibi
finem di dederint, Leuconoe, nec Babylonios
temptaris numeros. ut melius, quidquid erit, pati,
seu pluris hiemes seu tribuit Iuppiter ultimam,
quae nunc oppositis debilitat pumicibus mare 5
Tyrrhenum: sapias, vina liques, et spatio brevi
spem longam reseces. dum loquimur, fugerit invida
aetas: carpe diem, quam minimum credula postero.
(*Horace*, Odes *I 11*)

52

Parcus deorum cultor et infrequens
insanientis dum sapientiae
consultus erro, nunc retrorsum
vela dare atque iterare cursus

cogor relictos: namque Diespiter, 5
igni corusco nubila dividens
plerumque, per purum tonantis
egit equos volucremque currum,

quo bruta tellus et vaga flumina,
quo Styx et invisi horrida Taenari
    sedes Atlanteusque finis
        concutitur. valet ima summis

mutare et insignem attenuat deus,
obscura promens; hinc apicem rapax
    fortuna cum stridore acuto
        sustulit, hic posuisse gaudet.

(*Horace*, Odes *I 34*)

53

Aequam memento rebus in arduis
servare mentem, non secus in bonis
    ab insolenti temperatam
        laetitia, moriture Delli,

seu maestus omni tempore vixeris,
seu te in remoto gramine per dies
    festos reclinatum bearis
        interiore nota Falerni.

quo pinus ingens albaque populus
umbram hospitalem consociare amant
    ramis? quid obliquo laborat
        lympha fugax trepidare rivo?

huc vina et unguenta et nimium brevis
flores amoenae ferre iube rosae,
    dum res et aetas et sororum
        fila trium patiuntur atra.

cedes coemptis saltibus et domo
villaque flavus quam Tiberis lavit;
    cedes, et exstructis in altum
        divitiis potietur heres.

divesne prisco natus ab Inacho
nil interest an pauper et infima
    de gente sub divo moreris,
        victima nil miserantis Orci.

omnes eodem cogimur, omnium25
versatur urna serius ocius
  sors exitura et nos in aeternum
    exsilium impositura cumbae.
          (*Horace*, Odes *II 3*)

54

Rectius vives, Licini, neque altum
semper urgendo neque, dum procellas
  cautus horrescis, nimium premendo
    litus iniquum.

auream quisquis mediocritatem5
diligit, tutus caret obsoleti
  sordibus tecti, caret invidenda
    sobrius aula.

saepius ventis agitatur ingens
pinus et celsae graviore casu10
  decidunt turres feriuntque summos
    fulgura montis.

sperat infestis, metuit secundis
alteram sortem bene praeparatum
  pectus. informis hiemes reducit15
    Iuppiter, idem

summovet. non, si male nunc, et olim
sic erit: quondam cithara tacentem
  suscitat Musam neque semper arcum
    tendit Apollo.20

rebus angustis animosus atque
fortis appare; sapienter idem
  contrahes vento nimium secundo
    turgida vela.
          (*Horace*, Odes *II 10*)

55

Eheu fugaces, Postume, Postume,
labuntur anni nec pietas moram
  rugis et instanti senectae
    adferet indomitaeque morti:

>   non si trecenis quotquot eunt dies, 5
>   amice, places illacrimabilem
>   Plutona tauris, qui ter amplum
>   Geryonen Tityonque tristi
>
>   compescit unda, scilicet omnibus,
>   quicumque terrae munere vescimur, 10
>   enaviganda, sive reges
>   sive inopes erimus coloni.
>
>   frustra cruento Marte carebimus
>   fractisque rauci fluctibus Hadriae,
>   frustra per autumnos nocentem 15
>   corporibus metuemus Austrum:
>
>   visendus ater flumine languido
>   Cocytos errans et Danai genus
>   infame damnatusque longi
>   Sisyphus Aeolides laboris: 20
>
>   linquenda tellus et domus et placens
>   uxor, neque harum quas colis arborum
>   te praeter invisas cupressos
>   ulla brevem dominum sequetur:
>
>   absumet heres Caecuba dignior 25
>   servata centum clavibus et mero
>   tinget pavimentum superbo,
>   pontificum potiore cenis.
>   (*Horace*, Odes *II 14*)

56

Otium divos rogat in patenti
prensus Aegaeo, simul atra nubes
condidit lunam neque certa fulgent
    sidera nautis;

otium bello furiosa Thrace, 5
otium Medi pharetra decori,
Grosphe, non gemmis neque purpura ve-
    nale neque auro.

non enim gazae neque consularis
summovet lictor miseros tumultus 10
mentis et curas laqueata circum
    tecta volantis.

vivitur parvo bene, cui paternum
splendet in mensa tenui salinum
nec levis somnos timor aut cupido
    sordidus aufert.

quid brevi fortes iaculamur aevo
multa? quid terras alio calentis
sole mutamus? patriae quis exsul
    se quoque fugit?

scandit aeratas vitiosa navis
Cura nec turmas equitum relinquit,
ocior cervis et agente nimbos
    ocior Euro.

laetus in praesens animus quod ultra est
oderit curare et amara lento
temperet risu; nihil est ab omni
    parte beatum.

abstulit clarum cita mors Achillem,
longa Tithonum minuit senectus,
et mihi forsan, tibi quod negarit,
    porriget hora.

te greges centum Siculaeque circum
mugiunt vaccae, tibi tollit hinnitum
apta quadrigis equa, te bis Afro
    murice tinctae

vestiunt lanae: mihi parva rura et
spiritum Graiae tenuem Camenae
Parca non mendax dedit et malignum
    spernere vulgus.

                (*Horace*, Odes *II 16*)

57

Diffugere nives, redeunt iam gramina campis
    arboribusque comae;
mutat terra vices, et decrescentia ripas
    flumina praetereunt;
Gratia cum Nymphis geminisque sororibus audet
    ducere nuda choros.
immortalia ne speres, monet annus et almum
    quae rapit hora diem:

frigora mitescunt Zephyris, ver proterit aestas
    interitura simul   10
pomifer Autumnus fruges effuderit, et mox
    bruma recurrit iners.
damna tamen celeres reparant caelestia lunae:
    nos ubi decidimus
quo pater Aeneas, quo Tullus dives et Ancus,   15
    pulvis et umbra sumus.
quis scit an adiciant hodiernae crastina summae
    tempora di superi?
cuncta manus avidas fugient heredis, amico
    quae dederis animo.   20
cum semel occideris et de te splendida Minos
    fecerit arbitria,
non, Torquate, genus, non te facundia, non te
    restituet pietas;
infernis neque enim tenebris Diana pudicum   25
    liberat Hippolytum,
nec Lethaea valet Theseus abrumpere caro
    vincula Perithoo.

                              (*Horace*, Odes *IV* 7)

HYMNS – EPITHALAMIA – PRAYERS

The hymn in ancient poetry is not necessarily an expression of any deeply held religious sentiment. In the case of almost the earliest examples of the form in Greek literature, the hymn was more a literary than a devotional exercise. Although occasional examples of hymns exist which were composed for actual performance (the 'victory hymns' of Pindar, for example – which, however, celebrate human achievement rather than divine power and greatness), the form was eagerly taken up by poets for purely literary ends. The hymns selected from the lyric poetry of Catullus and Horace for this collection are wholly Greek in form, and almost wholly Greek in inspiration also. Of the many hymns in Horace's work, only one, the *Carmen Saeculare* of 17 B.C., was composed for public performance.

    The ancient hymn took many forms; its categories of types were based on the (often hypothetical) occasion for which it was composed, the object to be attained, or the manner of its performances (chorus or single singer; chorus of young men and women, or of women alone, etc.). But even though actual performance may have been the thing furthest from the poet's mind, he still tended to preserve the conventions of actual performance (e.g. Catullus seems to write his hymn to Diana [34 (58)] for antiphonal performance of a chorus of young boys and girls).

In spite of the many varieties of hymn which developed, an almost standard pattern was preserved: opening address to the deity, usually attended by some reference to his origins; a *laudatio*, or catalogue of his powers, provinces, deeds (often illustrated by a few concrete examples of the god at work); finally (though not invariably) a prayer.

Horace was particularly attracted, it would seem, by the hymn-form. He even adapts it for his addresses to human subjects on occasion, especially for Augustus. His famous ode [III 21 (63)] *O nata mecum consule Manlio*, addressed to a wine-jar, clearly adheres to the same hymn-form. Horace's attraction to the hymn was undoubtedly due to the opportunity it gave him to employ the riches of the mythological tradition within a form which was clear and ready-made.

Of the two other forms represented in this section, less needs to be said; the prayer differs little in form from the hymn, and often is just the conclusion of a hymn. In fact, the example offered here is not strictly a prayer, but rather reflections on prayer and what to pray for.

The marriage-song (*epithalamium*) was a Greek custom, sometimes, but not one imagines often, grafted on to the Roman marriage ceremony. Intended originally for singing outside the marriage chamber itself, it seems to have been performed sometimes at the bride's house before she left on her journey to her new home, or as an accompaniment to the actual procession. Of the two marriage-songs of Catullus, one (61), not included in this collection, was composed for a friend, but probably not for performance, while the other [62 (59)] was an exercise in this attractive form.

58

Dianae sumus in fide
puellae et pueri integri:
[Dianam pueri integri]
    puellaeque canamus.
o Latonia, maximi   5
magna progenies Iovis,

  quam mater prope Deliam
   deposivit olivam,
  montium domina ut fores
  silvarumque virentium   10
  saltuumque reconditorum
   amniumque sonantum:
  tu Lucina dolentibus
  Iuno dicta puerperis,
  tu potens Trivia et notho es   15
   dicta lumine Luna.
  tu cursu, dea, menstruo
  metiens iter annuum,
  rustica agricolae bonis
   tecta frugibus exples.   20
  sis quocumque tibi placet
  sancta nomine, Romulique,
  antique ut solita es, bona
   sospites ope gentem.
        (*Catullus 34*)

59

Vesper adest, iuvenes, consurgite: Vesper Olympo
exspectata diu vix tandem lumina tollit.
surgere iam tempus, iam pinguis linquere mensas,
iam veniet virgo, iam dicetur hymenaeus.
Hymen o Hymenaee, Hymen ades o Hymenaee!   5

Cernitis, innuptae, iuvenes? consurgite contra;
nimirum Oetaeos ostendit Noctifer ignes.
sic certest; viden ut perniciter exsiluere?
non temere exsiluere, canent quod vincere par est.
Hymen o Hymenaee, Hymen ades o Hymenaee!   10

Non facilis nobis, aequales, palma parata est;
aspicite, innuptae secum ut meditata requirunt.
non frustra meditantur: habent memorabile quod sit;
nec mirum, penitus quae tota mente laborant.
nos alio mentes, alio divisimus aures;   15
iure igitur vincemur: amat victoria curam.
quare nunc animos saltem convertite vestros;
dicere iam incipient, iam respondere decebit.
Hymen o Hymenaee, Hymen ades o Hymenaee!

Hespere, quis caelo fertur crudelior ignis? 20
qui natam possis complexu avellere matris,
complexu matris retinentem avellere natam,
et iuveni ardenti castam donare puellam.
quid faciunt hostes capta crudelius urbe?
Hymen o Hymenaee, Hymen ades o Hymenaee! 25

Hespere, quis caelo lucet iucundior ignis?
qui desponsa tua firmes conubia flamma,
quae pepigere viri, pepigerunt ante parentes,
nec iunxere prius quam se tuus extulit ardor.
quid datur a divis felici optatius hora? 30
Hymen o Hymenaee, Hymen ades o Hymenaee!

Hesperus e nobis, aequales, abstulit unam.

. . .

namque tuo adventu vigilat custodia semper,
nocte latent fures, quos idem saepe revertens,
Hespere, mutato comprendis nomine Eous. 35
at lubet innuptis ficto te carpere questu.
quid tum, si carpunt, tacita quem mente requirunt?
Hymen o Hymenaee, Hymen ades o Hymenaee!

Ut flos in saeptis secretus nascitur hortis,
ignotus pecori, nullo convolsus aratro, 40
quem mulcent aurae, firmat sol, educat imber;
multi illum pueri, multae optavere puellae:
idem cum tenui carptus defloruit ungui,
nulli illum pueri, nullae optavere puellae:
sic virgo, dum intacta manet, dum cara suis est; 45
cum castum amisit polluto corpore florem,
nec pueris iucunda manet, nec cara puellis.
Hymen o Hymenaee, Hymen ades o Hymenaee!

Ut vidua in nudo vitis quae nascitur arvo,
numquam se extollit, numquam mitem educat uvam, 50
sed tenerum prono deflectens pondere corpus
iam iam contingit summum radice flagellum;
hanc nulli agricolae, nulli coluere iuvenci:
at si forte eadem est ulmo coniuncta marito,
multi illam agricolae, multi coluere iuvenci: 55

sic virgo dum intacta manet, dum inculta senescit;
cum par conubium maturo tempore adepta est,
cara viro magis et minus est invisa parenti.
[Hymen o Hymenaee, Hymen ades o Hymenaee!]   58b

Et tu ne pugna cum tali coniuge, virgo.
non aequom est pugnare, pater cui tradidit ipse,   60
ipse pater cum matre, quibus parere necesse est.
virginitas non tota tua est, ex parte parentum est,
tertia pars patrist, pars est data tertia matri,
tertia sola tua est: noli pugnare duobus,
qui genero sua iura simul cum dote dederunt.   65
Hymen o Hymenaee, Hymen ades o Hymenaee!
(Catullus 62)

60

Mercuri, facunde nepos Atlantis,
qui feros cultus hominum recentum
voce formasti catus et decorae
    more palaestrae,

te canam, magni Iovis et deorum   5
nuntium curvaeque lyrae parentem,
callidum quidquid placuit iocoso
    condere furto.

te, boves olim nisi reddidisses
per dolum amotas, puerum minaci   10
voce dum terret, viduus pharetra
    risit Apollo.

quin et Atridas duce te superbos
Ilio dives Priamus relicto
Thessalosque ignis et iniqua Troiae   15
    castra fefellit.

tu pias laetis animas reponis
sedibus virgaque levem coerces
aurea turbam, superis deorum
    gratus et imis.   20
        (Horace, Odes *I 10)*

61

Dianam tenerae dicite virgines,
intonsum, pueri, dicite Cynthium
    Latonamque supremo
        dilectam penitus Iovi.

vos laetam fluviis et nemorum coma,   5
quaecumque aut gelido prominet Algido
    nigris aut Erymanthi
        silvis aut viridis Cragi.

vos Tempe totidem tollite laudibus
natalemque, mares, Delon Apollinis,   10
    insignemque pharetra
        fraternaque umerum lyra.

hic bellum lacrimosum, hic miseram famem
pestemque a populo et principe Caesare in
    Persas atque Britannos   15
        vestra motus aget prece.
                (*Horace*, Odes *I 21*)

62

O fons Bandusiae splendidior vitro
dulci digne mero non sine floribus,
    cras donaberis haedo,
        cui frons turgida cornibus

primis et venerem et proelia destinat;   5
frustra: nam gelidos inficiet tibi
    rubro sanguine rivos
        lascivi suboles gregis.

te flagrantis atrox hora Caniculae
nescit tangere, tu frigus amabile   10
    fessis vomere tauris
        praebes et pecori vago.

fies nobilium tu quoque fontium,
me dicente cavis impositam ilicem
    saxis, unde loquaces   15
        lymphae desiliunt tuae.
                (*Horace*, Odes *III 13*)

63

O nata mecum consule Manlio,
seu tu querelas sive geris iocos
   seu rixam et insanos amores
     seu facilem, pia testa, somnum,

quocumque lectum nomine Massicum 5
servas, moveri digna bono die,
   descende, Corvino iubente
     promere languidiora vina.

non ille, quamquam Socraticis madet
sermonibus, te negleget horridus: 10
   narratur et prisci Catonis
     saepe mero caluisse virtus.

tu lene tormentum ingenio admoves
plerumque duro; tu sapientium
   curas et arcanum iocoso 15
     consilium retegis Lyaeo;

tu spem reducis mentibus anxiis,
virisque et addis cornua pauperi
   post te neque iratos trementi
     regum apices neque militum arma. 20

te Liber et, si laeta aderit, Venus
segnesque nodum solvere Gratiae
   vivaeque producent lucernae,
     dum rediens fugat astra Phoebus.
        (*Horace*, Odes *III 21*)

64

Caelo supinas si tuleris manus
nascente Luna, rustica Phidyle,
   si ture placaris et horna
     fruge Lares avidaque porca,

nec pestilentem sentiet Africum 5
fecunda vitis nec sterilem seges
   robiginem aut dulces alumni
     pomifero grave tempus anno.

nam quae nivali pascitur Algido
devota quercus inter et ilices
   aut crescit Albanis in herbis
      victima pontificum securis

cervice tinget: te nihil attinet
temptare multa caede bidentium
   parvos coronantem marino
      rore deos fragilique myrto.

immunis aram si tetigit manus,
non sumptuosa blandior hostia
   mollivit aversos Penatis
      farre pio et saliente mica.
        (*Horace*, Odes *III 23*)

65

Dive, quem proles Niobea magnae
vindicem linguae Tityosque raptor
sensit et Troiae prope victor altae
   Phthius Achilles,

ceteris maior, tibi miles impar,
filius quamvis Thetidis marinae
Dardanas turris quateret tremenda
   cuspide pugnax.

ille, mordaci velut icta ferro
pinus aut impulsa cupressus Euro,
procidit late posuitque collum in
   pulvere Teucro.

ille non inclusus equo Minervae
sacra mentito male feriatos
Troas et laetam Priami choreis
   falleret aulam;

sed palam captis gravis, heu nefas! !heu
nescios fari pueros Achivis
ureret flammis, etiam latentem
   matris in alvo,

ni tuis victus Venerisque gratae
vocibus divum pater adnuisset
rebus Aeneae potiore ductos
   alite muros.

doctor argutae fidicen Thaliae, 25
Phoebe, qui Xantho lavis amne crines,
Dauniae defende decus Camenae,
    levis Agyieu.

spiritum Phoebus mihi, Phoebus artem
carminis nomenque dedit poetae. 30
virginum primae puerique claris
    patribus orti,

Deliae tutela deae fugaces
lyncas et cervos cohibentis arcu,
Lesbium servate pedem meique 35
    pollicis ictum,

rite Latonae puerum canentes,
rite crescentem face Noctilucam,
prosperam frugum celeremque pronos
    volvere mensis. 40

nupta iam dices 'ego dis amicum,
saeculo festas referente luces,
reddidi carmen, docilis modorum
    vatis Horati.'
             (*Horace*, Odes *IV 6*)

III National and Political Lyric

Horace shared the defeat of Brutus and Cassius at Philippi in 42 B.C., and knew the ignominy and privations attaching to the losing side in the Civil War period. His property at Venusia was confiscated. However, through the clemency of Octavian and the Second Triumvirate he was able to find employment as a Treasury Clerk (*scriba quaestorius*) in the Temple of Saturn at Rome. After his admission to the circle of Maecenas *c.* 38 B.C., his art was ostensibly enlisted on the side of the Establishment, but not in practice. Though personally associated with Maecenas and the other peacemakers in 37 B.C. (*Sat.* I 5: The Journey to Brundisium), his political involvements were probably very limited. After Actium (31 B.C.), an event which Horace claims to have witnessed, the cool detachment of his earlier years, perhaps the product of his uncertainty about the respective merits of Antony and Octavian, perhaps too the result of his personal disaster, yielded to varying moods of excitement, anxiety and surrender, especially after the 'Restoration of the Republic' in 27 B.C. The *Odes*, Books I–III (30–23 B.C.) are marked by tension between Horace's Epicurean and Augustan sentiments, between *Respublica* and *Otium*, and between his Republican and Augustan sympathies. Though ready to accept the major changes after Philippi, he was never an avowed propagandist of the New Order, and always expressed his reluctance to write on heroic themes which might have magnified the architects of the New Rome and the formulators of its policies. Nevertheless Augustus remained the one hope of peace. The deeply ingrained and widely felt feeling of guilt, product of the century of civil war, required a redeemer, and only Augustus had survived. So in *Odes* I 2 (66) Horace proclaims that only Octavian can expiate the Civil Wars and usher in the Golden Age, a dream which Horace had imagined as early as *Epode* 16, where the Isles of the Blest symbolized his hopes of one day entering upon a land of wisdom and poetry and peace.

Of the eighty-eight odes in Books I–III only thirteen refer directly to the Princeps; and in *Odes* I 12 Augustus is measured against the celebrated heroes of the past with no positive affirmation of hope or eulogy of the Emperor's achievements. Repeatedly in the *Odes* [I 6 (5); II 12; II 1 (6); III 3] Horace asserts that his Muse is incapable of flattering Augustus. And the critical note frequently enters into his *Odes*, implying that Augustus has major responsibilities to perform on behalf of the state: that he should abandon the Arabian campaign to chastise the Parthians [*Odes* I 29(44)], that he should end the menace of a recurrence of civil war, rehabilitate religion, and restore morality. Besides there are frequent mentions of dire acts by the princeps: the crushing of *virtus* at Philippi (*Odes* II 7 (45), lines 9 f.), confiscations after the victory (*Odes* II 18, lines 26 f.), and the appropriation of Egyptian wealth (*Odes* II 2, lines 21 f.).

It is hard to tell when Horace is giving voice to his own personal estimate of the principate, and when he is reflecting the popular view. But Horace's conception of himself as *vates* – priest-bard and visionary – lifted him to a higher plane, and as representative spokesman of popular feeling he is fully convinced of the efficacy of poetry to provide counsel and support to the imperial aims. Octavian, as he remarks in *Odes* III 4 (71), lines 41 f., should harken to the *lene consilium* of the Muses.

The Roman Odes (*Odes* III 1–6) are, of course, the major statement by Horace on the contemporary political situation. Together they form a kind of literary testament to the Augustan order, and the symmetry is suggestive. Both *Odes* III 1 (70) – Simplicity and Contentment – and III 2 – Military *Virtus* – are brilliant philosophical expositions of the salutary effects of work and discipline, suggesting that *paupertas* (limited means) provides the best training for a strict, disciplined life; *Odes* III 3 – *Iustitia* – and III 4 (71) – *Lene Consilium* – are central in the design, and emphasize the importance of Rome and Augustus; in *Odes* III 5 (72) – Military *Virtus* – Horace abandons the philosophical approach of *Odes* III 2 in favour of the historic, and contrasts the shame of the present with the glories of the past; and finally in *Odes* III 6 (73) – Piety and Chastity – Horace again adopts the historical viewpoint and draws an unflattering contrast between present and past morality.

Patterns easily emerge: the first three odes are general, dealing primarily with Rome; the remaining three are more specific, and are concerned with Augustus (III 4), his military (III 5) and religious and social policies (III 6). Both groups introduce Horace as *Musarum sacerdos* and both rise to a minatory and vaguely pessimistic note at the close: III 3 ends on a positive but warning note, while III 6 (73) is negative, with a strong word of warning, almost of reproach.

Horace seems much less enthusiastic than Vergil in his estimate and support of the Augustan regime. All the Roman Odes are critical and corrective, and protest that Augustus' record is less than perfect in 23 B.C. Horace is anxious to issue a warning against the dangers of power and its tendency to corrupt, and to assert the right of the private individual in the makeup of a stable and happy state.

Certainly no major conversion to Augustan ideas can be detected in *Odes* I–III. Reluctance and a perfunctory allegiance are more often present than are outright eulogy and acceptance. The publication of the first three books of *Odes* in 23 B.C. was not greeted with universal enthusiasm, and Marcus Agrippa may have been publicly antagonistic to the sentiments expressed and Horace's manner of expressing them (cf *Epist.* I 19: II 1). After Maecenas' eclipse and withdrawal from the political scene, and after the political dismay attendant on the death of Murena and of the young Marcellus, heir-apparent and son-in-law of Augustus in 23 B.C., Horace turned to literary criticism and philosophy as his major concerns. The recovery of the Parthian standards in 20 B.C. by diplomatic manoeuvres rather than by war, a case of Augustan 'peace with honour', must have encouraged Horace. The limited success of Augustus' social reforms in 18 B.C., reforms which Horace had advocated in the first three books of the *Odes*, may have induced him to affirm his enthusiasm and confidence in the regime, for in 17 B.C., two years after Vergil's death, he assumed the role of panegyrist of the State. The *Carmen Saeculare* is a hymn to the achievements of Augustus in the fields of morality, civic order, international politics, and religion. The fourth book of *Odes* is free of tension and markedly eulogistic in tone. The spectre of civil war which had disturbed him repeatedly in his earlier odes was now finally laid to rest (contrast *Odes* I 2 (66), lines 21-4; I 35, lines 33-8; I 21 (61), lines 1-8, 29-36; III 24, lines 25 f.). Horace seems to have become aware that the Civil Law was functioning effectively, and to the inhabitants of Italy this had always been a matter of prime concern. The Italians have always shown a disposition to believe not so much in any abstract theory of government as in a system that works, and the Augustan system did work. Horace was ready to admit that the Golden Age had dawned again, and that Augustus was in fact Apollo incarnate (*Odes* IV 2, line 6).

For additional discussion consult:

G. E. Duckworth, '*Animae dimidium meae*: two poets of Rome', in *TAPA* 87 (1956) 281-316.

B. Fenik, 'Horace's Roman Odes and the Second Georgic', in *Hermes* 90 (1962) 72-96.

R. J. Getty, 'Romulus, Roma and Augustus in the sixth book of the *Aeneid*', in *CP* 45 (1950) 1-12.

V. Pöschl, *Horaz und die Politik*. Heidelberg, 1956; 2nd edition, 1961.

66

Iam satis terris nivis atque dirae
grandinis misit Pater et rubente
dextera sacras iaculatus arces
    terruit urbem,

terruit gentis, grave ne rediret 5
saeculum Pyrrhae nova monstra questae,
omne cum Proteus pecus egit altos
    visere montis,

piscium et summa genus haesit ulmo
nota quae sedes fuerat columbis, 10
et superiecto pavidae natarunt
    aequore dammae.

NATIONAL AND POLITICAL LYRIC

vidimus flavum Tiberim retortis
litore Etrusco violenter undis
ire deiectum monumenta regis 15
    templaque Vestae,

Iliae dum se nimium querenti
iactat ultorem, vagus et sinistra
labitur ripa Iove non probante u-
    xorius amnis. 20

audiet civis acuisse ferrum
quo graves Persae melius perirent,
audiet pugnas vitio parentum
    rara iuventus.

quem vocet divum populus ruentis 25
imperi rebus? prece qua fatigent
virgines sanctae minus audientem
    carmina Vestam?

cui dabit partis scelus expiandi
Iuppiter? tandem venias precamur 30
nube candentis umeros amictus,
    augur Apollo;

sive tu mavis, Erycina ridens,
quam Iocus circum volat et Cupido;
sive neglectum genus et nepotes 35
    respicis auctor,

heu nimis longo satiate ludo,
quem iuvat clamor galeaeque leves
acer et Mauri peditis cruentum
    vultus in hostem; 40

sive mutata iuvenem figura
ales in terris imitaris almae
filius Maiae patiens vocari
    Caesaris ultor:

serus in caelum redeas diuque 45
laetus intersis populo Quirini,
neve te nostris vitiis iniquum
    ocior aura

tollat; hic magnos potius triumphos,
hic ames dici pater atque princeps, 50
neu sinas Medos equitare inultos
    te duce, Caesar.

        (*Horace*, Odes *I 2*)

67

Laudabunt alii claram Rhodon aut Mytilenen
    aut Epheson bimarisve Corinthi
moenia vel Baccho Thebas vel Apolline Delphos
    insignis aut Thessala Tempe:
sunt quibus unum opus est intactae Palladis urbem 5
    carmine perpetuo celebrare et
undique decerptam fronti praeponere olivam:
    plurimus in Iunonis honorem
aptum dicet equis Argos ditisque Mycenas:
    me nec tam patiens Lacedaemon 10
nec tam Larisae percussit campus opimae,
    quam domus Albuneae resonantis
et praeceps Anio ac Tiburni lucus et uda
    mobilibus pomaria rivis.
albus ut obscuro deterget nubila caelo 15
    saepe Notus neque parturit imbris
perpetuo, sic tu sapiens finire memento
    tristitiam vitaeque labores
molli, Plance, mero, seu te fulgentia signis
    castra tenent seu densa tenebit 20
Tiburis umbra tui. Teucer Salamina patremque
    cum fugeret, tamen uda Lyaeo
tempora populea fertur vinxisse corona,
    sic tristis adfatus amicos:
'quo nos cumque feret melior fortuna parente, 25
    ibimus, o socii comitesque.
nil desperandum Teucro duce et auspice: Teucri
    certus enim promisit Apollo
ambiguam tellure nova Salamina futuram.
    o fortes peioraque passi 30
mecum saepe viri, nunc vino pellite curas;
    cras ingens iterabimus aequor.'
(Horace, Odes I 7)

68

O navis, referent in mare te novi
    fluctus! o quid agis? fortiter occupa
        portum! nonne vides ut
            nudum remigio latus,

et malus celeri saucius Africo,
antennaeque gemant, ac sine funibus
    vix durare carinae
        possint imperiosius

aequor? non tibi sunt integra lintea,
non di quos iterum pressa voces malo.
    quamvis Pontica pinus,
        silvae filia nobilis,

iactes et genus et nomen inutile,
nil pictis timidus navita puppibus
    fidit. tu, nisi ventis
        debes ludibrium, cave.

nuper sollicitum quae mihi taedium,
nunc desiderium curaque non levis,
    interfusa nitentis
        vites aequora Cycladas.
            (*Horace*, Odes *I 14*)

69

Nunc est bibendum, nunc pede libero
pulsanda tellus, nunc Saliaribus
    ornare pulvinar deorum
        tempus erat dapibus, sodales.

antehac nefas depromere Caecubum
cellis avitis, dum Capitolio
    regina dementis ruinas
        funus et imperio parabat

contaminato cum grege turpium
morbo virorum, quidlibet impotens
    sperare fortunaque dulci
        ebria. sed minuit furorem

vix una sospes navis ab ignibus,
mentemque lymphatam Mareotico
    redegit in veros timores
        Caesar ab Italia volantem

remis adurgens, accipiter velut
mollis columbas aut leporem citus
    venator in campis nivalis
        Haemoniae, daret ut catenis

fatale monstrum; quae generosius
perire quaerens nec muliebriter
　　expavit ensem nec latentis
　　　　classe cita reparavit oras;

ausa et iacentem visere regiam　　　　　　　　　25
vultu sereno, fortis et asperas
　　tractare serpentis, ut atrum
　　　　corpore combiberet venenum,

deliberata morte ferocior,
saevis Liburnis scilicet invidens　　　　　　　　30
　　privata deduci superbo
　　　　non humilis mulier triumpho.

　　　　　　　　(*Horace*, Odes *I 37*)

70

Odi profanum vulgus et arceo;
favete linguis: carmina non prius
　　audita Musarum sacerdos
　　　　virginibus puerisque canto.

regum timendorum in proprios greges,　　　　5
reges in ipsos imperium est Iovis,
　　clari Giganteo triumpho,
　　　　cuncta supercilio moventis.

est ut viro vir latius ordinet
arbusta sulcis, hic generosior　　　　　　　　　10
　　descendat in Campum petitor,
　　　　moribus hic meliorque fama

contendat, illi turba clientium
sit maior: aequa lege Necessitas
　　sortitur insignis et imos;　　　　　　　　　15
　　　　omne capax movet urna nomen.

destrictus ensis cui super impia
cervice pendet, non Siculae dapes
　　dulcem elaborabunt saporem,
　　　　non avium citharaeque cantus　　　　20

somnum reducent: somnus agrestium
lenis virorum non humilis domos
　　fastidit umbrosamque ripam,
　　　　non Zephyris agitata Tempe.

desiderantem quod satis est neque 25
tumultuosum sollicitat mare
   nec saevus Arcturi cadentis
      impetus aut orientis Haedi,
non verberatae grandine vineae
fundusque mendax, arbore nunc aquas 30
   culpante, nunc torrentia agros
      sidera, nunc hiemes iniquas.
contracta pisces aequora sentiunt
iactis in altum molibus; huc frequens
   caementa demittit redemptor 35
      cum famulis dominusque terrae
fastidiosus: sed Timor et Minae
scandunt eodem quo dominus, neque
   decedit aerata triremi et
      post equitem sedet atra Cura. 40
quodsi dolentem nec Phrygius lapis
nec purpurarum sidere clarior
   delenit usus nec Falerna
      vitis Achaemeniumque costum,
cur invidendis postibus et novo 45
sublime ritu moliar atrium?
   cur valle permutem Sabina
      divitias operosiores?
         (*Horace*, Odes *III 1*)

71

Descende caelo et dic age tibia
regina longum Calliope melos,
   seu voce nunc mavis acuta,
      seu fidibus citharave Phoebi.
auditis an me ludit amabilis 5
insania? audire et videor pios
   errare per lucos, amoenae
      quos et aquae subeunt et aurae.
me fabulosae Vulture in Apulo
nutricis extra limen Apuliae 10
   ludo fatigatumque somno
      fronde nova puerum palumbes

texere, mirum quod foret omnibus,
quicumque celsae nidum Acherontiae
    saltusque Bantinos et arvum 15
        pingue tenent humilis Forenti,

ut tuto ab atris corpore viperis
dormirem et ursis, ut premerer sacra
    lauroque collataque myrto,
        non sine dis animosus infans. 20

vester, Camenae, vester in arduos
tollor Sabinos, seu mihi frigidum
    Praeneste seu Tibur supinum
        seu liquidae placuere Baiae.

vestris amicum fontibus et choris 25
non me Philippis versa acies retro,
    devota non exstinxit arbos,
        nec Sicula Palinurus unda.

utcumque mecum vos eritis, libens
insanientem navita Bosphorum 30
    temptabo et urentis harenas
        litoris Assyrii viator,

visam Britannos hospitibus feros
et laetum equino sanguine Concanum,
    visam pharetratos Gelonos 35
        et Scythicum inviolatus amnem.

vos Caesarem altum, militia simul
fessas cohortis abdidit oppidis,
    finire quaerentem labores
        Pierio recreatis antro. 40

vos lene consilium et datis et dato
gaudetis almae. scimus ut impios
    Titanas immanemque turbam
        fulmine sustulerit caduco,

qui terram inertem, qui mare temperat 45
ventosum, et urbes regnaque tristia
    divosque mortalisque turmas
        imperio regit unus aequo.

magnum illa terrorem intulerat Iovi
fidens iuventus horrida bracchiis 50
    fratresque tendentes opaco
        Pelion imposuisse Olympo.

sed quid Typhoeus et validus Mimas,
aut quid minaci Porphyrion statu,
    quid Rhoetus evulsisque truncis 55
        Enceladus iaculator audax

contra sonantem Palladis aegida
possent ruentes ? hinc avidus stetit
    Vulcanus, hinc matrona Iuno et
        numquam umeris positurus arcum, 60

qui rore puro Castaliae lavit
crinis solutos, qui Lyciae tenet
    dumeta natalemque silvam,
        Delius et Patareus Apollo.

vis consili expers mole ruit sua: 65
vim temperatam di quoque provehunt
    in maius; idem odere viris
        omne nefas animo moventis.

testis mearum centimanus Gyas
sententiarum, notus et integrae 70
    temptator Orion Dianae,
        virginea domitus sagitta.

iniecta monstris Terra dolet suis
maeretque partus fulmine luridum
    missos ad Orcum; nec peredit 75
        impositam celer ignis Aetnen,

incontinentis nec Tityi iecur
reliquit ales, nequitiae additus
    custos; amatorem trecentae
        Perithoum cohibent catenae. 80
           (*Horace*, *Odes III 4*)

72

Caelo tonantem credidimus Iovem
regnare: praesens divus habebitur
    Augustus adiectis Britannis
        imperio gravibusque Persis.

milesne Crassi coniuge barbara 5
turpis maritus vixit et hostium –
 pro curia inversique mores! –
  consenuit socerorum in armis

sub rege Medo Marsus et Apulus,
anciliorum et nominis et togae 10
 oblitus aeternaeque Vestae,
  incolumi Iove et urbe Roma?

hoc caverat mens provida Reguli
dissentientis condicionibus
 foedis et exemplo trahentis 15
  perniciem veniens in aevum,

si non periret immiserabilis
captiva pubes. 'signa ego Punicis
 adfixa delubris et arma
  militibus sine caede' dixit 20

'derepta vidi; vidi ego civium
retorta tergo bracchia libero
 portasque non clausas et arva
  Marte coli populata nostro.

auro repensus scilicet acrior 25
miles redibit. flagitio additis
 damnum: neque amissos colores
  lana refert medicata fuco,

nec vera virtus, cum semel excidit,
curat reponi deterioribus. 30
 si pugnat extricata densis
  cerva plagis, erit ille fortis

qui perfidis se credidit hostibus,
et Marte Poenos proteret altero,
 qui lora restrictis lacertis 35
  sensit iners timuitque mortem.

hic, unde vitam sumeret inscius,
pacem duello miscuit. o pudor!
 o magna Carthago, probrosis
  altior Italiae ruinis!' 40

fertur pudicae coniugis osculum
parvosque natos ut capitis minor
 ab se removisse et virilem
  torvus humi posuisse vultum,

donec labantis consilio patres 45
firmaret auctor numquam alias dato,
 interque maerentis amicos
  egregius properaret exsul.

atqui sciebat quae sibi barbarus
tortor pararet; non aliter tamen 50
 dimovit obstantis propinquos
  et populum reditus morantem

quam si clientum longa negotia
diiudicata lite relinqueret,
 tendens Venafranos in agros 55
  aut Lacedaemonium Tarentum.
   (*Horace*, Odes *III* 5)

73

Delicta maiorum immeritus lues,
Romane, donec templa refeceris
 aedesque labentis deorum et
  foeda nigro simulacra fumo.

dis te minorem quod geris, imperas: 5
hinc omne principium, huc refer exitum:
 di multa neglecti dederunt
  Hesperiae mala luctuosae.

iam bis Monaeses et Pacori manus
non auspicatos contudit impetus 10
 nostros et adiecisse praedam
  torquibus exiguis renidet.

paene occupatam seditionibus
delevit urbem Dacus et Aethiops,
 hic classe formidatus, ille 15
  missilibus melior sagittis.

fecunda culpae saecula nuptias
primum inquinavere et genus et domos;
 hoc fonte derivata clades
  in patriam populumque fluxit. 20

motus doceri gaudet Ionicos
matura virgo et fingitur artibus
    iam nunc et incestos amores
        de tenero meditatur ungui;

mox iuniores quaerit adulteros   25
inter mariti vina, neque eligit
    cui donet impermissa raptim
        gaudia luminibus remotis,

sed iussa coram non sine conscio
surgit marito, seu vocat institor   30
    seu navis Hispanae magister,
        dedecorum pretiosus emptor.

non his iuventus orta parentibus
infecit aequor sanguine Punico,
    Pyrrhumque et ingentem cecidit   35
        Antiochum Hannibalemque dirum,

sed rusticorum mascula militum
proles, Sabellis docta ligonibus
    versare glebas et severae
        matris ad arbitrium recisos   40

portare fustis, sol ubi montium
mutaret umbras et iuga demeret
    bobus fatigatis, amicum
        tempus agens abeunte curru.

damnosa quid non imminuit dies?   45
aetas parentum peior avis tulit
    nos nequiores, mox daturos
        progeniem vitiosiorem.
                    (*Horace*, Odes *III 6*)

74

Herculis ritu modo dictus, o plebs,
morte venalem petiisse laurum
Caesar Hispana repetit penatis
    victor ab ora.

unico gaudens mulier marito   5
prodeat iustis operata divis,
et soror clari ducis et decorae
    supplice vitta

virginum matres iuvenumque nuper
sospitum. vos, o pueri et puellae   10
iam virum expertae, male ominatis
    parcite verbis.

hic dies vere mihi festus atras
eximet curas; ego nec tumultum
nec mori per vim metuam tenente   15
    Caesare terras.

i pete unguentum, puer, et coronas
et cadum Marsi memorem duelli,
Spartacum si qua potuit vagantem
    fallere testa.   20

dic et argutae properet Neaerae
murreum nodo cohibere crinem;
si per invisum mora ianitorem
    fiet, abito.

lenit albescens animos capillus   25
litium et rixae cupidos protervae;
non ego hoc ferrem calidus iuventa
    consule Planco.

          (*Horace*, Odes *III 14*)

75

Divis orte bonis, optime Romulae
custos gentis, abes iam nimium diu;
maturum reditum pollicitus patrum
    sancto concilio, redi.

lucem redde tuae, dux bone, patriae: 5
instar veris enim vultus ubi tuus
adfulsit populo, gratior it dies
    et soles melius nitent.

ut mater iuvenem, quem Notus invido
flatu Carpathii trans maris aequora   10
cunctantem spatio longius annuo
    dulci distinet a domo,

votis ominibusque et precibus vocat,
curvo nec faciem litore dimovet:
sic desideriis icta fidelibus   15
    quaerit patria Caesarem.

tutus bos etenim rura perambulat,
nutrit rura Ceres almaque Faustitas,
pacatum volitant per mare navitae,
    culpari metuit fides, 20

nullis polluitur casta domus stupris,
mos et lex maculosum edomuit nefas,
laudantur simili prole puerperae,
    culpam poena premit comes.

quis Parthum paveat, quis gelidum Scythen, 25
quis Germania quos horrida parturit
fetus, incolumi Caesare? quis ferae
    bellum curet Hiberiae?

condit quisque diem collibus in suis,
et vitem viduas ducit ad arbores; 30
hinc ad vina redit laetus et alteris
    te mensis adhibet deum;

te multa prece, te prosequitur mero
defuso pateris et Laribus tuum
miscet numen, uti Graecia Castoris 35
    et magni memor Herculis.

'longas o utinam, dux bone, ferias
praestes Hesperiae!' dicimus integro
sicci mane die, dicimus uvidi,
    cum sol Oceano subest. 40
              (*Horace*, Odes *IV* 5)

76

Phoebus volentem proelia me loqui
victas et urbis increpuit lyra,
    ne parva Tyrrhenum per aequor
        vela darem. tua, Caesar, aetas

fruges et agris rettulit uberes, 5
et signa nostro restituit Iovi
    derepta Parthorum superbis
        postibus et vacuum duellis

Ianum Quirini clausit et ordinem
rectum evaganti frena licentiae 10
    iniecit emovitque culpas
        et veteres revocavit artis,

per quas Latinum nomen et Italae
crevere vires, famaque et imperi
    porrecta maiestas ad ortus 15
        solis ab Hesperio cubili.

custode rerum Caesare non furor
civilis aut vis exiget otium,
    non ira, quae procudit ensis
        et miseras inimicat urbis. 20

non qui profundum Danuvium bibunt
edicta rumpent Iulia, non Getae,
    non Seres infidive Persae,
        non Tanain prope flumen orti.

nosque et profestis lucibus et sacris 25
inter iocosi munera Liberi
    cum prole matronisque nostris,
        rite deos prius apprecati,

virtute functos more patrum duces
Lydis remixto carmine tibiis 30
    Troiamque et Anchisen et almae
        progeniem Veneris canemus.
                (*Horace*, Odes *IV 15*)

IV Humorous and Experimental Lyric

    Scribens versiculos uterque nostrum
    ludebat numero modo hoc modo illoc,
    reddens mutua per iocum atque vinum.
               (Catullus 50 (2), lines 4–6)

For Catullus and his friends poetry was almost a way of life, and life was not always lived at its fullest and deepest; it had many lighter moments. Poetry became, at times, a game, a form of play, a friendly competition; experiment in new forms and untried metres offered challenges for developing talents.

    The members of the circle regarded themselves with a certain seriousness; they were perhaps somewhat consciously sophisticated, *avant-garde*. Having little time or use for politics themselves, they looked upon the scrambling politicians of their time as fit butts for their invective. Social misfits and literary hacks who offended their standards of what was *venustum, lepidum, urbanum* and *facetum,* drew their satiric fire. The level of most of Catullus' efforts in this line is not high; much is little more than versified anecdote; still it affords us amusing insights into the personalities of the society in which he and his friends moved and into the values of their circle.

In the rich heritage of the Alexandrians Catullus found many models to tempt him to experiment – new forms, untried metres. His most ambitious essays – *The Marriage of Peleus and Thetis* (64), in which he attempted the epic manner after the Alexandrian *epyllion*, and *Attis* (63), an excited treatment in galliambics of the self-castration of a youth in honour of the Oriental goddess Cybele – have not been included here because of their length. But *Phaselus ille* [4 (77)] is a notably successful experiment in pure iambic trimeter, which has stirred scholarly debate about both its intentions and its literary antecedents; *O Colonia* [17 (79)] is one of the few surviving poems in Latin in the Priapean metre; while in *Acme and Septimius* [45 (83)], with its careful balance and refrain, he seems to be reaching towards the ballad form.

While it was Horace's proud boast that he was the first to introduce Aeolian measures to Italian song, he also experimented in new forms. In spite of his modest denial that epic was for him, he attempts the epic manner in *Pastor cum traheret* [*Odes* I 15]; *O matre pulchra* [*Odes* I 16 (88)] may represent an experiment in the palinode, looking back to the early Greek poet Stesichorus; in *Donec gratus* [*Odes* III 9 (91)] he may owe inspiration to Catullus' *Acme and Septimius*.

77

Phaselus ille, quem videtis, hospites,
ait fuisse navium celerrimus,
neque ullius natantis impetum trabis
nequisse praeterire, sive palmulis
opus foret volare sive linteo.   5
et hoc negat minacis Hadriatici
negare litus insulasve Cycladas
Rhodumque nobilem horridamque Thraciam
Propontida trucemve Ponticum sinum,
ubi iste post phaselus antea fuit   10
comata silva; nam Cytorio in iugo
loquente saepe sibilum edidit coma.
Amastri Pontica et Cytore buxifer,
tibi haec fuisse et esse cognitissima

ait phaselus: ultima ex origine
tuo stetisse dicit in cacumine,
tuo imbuisse palmulas in aequore,
et inde tot per impotentia freta
erum tulisse, laeva sive dextera
vocaret aura, sive utrumque Iuppiter
simul secundus incidisset in pedem;
neque ulla vota litoralibus deis
sibi esse facta, cum veniret a mari
novissimo hunc ad usque limpidum lacum.
sed haec prius fuere: nunc recondita
senet quiete seque dedicat tibi,
gemelle Castor et gemelle Castoris.
(Catullus 4)

78

Varus me meus ad suos amores
visum duxerat e foro otiosum,
scortillum, ut mihi tum repente visum est,
non sane illepidum neque invenustum.
huc ut venimus, incidere nobis
sermones varii, in quibus, quid esset
iam Bithynia, quo modo se haberet,
et quonam mihi profuisset aere.
respondi id quod erat, nihil neque ipsis
nec praetoribus esse nec cohorti,
cur quisquam caput unctius referret,
praesertim quibus esset irrumator
praetor, nec faceret pili cohortem.
'at certe tamen,' inquiunt 'quod illic
natum dicitur esse, comparasti
ad lecticam homines.' ego, ut puellae
unum me facerem beatiorem,
'non' inquam 'mihi tam fuit maligne,
ut, provincia quod mala incidisset,
non possem octo homines parare rectos.'
at mi nullus erat nec hic neque illic,
fractum qui veteris pedem grabati
in collo sibi collocare posset.
hic illa, ut decuit cinaediorem,
'quaeso', inquit 'mihi, mi Catulle, paulum

istos commoda: nam volo ad Serapim
deferri.' 'mane,' inquii puellae,
'istud quod modo dixeram me habere,
fugit me ratio: meus sodalis –
Cinna est Gaius, – is sibi paravit. 30
verum, utrum illius an mei, quid ad me?
utor tam bene quam mihi pararim.
sed tu insulsa male et molesta vivis,
per quam non licet esse neglegentem.'
(*Catullus 10*)

79

O Colonia, quae cupis ponte ludere longo
et salire paratum habes, sed vereris inepta
crura ponticuli axulis stantis in redivivis,
ne supinus eat cavaque in palude recumbat:
sic tibi bonus ex tua pons libidine fiat, 5
in quo vel Salisubsali sacra suscipiantur,
munus hoc mihi maximi da, Colonia, risus.
quendam municipem meum de tuo volo ponte
ire praecipitem in lutum per caputque pedesque,
verum totius ut lacus putidaeque paludis 10
lividissima maximeque est profunda vorago.
insulsissimus est homo, nec sapit pueri instar
bimuli tremula patris dormientis in ulna.
cui cum sit viridissimo nupta flore puella
et puella tenellulo delicatior haedo, 15
adservanda nigerrimis diligentius uvis,
ludere hanc sinit ut lubet, nec pili facit uni,
nec se sublevat ex sua parte, sed velut alnus
in fossa Liguri iacet suppernata securi,
tantundem omnia sentiens quam si nulla sit usquam; 20
talis iste meus stupor nil videt, nihil audit,
ipse qui sit, utrum sit an non sit, id quoque nescit.
nunc eum volo de tuo ponte mittere pronum,
si pote stolidum repente excitare veternum,
et supinum animum in gravi derelinquere caeno, 25
ferream ut soleam tenaci in voragine mula.
(*Catullus 17*)

80

Furi, villula vestra non ad Austri
flatus opposita est neque ad Favoni
nec saevi Boreae aut Apheliotae,
verum ad milia quindecim et ducentos.
o ventum horribilem atque pestilentem! 5
              (*Catullus 26*)

81

Egnatius, quod candidos habet dentes,
renidet usque quaque. si ad rei ventum est
subsellium, cum orator excitat fletum,
renidet ille; si ad pii rogum fili
lugetur, orba cum flet unicum mater, 5
renidet ille. quidquid est, ubicumque est,
quodcumque agit, renidet: hunc habet morbum,
neque elegantem, ut arbitror, neque urbanum.
quare monendum est (te) mihi, bone Egnati.
si urbanus esses aut Sabinus aut Tiburs 10
aut pinguis Umber aut obesus Etruscus
aut Lanuvinus ater atque dentatus
aut Transpadanus, ut meos quoque attingam,
aut quilubet, qui puriter lavit dentes,
tamen renidere usque quaque te nollem: 15
nam risu inepto res ineptior nulla est.
nunc Celtiber (es): Celtiberia in terra,
quod quisque minxit, hoc sibi solet mane
dentem atque russam defricare gingivam,
ut, quo iste vester expolitior dens est, 20
hoc te amplius bibisse praedicet loti.
              (*Catullus 39*)

82

O funde noster seu Sabine seu Tiburs
(nam te esse Tiburtem autumant, quibus non est
cordi Catullum laedere; at quibus cordi est,
quovis Sabinum pignore esse contendunt),
sed seu Sabine sive verius Tiburs, 5

fui libenter in tua suburbana
villa, malamque pectore expuli tussim,
non inmerenti quam mihi meus venter,
dum sumptuosas appeto, dedit, cenas.
nam, Sestianus dum volo esse conviva, 10
orationem in Antium petitorem
plenam veneni et pestilentiae legi.
hic me gravedo frigida et frequens tussis
quassavit usque, dum in tuum sinum fugi,
et me recuravi otioque et urtica. 15
quare refectus maximas tibi grates
ago, meum quod non es ulta peccatum.
nec deprecor iam, si nefaria scripta
Sesti recepso, quin gravedinem et tussim
non mi, sed ipsi Sestio ferat frigus, 20
qui tunc vocat me, cum malum librum legi.

(*Catullus 44*)

83

Acmen Septimius suos amores
tenens in gremio 'mea' inquit 'Acme,
ni te perdite amo atque amare porro
omnes sum assidue paratus annos,
quantum qui pote plurimum perire, 5
solus in Libya Indiaque tosta
caesio veniam obvius leoni.'
hoc ut dixit, Amor sinistra ut ante
dextra sternuit approbationem.
  at Acme leviter caput reflectens 10
et dulcis pueri ebrios ocellos
illo purpureo ore suaviata,
'sic', inquit 'mea vita Septimille,
huic uni domino usque serviamus,
ut multo mihi maior acriorque 15
ignis mollibus ardet in medullis.'
hoc ut dixit, Amor sinistra ut ante
dextra sternuit approbationem.
  nunc ab auspicio bono profecti
mutuis animis amant amantur. 20
unam Septimius misellus Acmen
mavult quam Syrias Britanniasque:

HUMOROUS AND EXPERIMENTAL LYRIC

uno in Septimio fidelis Acme
facit delicias libidinesque.
quis ullos homines beatiores   25
vidit, quis Venerem auspicatiorem?
   (*Catullus 45*)

84

Disertissime Romuli nepotum,
quot sunt quotque fuere, Marce Tulli,
quotque post aliis erunt in annis,
gratias tibi maximas Catullus
agit pessimus omnium poeta,   5
tanto pessimus omnium poeta,
quanto tu optimus omnium patronus.
   (*Catullus 49*)

85

Risi nescio quem modo e corona,
qui, cum mirifice Vatiniana
meus crimina Calvos explicasset,
admirans ait haec manusque tollens,
'di magni, salaputium disertum!'   5
   (*Catullus 53*)

86

Chommoda dicebat, si quando commoda vellet
   dicere, et insidias Arrius hinsidias,
et tum mirifice sperabat se esse locutum,
   cum quantum poterat dixerat hinsidias.
credo, sic mater, sic liber avunculus eius,   5
   sic maternus avus dixerat atque avia.
hoc misso in Syriam requierant omnibus aures:
   audibant eadem haec leniter et leviter,
nec sibi postilla metuebant talia verba,
   cum subito affertur nuntius horribilis,   10
Ionios fluctus, postquam illuc Arrius isset,
   iam non Ionios esse sed Hionios.
   (*Catullus 84*)

87

Nil nimium studeo, Caesar, tibi velle placere,
nec scire utrum sis albus an ater homo.
(Catullus 93)

88

O matre pulchra filia pulchrior,
quem criminosis cumque voles modum
    pones iambis, sive flamma
        sive mari libet Hadriano.

non Dindymene, non adytis quatit   5
mentem sacerdotum incola Pythius,
    non Liber aeque, non acuta
        sic geminant Corybantes aera,

tristes ut irae, quas neque Noricus
deterret ensis nec mare naufragum   10
    nec saevus ignis nec tremendo
        Iuppiter ipse ruens tumultu.

fertur Prometheus addere principi
limo coactus particulam undique
    desectam et insani leonis   15
        vim stomacho apposuisse nostro.

irae Thyesten exitio gravi
stravere et altis urbibus ultimae
    stetere causae cur perirent
        funditus imprimeretque muris   20

hostile aratrum exercitus insolens.
compesce mentem: me quoque pectoris
    temptavit in dulci iuventa
        fervor et in celeris iambos

misit furentem: nunc ego mitibus   25
mutare quaero tristia, dum mihi
    fias recantatis amica
        opprobriis animumque reddas.
(Horace, Odes I 16)

89

O Venus, regina Cnidi Paphique,
sperne dilectam Cypron et vocantis
ture te multo Glycerae decoram
    transfer in aedem.

fervidus tecum puer et solutis 5
Gratiae zonis properentque Nymphae
et parum comis sine te Iuventas
    Mercuriusque.
              (*Horace*, Odes *I 30*)

90

Persicos odi, puer, apparatus,
displicent nexae philyra coronae;
mitte sectari, rosa quo locorum
    sera moretur.

simplici myrto nihil allabores 5
sedulus curo: neque te ministrum
dedecet myrtus neque me sub arta
    vite bibentem.
              (*Horace*, Odes *I 38*)

91

    Donec gratus eram tibi
nec quisquam potior bracchia candidae
    cervici iuvenis dabat,
Persarum vigui rege beatior.
    'donec non alia magis 5
arsisti neque erat Lydia post Chloen,
    multi Lydia nominis
Romana vigui clarior Ilia.'
    me nunc Thraessa Chloe regit,
dulcis docta modos et citharae sciens, 10
    pro qua non metuam mori,
si parcent animae fata superstiti.
    'me torret face mutua
Thurini Calais filius Ornyti,

> pro quo bis patiar mori, 15
> si parcent puero fata superstiti.'
> quid si prisca redit Venus
> diductosque iugo cogit aeneo,
> si flava excutitur Chloe
> reiectaeque patet ianua Lydiae? 20
> 'quamquam sidere pulchrior
> ille est, tu levior cortice et improbo
> iracundior Hadria,
> tecum vivere amem, tecum obeam libens.'
> (*Horace*, Odes *III 9*)

COMMENTARY

Note: *All references to the poems of Catullus and to the* Odes *of Horace within this Commentary are to the traditional numbers; when the poem also occurs in this collection, its number in this collection appears in brackets: e.g.* Cat. 1 (1); Horace, Odes I, 1 (4).

Roman Lyric Poetry

1 (CATULLUS 1) *Cui dono lepidum novum libellum*

Metre: Hendecasyllabic
Catullus dedicates his book of poems to Cornelius Nepos, the historian.

1 **dono** 'deliberative' present, a rhetorical question.
lepidum novum libellum *lepidum* is applied to behaviour and personality among Catullus' friends. *novum* suggests the freshness of the newly released volume and the novelty of its subject-matter and expression. Catullus offers lyrics in a light vein and popular idiom. *libellum* the first of many diminutives in Catullus, suggests that the 'modest' collection dedicated to Nepos was smaller than the present compilation which would fill three or four papyrus rolls. Catullus probably consigned to Nepos a collection of the shorter poems and epigrams.

2 **arida modo pumice expolitum** an allusion to book publishing. After the separate sheets (*cartae*) of papyrus had been glued together to form a roll (*volumen*), the rough ends (*frontes*) of the sheets were smoothed off with pumice and abrasive lava; then the roller (*umbilicus*) with tips (*cornua*) for handling and unrolling was inserted.

3 **Corneli, tibi** emphatic, by position.
namque tu solebas the imperfect tense suggests repeated and continuing support and encouragement of Catullus by Nepos in the face of criticism and scorn for his *nugae*.

4 **aliquid putare** 'to think (that my trifles) were really something'.
nugas 'stuff, trifles', another colloquial expression of contempt for anything stupid or worthless.

5 **iam tum** though engaged with an important work, Nepos kept insisting on Catullus' merits and rights. Nepos may have supported or patronized Catullus during his residence in Rome.

5 **unus Italorum** before Nepos, Roman history consisted of annalistic accounts of Italy or general histories of limited periods.

6 **omne aevum tribus explicare cartis** Catullus, perhaps ironically, compliments Nepos on his courageous innovation in prose of a synopsis of universal history. *explicare*, lit. 'to unfold, unroll, give a comprehensive view' in three *volumina*.

7 **doctis, Iuppiter, et laboriosis** Catullus' exclamation mingles compliment and awe with humour and candid comment. Nepos, scholarly, pedantic and industrious, has packed 'all history' into the brief compass of three rolls.

8 **quidquid hoc libelli** notice the modesty and self-effacement in expression (cf line 1: *libellum*). This apologetic tone continues with *qualecumque* (9). For the partitive genitive with *hoc* cf Vergil, *Aen.* 1, line 78: *quodcumque hoc regni*.

9 **quod, o patrona virgo** the poet does not presume to name a deity but merely requests divine favour to ensure that his work will outlive his own age and belong to posterity. The modesty is apt and Roman, for the relationship between *patronus* and *cliens* was deep-rooted in the Roman way of life, and the compliment and modest request apply to Nepos as much as the Muse.

10 **plus uno maneat** a common topic: cf Catullus 95, line 6: *Zmyrnam cana diu saecula pervoluent*.

F. O. Copley, 'Catullus i', in *TAPA* 82 (1951) 200–6.

The structural pattern of the dedicatory poem, excluding the prayer, is much favoured by Catullus [cf 6, 21, 23, 35, 44 (82), 69, 76 (26)] and lends directness and a logical reflective order to the basic simplicity of expression.

1–2 *Question:*   Cui dono...
3–4 *Answer:*   Corneli tibi...
5–7 *Reason:*   namque tu solebas...
8–9 *Conclusion:* quare habe tibi...
9–10 *Prayer:*   quod o patrona...

The poem is a superb example of Catullus' craft and language. Examine the poem for instances of anaphora, end-rhymes, alliteration, use of diminutives, colloquialisms, and mock usages. What effect do these various factors have on the poem's progress and unity?

Language, style, and sentiment combine in this poem to proclaim

Catullus' theory of lyric. Try to define his theory by a careful rereading of the poem.

2 (CATULLUS 50) *Hesterno, Licini, die otiosi*

Metre: Hendecasyllabic
Catullus writes to his friend Calvus after a meeting when they had composed epigrams in friendly competition. Catullus admired and envied his friend's lines to such a degree that he could neither eat nor sleep.

1 **otiosi** 'relaxed' cf Catullus 10 (78), line 2; 51 (10), lines 13–16.

2 **lusimus** *ludere* applied to poetry denotes the lighter forms of verse as opposed to serious poetry, epic or tragedy, or *any* poetry as distinct from the active life (*negotium, labor*). Amusement is evidently part of the poetic act. Cf Vergil, *Georg.* 4, line 565: *carmina qui lusi pastorum.*

in meis tabellis a pair or set of waxed wooden tablets designed for easy erasures and return messages and frequently used as notebooks.

3 **convenerat** impersonal ironic use. The term suggests that Catullus and Calvus will strike a formal compact for their informal behaviour.

delicatos applied to the Bohemian society of the day (cf Cicero, *Att.* I 19, 8) and denoting behaviour which is sophisticated, naughty, frivolous, and uninhibited.

5 **illoc** the suffix *c*(e) derives from earlier Latin and simply intensifies the demonstrative *illo*. Cf Catullus 3 (12), line 9: *sed circumsiliens modo huc modo illuc*; 50 (2), line 7: *illinc.*

6 **reddens mutua** implies payment of debts to one another, here a retaliatory give-and-take in poetic composition wherein one line 'caps' another.

per iocum atque vinum cf Catullus 12 (29), line 2: *in ioco atque vino.*

7 **atque** regular comic usage, 'and then, and so' to help quicken and enliven a story or account.

7–8 **lepore/incensus... facetiisque** *incensus* is part of the vocabulary of love [cf *ardor* and *dolor* (Catullus 2 (11), lines 7–8; 50 (2), line 17)], and reflects Catullus' deep-seated affection for his *amicus.* Cf the compliment to Asinius Pollio in Catullus 12 (29), lines 9–10: *leporum differtus puer ac facetiarum.* Sallust (*Catilina* 25, 5) uses similar

D

terms in connection with Sempronia: *prorsus multae facetiae multusque lepos inerat.*

11 indomitus furore passionate vocabulary more expressive of emotion than of nervous breakdown.

13 simulque ut essem colloquial. Cf Catullus 21, line 5: *simul es.*

14 labore cf Catullus 38 (33), line 2: *laboriose.*

18 audax cave sis *audax*, here equivalent to *superbus*, recalls the notion that rejection of a genuine supplication (*precesque nostras*, 18) entails punishment or ruin. *Cave*, short *e* (cf 19), frequently in the comedians and later. After *cave* Catullus uses either the simple subjunctive (18), the present infinitive (21), or the subjunctive with *ne* (61, line 145).

20 poenas Nemesis reposcat a te Nemesis is goddess of Divine Retribution required for an act of impiety or *hybris* (wanton arrogance). There is retaliation or give-and-take in Heaven as much as in the world of poetic improvisation (cf line 6: *reddens mutua*). Nemesis appears later in Ovid as the avenger of slighted love which is also suggested here (*Met.* 3, lines 406 ff.). Cf Catullus 66, line 71; 68, line 77.

Does the poet's use of the language of love add distinction to the poem?

What are the imaginative links between love-making and writing poetry?

Trace the thought-progression of the poem by a study of linkwords, repetitions, and recurrent theme.

Examine the lines for significant use of anaphora, alliteration, diminutives, colloquialisms, and formal expressions.

3 (CATULLUS 65) *Etsi me assiduo confectum cura dolore*

Metre: Elegiac Couplet

Catullus sends a poetic epistle to his friend Q. Hortensius (H)ortalus enlarging on his sorrow over his brother's death. Unable to compose the sort of poem (H)ortalus had requested, Catullus presents as substitute a translation from Callimachus, presumably his translation of the *Lock of Berenice* (66).

2 doctis ... virginibus the Muses. Cf Catullus 35, lines 16–17: *Sapphica puella,/musa doctior.*

COMMENTARY

3 **potis est** preclassical form of *potest*.

dulcis Musarum expromere fetus the offspring of the Muses defy Catullus' efforts to 'deliver' them, to bring them forth. The imagery is almost certainly related to childbirth. Others interpret *expromere* as the act of bringing out sweet fruits from a store (cf Catullus 64, line 223).

4 **mens animi** 'feelings'. Provide an emphatic meaning for the reflexive *ipsa*.

fluctuat cf Catullus 64, line 62: *magnis curarum fluctuat undis*.

5 **Lethaeo gurgite** an elaborate phrase for the 'stream' of Forgetfulness, implying the oblivion of death.

7 **Troia ... tellus** alludes to his brother's death near Troy. Cf Catullus 68, lines 89 ff.

8 **obterit** contrast the usual epitaph formula: *sit terra tibi levis*.

9 Line missing in the manuscript.

10 **vita frater amabilior** cf Catullus 64, line 215: *gnate mihi longa iucundior unice vita*.

12 **tua ... morte** governed either by *maesta* or by *canam* (ablative of external cause). Cf Catullus 14 (31), lines 2–3: *munere isto/odissem*.

13–14 The simile of the nightingale's lament is Homeric (*Odys.* 19, lines 518–23).

16 **expressa** 'translated'. Contrast *expromere* (1) 'to bring forth something new, newborn'. The metaphor in *exprimo* implies the imprint of a seal-stone, or, more likely, the modelling of a statue or *imago* (likeness) in terracotta or marble. Translation is, partly at least, an impression or likeness of the original. Cf Cicero, *Pro Archia* 6, 14: *multas nobis imagines fortissimorum virorum expressas scriptores Graeci et Latini reliquerunt*. Cf ibid., 12, 30.

carmina Battiadae Catullus submitted his translation of Callimachus' *Lock of Berenice* with his poetic apology to Hortalus.

17 **nequiquam credita** for similar pathos cf Horace, *Odes* I 3 (35), lines 5–6: *navis, quae tibi creditum/debes Vergilium*; and *Odes* I 24 (43), lines 11–12: *tu frustra pius heu non ita creditum/poscis Quintilium deos.* Horace seems indebted to Catullus in both instances.

19 **ut missum sponsi ... malum** the apple, frequently associated with Venus, is a gift from a secret lover and probably symbolizes the freshness of young love. The simile, introduced by *ut*, seems designed to suggest the tenderness and affection attached to Catullus' poetic obligations, and Hortalus' affection for the poet.

19 **furtivo munere** ablative, 'by way of a secret gift'. Cf Catullus 7 (14), line 8, *furtivos amores*; Catullus 101 (48), line 8 *tristi munere ad inferias*.

20, 21 **casto virginis e gremio ... molli sub veste locatum** the adjectives emphasize the gentle innocence of the girl; *gremio* must refer to the fold of a garment over the bosom, not to the lap.

23 **atque** for similar abruptness cf Catullus 50 (2), line 7.

23-4 **illud ... huic** the demonstratives direct the glance and point the analogy between the girl (*huic*) and the apple (*illud*).

23 **atque illud prono** Vergil, *Georg.* 1, line 203, was evidently inspired by Catullus' alliteration: *atque illum in praeceps prono rapit alveus amni*.

24 **conscius ore rubor** instance of transferred epithet. How effective? The simile may derive from Callimachus' *Aetia* ('Causes') published in 270 B.C. Borrowed or original, the simile is a masterpiece of Catullus' poetic artistry. Examine the lines (19-24) to discover effective use of metre to support sound and sense, clever use of alliteration, and linkwords of similarity and contrast. How does the simile relate to the rest of the poem?

The structure of the poem is simple, compact and balanced.

1-4 *Direct address*: grief dispels creative writing.
5-12 *Parenthesis*: My brother lies buried near Troy, an object of love and mourning.
12-14 *Simile*: the myth of Philomela and Procne.
15-18 *Direct address*: the translation of Callimachus follows; Catullus has not forgotten.
19-24 *Simile*: the forgetful girl and the apple.

Examine the entire poem for word-links, use of diminutives, alliteration, internal rhyme, and assonance, and assess their contribution to the unity and thought-sequence of the poem.

The imagery of water is persistent throughout the poem. What structural and emotional effects are gained by its use?

Do the 'learned' allusions detract from or enhance the total effect of the poem?

4 (HORACE, *Odes* I 1) *Maecenas atavis edite regibus*
Metre: First Asclepiadean

Horace's introductory poem is also an apology to Maecenas for attempting lyric poetry. In the opening verses of the prologue Horace dedicates the three books to Maecenas, his literary patron.

1 **atavis edite regibus** Horace opens with deliberate formal rhetoric. Gaius Cilnius Maecenas, an equestrian, traced his descent to Etruscan rulers at Arretium.

2 **praesidium et dulce decus meum** a tribute to the material and moral support and the distinction which friendship with Maecenas conferred on Horace. Cf Lucretius 2, line 643: *praesidioque parent decorique parentibus esse.*

3 **pulverem Olympicum** *Olympicum* is typical for Greek games generally. Here, as elsewhere, Horace juxtaposes the trivial and the grandiose (cf *Odes* I 6 (5), line 9: *tenues grandia*).

4 **metaque** 'turning-post'. Chariot races were held in the hippodrome or circus in Greek and Roman society. The charioteers drove their vehicles around a long low structure, technically the *spina* ('thorn'), and at each end of the *spina* was a semicircular base surmounted usually by three columns. The charioteer sought to wheel around the columnar turning-post at maximum speed and sometimes grazed the platform if he were on the inside track.

fervidis implications of friction, extreme speed, and ardent determination on the part of the charioteer.

6 **terrarum dominos** further ambiguity. The expression may refer to the charioteers whose victories are passports to divinity, or may equally well enlarge the status of the gods (*deos*), an elect company receptive to successful chariot-racers.

7 **mobilium turba Quiritium** Horace refers cynically to the uncertain and fickle nature of the political temper. Cf *Odes* III 1 (70), lines 1–4; *Epist.* I 19, line 37: *ventosae plebis.*

8 **tergeminis honoribus** the last three stages of the *cursus honorum*: curule aedile, praetor, and consul. Ablative of means.

9 **proprio condidit horreo** ablative of place. Notice the contrast between public *honores* and private *horreum*. Public granaries (*horrea*) and warehouses were numerous in Rome and particularly in Ostia.

10 **Libycis** Africa was a major 'grain supplier' for the Augustan Empire, together with Asia and Sicily.

area the circular threshing-floor where grain was trampled by cattle, horses, or mules as today in South Italy and Sicily, and in

Greece. The grain was winnowed by tossing it into the breeze with shovels until the chaff blew away, whereupon the grain was swept (*verritur*) into bags.

verritur implies sweeping up the last morsel, a clean sweep of the grain tribute.

11–12 **patrios findere sarculo/agros** the modest but independent *colonus*, a vanishing class in Horace's time, 'splits' the hard unproductive earth of his ancestral holdings with a hoe rather than a plough.

12 **Attalicis condicionibus** the wealth of the Attalids of Pergamum was proverbial. The Stoa of Attalus II, a splendid porticus and shopping centre in the Agora of Athens, is a token of their wealth and largesse. Attalus III willed his kingdom and wealth to the Roman people and Tiberius Gracchus diverted the funds to assist his agrarian reforms in 133 B.C. Pergamum was later organized as the province of Asia.

13 **trabe Cypria** Horace uses the particular rather than the general adjective. Cyprus was a major centre for Mediterranean shipbuilding. Cf *Myrtoum* (14) *and Icariis* (15) for similar picturesque effect.

14 **pavidus nauta** the non-professional sailor as opposed to the professional trader (*mercator*).

15 **luctantem** observe the metaphor. Cf Horace, *Odes* I 3 (35), line 13: *decertantem*.

18 **pauperiem** implies modest circumstances rather than privation or penury. Cf *Odes* III 2, line 1.

20 **solido de die** the 'business day' started at dawn and continued until the ninth hour (3 p.m.).

21 **arbutus** the wild strawberry tree was highly prized for its shade.

22 **stratus** reflexive use.

aquae ... sacrae considerable superstition attached to springs and streams, thought to be the home of nymphs and divinities. Cf *Odes* III 13 (62), lines 1–5.

24 **matribus** dative of agency, with perfect participle passive.

25 **sub Iove frigido** Jupiter (cf *Odes* I 34 (52), line 5) was originally conceived as a sky-god, a deity of the elements, thunder, lightning, rain and light. Cf *sub divo*: *Odes* II 3 (53), line 23; III 2, line 5.

28 teretes Marsus aper plagas *teretes . . . plagas* used to trap and confine the wild boar may be translated 'close-twisted' or 'close-meshed' (of texture) or more likely, with the idea of curvature, 'the curves of the nets'.

29 me emphatic, by position, at the climax of the Ode.

doctarum . . . frontium Horace did not entirely dissociate himself from 'intellectual' poetry, but he was sceptical about any parade of learning for its own sake.

hederae ivy was sacred to Bacchus, patron of poets, a source of inspiration.

30 dis miscent cf *evehit ad deos* (6). There is a striking correspondence between the victorious charioteer destined for heroic apotheosis (3–6) and the poet (29–34). Both earn immortality and everlasting fame as winners, one of the palm branch (5) the other of the ivy wreath (29).

31 leves 'lightly-stepping, light-footed'.

32 secernunt populo for the poet's isolation cf *Odes* III 1 (70), line 1: *odi profanum vulgus et arceo*.

34 Lesboum . . . barbiton the lyre of Sappho and Alcaeus, both of Lesbos, his chief metrical models and the inspiration for his verse on several occasions.

35 quodsi me lyricis vatibus inseres Horace asks for inclusion among the company of the nine accepted Greek lyric poets.

36 sublimi feriam sidera vertice cf *Odes* I 18, line 15: *et tollens vacuum plus nimio gloria verticem*. Horace here implies that he will become a towering figure which rises far above the populace. But there are also suggestions of apotheosis and of a colossal figure (cf Colossus of Rhodes). See also Vergil, *Georg.* 2, line 292; 1, lines 242–3.

D. Norberg, *L'Olympionique, le poète et leur renon éternel*: Uppsala, 1945.
H. Musurillo, 'The poet's apotheosis (c. I, 1)', in *TAPA* 93 (1961) 230–9.

The structure of the ode is intricate but in many ways typical of Horace's craft and thought-progression through associational links:

   1–2   *Prologue*: To Maecenas.
   3–18 *Catalogue*, of typical aims and careers (GROUP I)
         3–6.   chariot-racing.
         7–10.   politics; grain market.

11–14. farming; sea-faring (passive).
15–18. sea trade (restless).
19–22 RESPONSE A: The Country Life (*otium*).
23–28 *Catalogue*, of typical preoccupations (GROUP II).
23–25. warfare.
25–28. hunting.
29–31 RESPONSE B: Country retreat (*poetry*).
32–34 *Horace's aim and preoccupation*: lyric poetry.
35–36 *Epilogue*: to Maecenas.

The poetic texture of this ode, probably one of the last to be written before publication, is intricate and close-knit. The balance of theme and mood and motif is subtle and very neatly contrived. Notice, for example, how the themes of absorption and strain are answered by the themes of relaxation (19–22). List as many as possible of these contrasts in an effort to appreciate one of Horace's favourite devices for poetic unity.

There are many instances of assonance, alliteration, internal and end-rhymes in the ode. Study the poem closely to help develop an awareness of these constant ingredients in Horace's poetry.

Why does Horace refer to Greek mythology and use predominantly Greek allusions when he describes his own vocation? What verbal or sound effects does he gain by the Greek usages?

Horace's concrete illustrations and choice of epithets help determine his values and preferences. How much of Horace's manner of life and scale of values and preferences can be detected in this poem?

Discover differences in range of thought, coherence, invention and confidence between the dedicatory poems of Catullus (1) and Horace (4).

5 (HORACE, *Odes* I 6) *Scriberis Vario fortis et hostium*

Metre: Third Asclepiadean

Horace addresses Marcus Vipsanius Agrippa, victor over Sextus Pompey at Naulochus in 36 B.C., and commander at Actium in 31 B.C. Agrippa was also friend, adviser, and son-in-law of Augustus. The poet declines an invitation to celebrate Agrippa's achievements because he regards his talents as unequal to the undertaking.

1 **scriberis Vario fortis et hostium** See *Index Nominum*.

2 **Maeonii** Smyrna, in Lydia (Maeonia), claimed Homer as citizen. *Maeonii carminis alite* the bird-bard association also appears in

COMMENTARY

Odes II 20 (7), which relates Horace's metamorphosis into a swan, sacred to Apollo. *alite* ablative of agency without *ab*, in apposition with *Vario* 'by Varius'. Some editors regard *Vario... alite* as an ablative absolute construction.

3 **quam rem cumque** tmesis (*quamcumque rem*). Agrippa's accomplishments (*res gestae*) on land and sea, were significant and ensured the victory and stability of the Augustan Order and Peace.

5–6 **gravem/Pelidae stomachum cedere nescii** a reference to the wrath of Achilles, son of Peleus. Cf Homer, *Iliad* I 1. *Stomachum* is Horace's colloquial, perhaps ironical version of the Homeric wrath (*mēnin*); *cedere nescii* is an ambiguous allusion to Achilles' courage in the field and to his inability to compromise or accept supplication from friend or foe.

7 **cursus duplicis per mare Ulixei** alludes to the theme of Homer's *Odyssey*. *Duplicis*, Horace's version of the Homeric 'wily, versatile' Odysseus suggests 'double-minded, treacherous, false, deceitful' in Latin.

8 **saevam Pelopis domum** a glance at the legendary House of Atreus, son of Pelops, and a compliment, probably, to Varius' *Thyestes* which dealt with the travails of the House.

9 **tenues grandia** a concise antithesis or oxymoron implying that Horace's slender talent is inadequate to contemporary (3–4) or legendary (6–8) themes. Horace associates Agrippa's achievements with exalted subject matter.

10 **imbellis lyrae** governed by *potens*. Cf *Odes* I 3 (35), line 1; I 5 (36), line 15.

11 **Caesaris** C. Julius Caesar Octavianus, named Augustus after 27 B.C.

13 **quis Martem**... rhetorical question. Obviously no ordinary person is required, and Varius is the proper epic poet. Ironically, after lines 9–12, Horace might equally well be the proper answer.

14 **scripserit** potential subjunctive.

16 **superis parem** 'godlike'.

17 **nos convivia, nos proelia virginum** *nos*, emphatic by repetitions (cf 5), reaffirms Horace's inability to cope with the exploits of Agrippa as subject-matter. *proelia virginum* gives a mock-heroic tone.

19 **vacui** cf *Odes* I 5 (36), line 10.
   quid adverbial, with *urimur*, supply *amore*.

20 non praeter solitum litotes for 'always, habitually, normally'. **leves** cf *tenues* (9).

The tone of the apology expressed in this poetic epistle is debatable. Some authorities regard it as a graceful compliment to the great admiral and statesman, and a genuinely regretful and tactful *recusatio* on the grounds of limited poetic talent. But there are places in the ode where ambiguity with a less favourable slant seems to come to the surface. Horace's possible dislike of Agrippa may stem from the events of 23 B.C., the year of publication, when Maecenas lost favour and influence. Agrippa, long engaged in a secret power struggle with Maecenas, emerged as victor. Examine the ode carefully for indications of sincere eulogy or muted criticism and possible dislike of Agrippa. The epic heroes are curious examples of behaviour for the poet to choose. The choice of epithets for his heroic *exempla* may either indicate his ineptitude for epic or his aversion to the suggested hero. The next poem, *Odes* I 7 (67), which is dedicated to L. Munatius Plancus, adopts the dactylic hexameter and relates a heroic myth (lines 21–32).

The strophic structure of five four-line stanzas in the present ode is obvious. Observe Horace's clever balance of opposites throughout the ode, and also his use of military metaphors as a device for structural unity.

6 (HORACE, *Odes* II 1) *Motum ex Metello consule civicum*

Metre: Alcaic

Horace addresses Gaius Asinius Pollio [the Pollio of Vergil's Messianic Eclogue and Catullus 12 (29)], one of the most versatile men of the age. He introduced the practice of the *recitatio*, where an author read a new work to an audience. Horace seems to allude to the innovation and practice in this ode. Pollio is engaged with a history of the Civil War which Horace eagerly awaits.

1 **Motum ex Metello** 'civil war from the consulship of Metellus' (60 B.C.).

2 **belli causas** almost certainly a reference to the death of Julia, Caesar's daughter, and Pompey's wife in 55 B.C.; and the defeat and death of Crassus at Carrhae at the hands of the Parthians (53 B.C.).

vitia ... modos 'military mistakes, blunders' and 'vicissitudes of war'.

4, 5 **arma/nondum expiatis uncta cruoribus** Horace is repeatedly conscious of the impiety attaching to civil war. Cf *Odes* I 2 (66), line 29.

6 **periculosae plenum opus aleae** the allusion to dice-playing recalls Caesar's gambling expression at the Rubicon crossing in 49 B.C.: *iacta alea est* (or, *esto*). Asinius Pollio was among the intimate friends Caesar addressed on that occasion (Suet. *Divus Julius* 32, 5–6).

7 **tractas** cf usage in *Odes* I 37 (69), lines 26–7: *fortis et asperas/ tractare serpentes*.

7–8 **incedis per ignes . . .** Macaulay captured the meaning of the phrase in a comparable circumstance: 'When the historian of this troubled reign (James II) turns to Ireland, his task becomes peculiarly difficult and delicate. His steps – to borrow the fine image used on a similar occasion by a Roman poet – are on the thin crust of ashes beneath which the lava is still glowing.' (*History of England*, chapter 6.) Cf 'skating on thin ice'.

9 **severae Musa tragoediae** Pollio's reputation as tragic playwright was well established, but not a line survives today.

10 **theatris** Rome's only permanent stone theatre at this time was built by Pompey and dedicated in 52 B.C. (Plutarch, *Pompey* 42; Cassius Dio. 39, 38).

10, 11 **publicas/res ordinaris** an allusion to Pollio's annalistic 'ordering' of recent events. The verb is frequently used of the 'orderly planting' of vines.

11 **grande munus** may refer to Pollio's celebrated literary endowments, or to the impressive entertainment and public show associated with theatrical games. Public officials were frequently required to underwrite the costs of public spectacles. Cf Greek, *leitourgia*: liturgy, compulsory public service for the state.

12 **Cecropio repetes cothurno** 'resume your exalted vocation with the Attic buskin'. Pollio's reputation as tragedian was established before he turned his hand to history. The tragic shoe, with elevated sole, became the symbol of the tragic actor.

13 **insigne maestis praesidium reis** Horace obtains a fine visual effect of the distinguished defence lawyer (*patronus*) serving as 'bulwark' to his clients, intervening literally between their sorrow and the machinery of the lawcourts (cf *Odes* I 1 (4), line 2, Maecenas' relationship to Horace). Pollio was noted for the success of his interventions and arbitrations politically as well as legally, on behalf of Vergil, and on behalf of Antony and Octavian at Brundisium (cf Horace, *Satires* I 5).

14 **consulenti ... curiae** Pollio's was a respected voice in the deliberations of the Senate.

16 **Delmatico ... triumpho** after his consulship (40 B.C.) Pollio served as proconsul of Macedonia and subdued a revolt of the Illyrian Parthini. He returned to Rome to celebrate a triumph and built the *Atrium Libertatis*, Rome's first public library, out of the booty.

17 **iam nunc ...** signals the abrupt transfer from Pollio's professional and military successes to a colourful impression of his latest publication, the History of the Civil Wars. Repetition of *iam* (17, 18, 19) adds to the vividness and excitement of the account. Cf Catullus 46 (34), lines 1-2, 7-8.

18 **auris**, with *audire* and *videor* (21), gives the impression that Horace actually is listening to, or has already heard a *recitatio*, a preview or public reading of Pollio's History. Pollio introduced the practice from Greece to Rome (Seneca, *Contr.* 4, 1).

19, 20 **iam fulgor armorum fugaces.** *fugaces*: proleptic use. 'Now the flash of steel terrifies the horses into flight, and terrifies the faces of the riders.' An instance of the epic manner. This highly condensed passage is regarded by some as an allusion to Julius Caesar's command at Pharsalus (48 B.C.) that javelins be used as lances and thrust at the faces of Pompey's cavalry corps. Pollio served under Caesar at Pharsalus and may have recalled the incident in his History.

22 **non indecoro pulvere sordidos** Horace (or Pollio) suggests that 'the glorious dust' of heroic defeat erases all ignominy. Cf *Odes* III 2, line 13: *dulce et decorum est pro patria mori*.

23 **cuncta terrarum** possessive genitive, 'everything in the world'.

24 **atrocem animum Catonis** the younger Cato's indomitable spirit and resolute death at Utica (46 B.C.) enshrined him in Imperial times as a Stoic 'political martyr', and the embodiment of the best and sternest instincts of the Republican past.

25 Horace moves from Cato's suicide at Utica and Roman carnage in Africa, where the losses were in the neighbourhood of ten thousand men, to Juno, the divine protectress of Carthage whose longing for vengeance on behalf of Hannibal and Jugurtha was grimly satisfied by the Roman 'sacrificial blood'.

26 **cesserat** the gods deserted Africa unable to prevent its doom. Cf Vergil, *Aen.* 2, lines 351-2: *excessere omnes adytis arisque relictis/di*.

COMMENTARY

29 **pinguior** the blood of sacrificed animals was regarded as an aid to fertility in agricultural rites, but the enrichment to which Horace refers is achieved by human bloodshed.

30 **impia proelia** cf lines 5–6.

31, 32 **Medis/Hesperiae** an allusion to the conflict between East and West with suggestions of longstanding enmity since both names are antique for Parthians and Italians.
  ruinae suggests the collapse of a great building.

34 **Dauniae** cf Hesperiae (32) for similar effect.

35 **decoloravere** Roman blood has 'discoloured' the sea.

37 **Musa procax** Horace abruptly checks and reprimands his Muse. Dirges (*neniae*) and solemn topics are alien to his lyrical inspiration which favours lighter themes. Cf *Odes* III 3, lines 69–72.

38 **Ceae...neniae** refers to the elegies of Simonides of Ceos (556–467 B.C.).

39 **Dionaeo sub antro** Horace appeals to his 'saucy' Muse to share Love's grotto (cf *Odes* I 5 (36), line 3).

40 **leviore plectro** for similar sentiment and reproof cf *Odes* III 3, lines 69–72 and *Odes* I 6 (5), lines 17–20.

H. Bennett, 'Vergil and Pollio', in *AJP* 51 (1930) 325–42:
Gaius Asinius Pollio embodies the traditional virtues of a Roman gentleman. Reexamine the Ode and Catullus 12 (29), lines 6–9, to delineate his character and accomplishments more fully.

Try to distinguish between rhetorical and dramatic (i.e., tragic) elements in the ode. Both are appropriate to the person addressed and both occur in the lines. Does the tragic element determine the choice of scene and incident?

Examine the thought-structure of the ode with particular attention to the diverse moods which pervade the stanza-groupings. Observe any special sound effects (anaphora, assonance, alliteration) and link-words.

What is the effect of the final stanza after the rhetorical crescendo which precedes it? Compare the final stanza of *Odes* I 6 (5). Both are recantations. Which is more effective?

How does the Alcaic metre contribute to the poem's effectiveness?

To what degree is Catullus' dedicatory poem to Cornelius Nepos (1) comparable with Horace's 'dedication' to Asinius Pollio?

7 (HORACE, *Odes* II 20) *Non usitata nec tenui ferar*

Metre: Alcaic

Horace's epilogue to Books One and Two provides an allegorical melodrama centring about his imaginary metamorphosis into a swan. His favourable reception by Maecenas as a lyric poet (cf *Odes* I 1 (4), line 35) initiates his change of form. Maecenas either attends or witnesses 'off-stage' and Horace describes in detail, with a realism which is almost offensive to modern ears, the stages of his metamorphosis into a swan, sacred to Apollo. His achievements and canonization as a lyric poet permit him to forecast his ultimate far-reaching fame and influence.

1 **non usitata nec tenui ferar** the adjectives probably refer also to the nature of his lyric achievement, 'uncommon and substantial' by reason of his introduction of Greek lyric metres into Rome. The future tense in the first line sets the imaginative tone of the entire ode and underlines its prophetic character.

2 **penna** a suggestion of Daedalus and Icarus.

2, 3 **biformis ... vates** an ambiguous phrase, suggesting either poet and swan in succession or a 'bard of double shape', a double citizen of the natural and supernatural worlds. But *biformis* may also suggest Horace's double capacity for important and light themes.

   liquidum aethera 'clear, translucent air' contrasted with *in terris* (3).

4 **invidia maior** Horace was subject to envy because of his intimate association with Maecenas but now he says that he is 'too high for envy'. Cf *Odes* II 16 (56), lines 39–40.

6 **quem vocas** 'whom you summon' i.e., to poetic endeavour (Page). Other editors prefer 'whom you invite', i.e. to dinner, to your house. Horace describes the latter situation in *Sat.* I 6, 45 ff.

7 **dilecte** 'dearly beloved'.

8 **unda** cf *Odes* II 14 (55), lines 8–9: *tristi/compescit unda.*

9 **iam iam** (cf 13): this idiomatic repeated use of *iam* in quick succession enhances the imminence of the event. Horace dramatizes the ensuing transformation by suggesting a rapid sequence of changes.

10 **alitem** recalls *Odes* I 6 (5), lines 1–2: the bird-bard equation is now complete.

13 Daedaleo notior Icaro Horace's poetic flight will bring him even more extensive fame than the disastrous flight of Icarus from Crete.

13–20 the future circulation of his newly published work will reach barbaric frontiers. Horace will travel in the guise of a tuneful swan.

17, 18 dissimulat metum/Marsae cohortis Dacus Horace's declaration that the provincials will be 'made learned' by his writings was probably true. Spain in the next generation produced an intellectual élite numbering two Senecas, Lucan, Martial, Columella, and Quintilian. *Peritus,* either 'instructed by me' and so a connoisseur of literature, or proleptic 'to his enlightenment'.

21–4 Horace reminds his audience abruptly that this is no funeral, merely his own intimations of immortality as lyric bard. Horace seems to compose a paraphrase or variation on Ennius' epitaph in this epilogue:

> *nemo me lacrumis decoret nec funera fletu*
> *faxit. cur? volito vivus per ora virum.*

Vergil was also attracted to the Ennian epitaph and recalls it in *Georg.* 3, lines 8–9:

> *temptanda via est, qua me quoque possim*
> *tollere humo victorque virum volitare per ora.*

21 inani funere suggests a cenotaph.

22 luctusque turpes et querimoniae the lamentations of family and friends, accompanied often by dirges (*neniae*) chanted by hired mourners, included gashing of cheeks, breast-beating, and all the outward disfiguring signs of grief.

23 clamorem witnesses to a death called three times on the deceased by name to determine whether life remained. Cf. Vergil, *Aen.* 4, line 674.

24 mitte supervacuos honores the omission of superfluous distinctions would include the funeral eulogy, procession, and tributes paid at the tomb.

G. L. Hendrickson, '*Vates biformis*', in *CP* 44 (1949) 30–2. E. T. Silk, 'A Fresh Approach to Horace II 20', in *AJP* 77 (1956) 255–63. K. Abel, 'Horace, c. 2.20', in *RhMus* 104 (1961) 81–94.

Critics frequently find fault with Horace's transformation-poem for the prosaic, often grotesque nature of its details. But the Romans had a fondness for such imaginative literature, witness Ovid's *Metamorphoses* and Catullus' translation of Callimachus' *Lock of Berenice* (66).

Determine the structure of the poem and criticize the dramatic situation.

Does the ode conceal elements of irony and humour? How serious is Horace about his metamorphosis?

Examine the extent of Horace's travels and far-reaching fame. Try to determine reasons for his choice of the various ports of call. Compare Catullus 46 (34): *Iam ver egelidos refert tepores* throughout, but especially lines 6–8, and Catullus 11 (27), lines 1–20: *Furi et Aureli, comites Catulli*.

8 (HORACE, *Odes* III 30) *Exegi monumentum aere perennius*

Metre: First Ascelepiadean

Horace provides an epilogue to the first three books of *Odes* in which he reviews his own achievements and appraises his position in the field of Latin verse.

1 **Exegi monumentum...** 'I have finished off, fashioned, a memorial'. The opening phrase is highly ambiguous. Horace appears to liken his achievement to a commemorative plaque or statue wrought in bronze, but at the same time *monumentum* implies that he and his Odes will be *remembered* in men's minds as long as his Odes are read. Probably the external symbol is stronger, but both are implied. The ensuing allusion to the pyramids might suggest that *monumentum aere perennius* could refer to the towering bronze Colossus of Rhodes, broken off at the knees by earthquake in 227/6 B.C.

2 **regalique situ** the usual interpretation is 'a situation befitting a king (or pharaoh)', but *situs* also means 'decay, rust, mould', and this sense seems equally acceptable in conjunction with the preceding *aere perennius* and the following *imber edax*, etc. Horace in effect may be saying: 'the monument I have completed will outlive any in bronze; it stands higher than the decaying pyramids of kings'. Also, the Old Wonders, like the Colossus and the Pyramids of Gizeh, give way now to a new kind of monument in a classic but more durable form.

3 **quod non imber edax, non Aquilo impotens** Horace's memorial is immune from the destructive and corrosive attacks of nature and perhaps, by implication, of personal detractors. For *impotens*, cf *Odes* I 37 (69), line 10, 'wild, unrestrained'.

COMMENTARY

5 **fuga temporum** cf *Odes* II 14 (55), line 1; III 29, line 48.

7 **Libitinam** a metonymy for Death. The Capitoline Hill with the Temple of the Capitoline Triad (Jupiter Optimus Maximus, Juno, and Minerva) was the symbol of Rome's primacy and eternity. Cf *Odes* III 3, line 42; I 2 (66), line 3; Vergil, *Aen.* 9, line 448.
  usque modifies *crescam*.

9 **scandet cum tacita virgine** Fraenkel calls this a 'legato passage'. Silence was enjoined on all participants in religious rites and processions. Ritual silence in fact became a symbol of the peace, religious and political, guaranteed by Augustus at home and abroad.

10 **qua,** sc. *parte* the construction of the relative clauses, introduced by *qua*, is ambiguous. Two different interpretations are permissible; Horace either says that he will be remembered in the area of his birth, or, less likely, that he regards himself as a thoroughly Italian poet who subscribes to a Greek tradition.
  qua violens obstrepit Aufidus cf *Odes* IV 9, line 2; IV 14, line 25: shows local pride in the torrential flow of the Aufidus (Ofanto) River in springtime. Less spectacular in other seasons, it watered Apulia near Venusia (his birthplace) and Cannae. Notice the contrast of this line with the quiet mood of line 9, and with the scarcity of water in line 11.

11 **pauper aquae Daunus** parched land was common in Horace's Apulia. *aquae* genitive, with *pauper*.

12 **regnavit populorum** Greek construction, with verbs of ruling. Cf *potens*, with genitive.
  ex humili potens almost certainly applies to Horace not to Daunus. Notice the deliberate contrast with *impotens* (3) which occupies exactly the same line position. Horace was very conscious of his prestige and status as a poet in the circle of Maecenas.

13 **princeps** = *primus*. But there is also an amusing juxtaposition with the preceding line. The connotations are personal and political (cf Princeps Senatus, and the title assumed by Augustus). Horace resembles a *novus homo* who has attained distinction and leadership in spite of his humble origins, in the realm of poetry, especially Latin Lyric.

13, 14 **carmen ad Italos/deduxisse modos** The preposition *ad* corresponds to the English 'to musical accompaniment', Horace might be expected to say 'compose Italian songs to Aeolic music' (cf Propertius III 1, line 4: *Itala per Graios orgia ferre choros*). But

Horace's *superbia* was that he would be celebrated as the first man to 'compose' Aeolic song to Italian music. (Cf. *Epist.* I 19, lines 26–34, especially 32–4.) *Deducere* 'to introduce' is used of establishing a colony (*coloniam deducere*), and Horace may perhaps emphasize his technical transfer of Greek metres to Italy. But *deducere* may also be applied to spinning, for the wool was held up high in the left hand and 'drawn down' by the fingers of the right which spun it into thread. Horace actually uses *deducere* with the meaning 'to refine, shape a poetic line' (*Epist.* II 1, line 155: *tenui deducta poemata filo*). Both interpretations make sense, and increase the significance of the poet's proud claim.

15, 16 **Delphica/lauro** the laurel was sacred to Apollo, god of prophetic bards and lyric poets.

16 **volens** 'graciously, according to thy will', probably a ritual formula of prayers.

Melpomene lit., 'muse of song'. See *Index Nominum, s.v. Musae.* Horace uses the first Asclepiadean metre only three times and on each occasion to celebrate his poetic accomplishments, for the prologue and epilogue of Books I and III, and for the central poem of Book IV (8), presumably because it can provide a dignified measure consonant with his pride of achievement and place.

The structure of the ode is most commonly regarded as comprising an uneven three-part progression (1–5; 6–9; 10–14) with a coda (14–16).

Re-examine the ode with this acceptable pattern in mind, and discover how Horace obtains a unified thought-progression.

Try to detect effective instances of assonance, alliteration, etc.

Compare *Odes* I 1 (4) and III 30 (8) with attention to formal structure, rhetorical elements, geographical allusions, Greek and Roman imagery and associations, tone, and intimations of immortality.

Re-examine Horace's progressive comment on his poetic achievement and the promise of immortal fame in *Odes* I 1 (4); II 20 (7), and III 30 (8).

9 (HORACE, *Odes* IV 3) *Quem tu, Melpomene, semel*

Metre: Second Asclepiadean

Horace celebrates the achievement of the aims expressed in the Prologue [*Odes* I 1 (4)]. The publication of the three books of Odes,

COMMENTARY

and his commission to compose the *Carmen Saeculare* (17 B.C.) have silenced his detractors.

1 **semel** suggests an inevitable consequence.

2 **nascentem placido lumine videris** 'regard with favorable eye at birth'. Cf Vergil, *Ecl.* 4 (Messianic), lines 62-3.

5 **curru ducet** the chariot race.

6-7 **Deliis/ornatum foliis** the laurel wreath, sacred to Apollo, born on the island of Delos in the mid-Aegean.

8 **regum tumidas contuderit minas** the metaphor extends to warfare [cf *Odes* III 6 (73), line 10: *non auspicatos contudit impetus*] and to boxing (4).

9 **ostendet Capitolio** the *triumphator* was brought to the temple of Jupiter Optimus Maximus on the Capitoline Hill and there exhibited to his gods and his people.

10 **Tibur** modern Tivoli, 18 miles E.N.E. of Rome where the Anio river emerges from the Sabine hills. Horace's affection for Tibur and the nearby Sabine Farm at Licenza (Digentia) grew from his affection for romantic landscapes, for isolated spots, springs, groves, cascades, rocks and woods. Such places had a mystical, inspiring power for Horace. Cf *Odes* III 25, line 13; III 4 (71), lines 6-8; 40; II 19, line 1; I 1 (4), line 30; III 19, line 25; I 21 (61), line 6. Consult Gilbert Highet, *Poets in a Landscape* (London, 1957) pp. 114-60.

11 **spissae nemorum comae** cf *Odes* I 21, (61), line 5; III 19, line 25; IV 7 (57), line 2; and Catullus 4 (77), line 11, *comata silva*.

13 **Romae principis urbium** cf *Odes* IV 14, line 44: *dominaeque Romae*.

14, 15 **dignatur suboles inter ... me choros** Horace's acceptance by the youth of Rome as their lyrical *vates* is probably to be associated with the recent performance of Horace's *Carmen Saeculare* commissioned for the Secular Games of 17 B.C., and sung by a chorus of boys and girls. Horace appears here as a *citharoedus*, choir master and bard (*vates*). Cf *Odes* IV 6 (65).

16 **dente ... mordeor invido** cf *Epode* 6, line 13; and *Satire* I 6, line 46. For the idea expressed earlier cf *Odes* II 20 (7), line 4, *invidiaque maior*.

17 **testudinis aureae** cf Pindar, *Pythian* I 1, addressed to Apollo's Golden Lyre.

19 **mutis** traditional epithet.

20 **cycni sonum** cf *Odes* II 20 (7).
 si libeat formulaic reverential expression in prayers.

22 **quod monstror digito praetereuntium** Horace's extrovert response to popular fame is quite distinct from Vergil's retreatist attitude: *siquando Romae, quo rarissime commeabat, viseretur in publico, sectantis demonstrantisque se subterfugeret in proximum tectum* (Donatus-Suetonius, *Vita*, 11).

23 **Romanae fidicen lyrae** *fidicen* is Latin, *lyrae* is Greek; 'tuner of a Roman lyre'.

24 **quod spiro et placeo...** continues the markedly devotional language of line 17 ff. Acknowledged as *vates* Horace finally ascribes his success and his popularity (which he partly discredits) to an external agency, the Muse, divine patroness of his new lyrics.

The structure of the ode is fairly straightforward:

1-2   *Prologue:*
3-12 *Catalogue:* men's ambitions in review.
      3-6.   Boxing, chariot-race (Greek setting).
      6-9.   Military conquest, triumphal procession (Roman setting).
      10-12. Horace, and lyric poetry (Italian setting).
13-16 *Horace's triumph:* Carmen Saeculare (17 B.C.).
17-20 *Invocation:* to the Muse.
21-24 *Thanksgiving:* to the Muse.

Examine the ode carefully for link-words and contrasts, alliteration, and concrete imagery.

Examine the hymnic elements of language, mood, and structure, in the ode. Trace and discuss parallelisms of thought and expression between *Odes* I 1 (4) and *Odes* IV 3 (9).

10 (CATULLUS 51) *Ille mi par esse deo videtur*

Metre: Sapphic

This poem – or rather, the first three stanzas of it – is a fairly close translation of a poem of Sappho, preserved in fragmentary form in

Longinus, *On The Sublime*. But this is more than a literary exercise for Catullus; he employs Sappho's highly personal and intimate confession of her emotions at the sight of her loved one in the company of her betrothed to convey his own excitement on seeing Lesbia with some male friend – perhaps her husband. The poem is generally acknowledged to have been the first in the cycle inspired by the ups and downs of that affair.

2 **si fas est** this Roman religious and legal formula is the most striking Catullian addition to Sappho's ode; elsewhere Catullus omits and adapts Sappho's words and sentiments. For a close analysis of the similarities and differences between the two poems, see D. A. Kidd, 'The Unity of Catullus 51', *AUMLA* 20 (1963), 298–309.

5 **dulce ridentem** Horace, *Odes* I 22 (41), lines 23–4, repeats this phrase and adds as well *dulce loquentem* from Sappho's original.

8 Various supplements for the missing line have been suggested; e.g. *vocis in ore, Lesbia, vocis,* etc.

10 **suopte** – *pte* is an enclitic employed for emphasis, and is an archaic usage; cf *tute, memet,* etc.

11 **gemina** the epithet is transferred from *lumina* to *nocte*, a night for each eye.

13 ff. **otium ... urbes** this much-disputed stanza is rejected as part of this poem by many scholars, who accept it as a fragment of a lost poem.* Can you justify its inclusion on emotional grounds? For a discussion of stylistic reasons for believing it to be a genuine part of the poem, see R. Lattimore, *CP* 39 (1944), pp. 184–7. The stanza clearly influenced Horace, *Odes* II 16 (56), lines 1–8.

13 **molestum** here it means 'your nagging trouble'; cf Macrobius, *Sat.* 2, 7, 6: super cena exorta quaestione, quidnam esset molestum otium, alio aliud opinante ille 'podagrici pedes' dixit.

14 **exsultas ... gestis** both verbs suggest unnatural excitement and emotion.

Cf Cicero, *Tusc.* 4. 13 (where he contrasts *gaudium* and *laetitia*): cum ratione animus movetur placide atque constanter, tum illud gaudium dicitur; cum autem inaniter et effuse animus *exsultat*.

---

* Among the reasons given for its rejection: Horace regularly imitates the beginning of a poem, not the end; if Catullus intended the poem for Lesbia's eyes, this final stanza would have been offensive.

tum illa laetitia *gestiens* vel nimia dici potest, quam ita definiunt: sine ratione animi elationem.

Again, *ibid.* 5. 16 (describing the man who is a slave to passion): illum, quem libidinibus inflammatum et furentem videmus, omnia rabide adpetentem cum inexplebili cupiditate, quoque affluentius voluptates hauriat, eo gravius ardentiusque sitientem, nonne recte miserrimum dixeris? quid? elatus ille levitate inanique laetitia *exsultans* et temere *gestiens* nonne tanto miserior, quanto sibi videtur *beatus*?

Do these passages from Cicero serve to strengthen the argument for regarding the lines 13-16 as an integral part of Catullus's poem?

15 f. **reges ... urbes** have you any suggestions as to what kings and cities Catullus may have had in mind?

Consult bibliography in Fordyce, *Catullus*, p. 219. D. A. Kidd, 'The unity of Catullus 51', in *AUMLA* 20 (1963) 298-309. H. A. Akbar Khan, '*Color Romanus* and Cat. 51,' *Latomus* 25 (1966) 448-60. E. Fredricksmeyer, 'On the unity of Catullus 51', in *TAPA* 96 (1965) 153-63.

Sappho of Lesbos, a contemporary of Alcaeus, was acclaimed by the ancients as the greatest lyricist, a veritable Tenth Muse, and mistress of the short lyric for solo recitation or private reading. Catullus' 'translation' becomes more meaningful when read in conjunction with the Greek model:

> Like the very gods in my sight is he who
> sits where he can look in your eyes, who listens
> close to you, to hear the soft voice, its sweetness
> murmur in love and
>
> laughter, all for him. But it breaks my spirit;
> underneath my breast all the heart is shaken.
> Let me only glance where you are, the voice dies,
> I can say nothing,
>
> but my lips are stricken to silence, under-
> neath my skin the tenuous flame suffuses;
> nothing shows in front of my eyes, my ears are
> muted in thunder.
>
> And the sweat breaks running upon me, fever
> shakes my body, paler I turn than grass is;

I can feel that I have been changed, I feel that
death has come near me.
(Richmond Lattimore, *Greek Lyrics*, Chicago, 1955)

Make a critical examination of Catullus' adaptation of the Sapphic original. Comment on the Roman poet's innovations and on the success or failure of his meditative poem in comparison with the model.

11 (CATULLUS 2) *Passer, deliciae meae puellae*

Metre: Hendecasyllabic (Phalaecean)
Catullus speaks of his envy of the bird's favoured position with Lesbia, and of the hope – vain, he fears – that he too might find relief from love's pangs, as Lesbia does, by playing with the bird.

1 **passer** variously identified as a sparrow, thrush or goldfinch. See Fordyce, *ad loc.*

2 **quicum** *qui* is an old instrumental ablative preserved in this combination with – *cum* as late as Quintilian (second century A.D.).

3 **primum ... digitum** her 'finger-tip'.

5 **desiderio ... nitenti** 'my shining light of love'. Horace (*Odes* I 14 (68), lines 18 ff.) may have had these words in mind:

> nunc *desiderium* curaque non levis,
>   interfusa *nitentis*
> vites aequora Cycladas.

7 **et solaciolum sui doloris** a difficult phrase; some would take it as a vocative, parallel to *deliciae* (line 1), in spite of the ungrammatical *sui* (for *eius*). Zicàri (see bibliography below) would with Guarini (1521) read *ut solaciolum*, 'as a sort of comfort'.

9 **tecum ludere** balances *quicum ... ludere* (line 2).
ipsa cf Cat. 3 (12), lines 6 f., *suam ... ipsam*.
possem 'would that I had the opportunity'.

M. Zicàri, 'Il secondo Carme di Catullo', *Studi Urbinati* n.s. 2 (1963) 205–32.

12 (CATULLUS 3) *Lugete, o Veneres Cupidinesque*

Metre: Hendecasyllabic (Phalaecean)

1 **Veneres Cupidinesque** cf Cat. 13 (30), line 12; 86 (15), line 6, for *Veneres* alone. No complicated explanation of these plurals seems called for; Catullus, in the extravagance of his grief, calls upon all the forces of Love and Desire, just as, in the following line, he summons all the humans subject to such forces.

2 **quantum** Catullus shows a fondness for this construction; cf Cat. 1 (1), line 8, 9 (28), line 10, 31 (32), line 14.

venustiorum clearly a fashionable word in the circle in which Catullus moved, it also describes a quality of which he and his friends highly approved: someone who was open to the power of love; cf Cat. 13 (30), line 6; 31 (32), line 12; for its opposite, see Cat. 12 (29), line 5.

8 **illius** short penult.

13 **at** often marks an abrupt change of mood or address; cf Cat. 8 (19), line 14.

15 **mihi** Catullus subtly assumes the role of chief mourner.

16 ff. Note the liquid effect of these lines, the result in part of the accumulation of diminutives.

Structure: 1–2 Catullus summons all sympathetic powers and mortals to mourn
3 a blunt announcement of the catastrophe
4–10 he expands upon the place the bird held in Lesbia's affections (delicately reminding the reader, by the repetition of the opening line of Cat. 2 (11) in the fourth line, of the special comfort the *passer* had offered)
11–12 the permanence of death for bird and mortal alike
13–16 imprecations against death
17–18 turns his sympathy to Lesbia, the chief mourner

The poem is a dirge, a *nenia* (cf Horace, *Odes* II 1 (6), line 28; II 20 (7), line 21,) and seems to preserve much of the traditional form while turning the poem at the same time into a graceful love-poem. See N. Herescu, 'Catulle 3: un écho des nénies dans la littérature latine?,' *Rev. des Études latines*, 25 (1947) 74–6.

Examine the sound-effects which Catullus achieves throughout the poem.

Note the word-repetitions. How do they serve to increase the poignancy of the poem?

13 (CATULLUS 5) *Vivamus, mea Lesbia, atque amemus*

Metre: Hendecasyllabic (Phalaecean)

1 **vivamus ... amemus** life is the keynote of the poem, life *now*, for death will come all too soon; for Catullus life and love are, for the moment, one and the same.

2 **rumores** 'grumblings'; the disapproving whispers are effectively conveyed by the repeated 's' sounds.

3 **unius ... assis** the commercial imagery of the poem, most apt to be associated with *senes severiores*, begins here and recurs throughout the poem.

4 **soles** cf Catullus 8 (19), lines 3, 8.

5 **lux** this final monosyllable gives the effect of a curtain dropping with a bump. Cf Horace, *Odes* I 28, line 15,

> ... sed omnes una manet nox
> et calcanda semel via leti.

7 ff. This counting-sequence has stirred much discussion; does it allude to the ancient method of reckoning on the abacus or to finger-counting? The regularity with which Catullus uses first *mille*, then *centum* seems to fit the former method best, for the abacus employs separate columns for thousands and hundreds, *deinde, dein*: the *ei* should be read aloud as a single syllable.

9 **usque** 'immediately', 'straight ahead'.

11 **conturbabimus** 'confuse the count', i.e. either disarrange the pebbles used in the abacus-operation, or wiggle the fingers which kept the count in the finger-counting method. But *conturbo* may also mean, 'to become bankrupt', and hints that the lovers will thus cheat the *malus* of his profit of disapproval.

ne sciamus unlike moderns, the ancients thought it unwise to 'count your blessings'.

12 **invidere** cf *fascinare*, Cat. 7 (14), line 12.

N. T. Pratt, 'The numerical Catullus 5', in *CP* 51 (1956) 99–100.
R. E. Grimm, 'Catullus 5 again', in *CJ* 59 (1963–4) 15–22. S. Commager, 'The structure of Catullus 5', in *CJ* 59 (1963–4) 361–4.
Indicate how the ideas of singleness and multiplicity provide unity to the poem.
What theme from popular Epicureanism does Catullus employ?
Discover how metrics and imagery combine to reinforce the poem's unity.

14 (CATULLUS 7) *Quaeris quot mihi basiationes*

Metre: Hendecasyllabic (Phalaecean)
An extravagant and quite different answer to Lesbia's perhaps impatient question.

3 **quam ... harenae** cf Horace, *Odes* I 28, line 1: *numero carentis harenae*.

4 **lasarpiciferis** the plant *lasarpicium* was also called *silphium*; its juice, *laser*, besides possessing therapeutic properties, seems also to have possessed, in ancient belief, power as an aphrodisiac (see V. Vikentiev, 'Le silphium et le rite du renouvellement de la vigeur', *Bull. de l'Institut d'Égypte* 37 (1954–5), 123–50). Its relative scarcity and the special powers attributed to it made it highly prized and expensive; hence Augustus, we are told, used it as a term of endearment, calling Maecenas 'laser Aretinum', 'my treasure from Arezzo' (Macrobius, *Sat.* II 4, 12). Silphium and grain provided Cyrene's chief exports.

Cyrenis the capital of Cyrenaica, founded *c*. 650 B.C. by Battus of Thera (*mod*. Santorini), according to legend (see line 6).

5 **oraclum Iovis** the famous shrine of Ammon, identified, after ancient practice, with Jupiter. Alexander the Great visited the shrine and received – he said – the answer he desired.

6 **Batti** see above on line 4. Battus was revered as a hero after his death; his tomb stood in the heart of Cyrene. In lines 5–6 Catullus spans the desert between Cyrene in the north-west of Cyrenaica and Ammonium in the south-east.

8 **furtivos ... amores** Catullus' own affair with Lesbia belongs to this class. Cf Cat. 68, line 145.

11 **pernumerare** cf Cat. 5 (13), line 11.

COMMENTARY

12 fascinare 'to bewitch' either by tongue, as here, or with the eye (as in Cat. 5 (13), line 12).

Structure: 1-2 the question
3-12 the answer

Compare the two kissing-poems of Catullus 5 (13), 7 (14); how does the treatment differ?

15 (CATULLUS 86) *Quintia formosa est multis, mihi candida, longa*

Metre: Elegiac

Cf Cat. 43 (16) for another more devastating poem about a woman who fails to measure up to Lesbia in beauty. Here Quintia's possession of many of the separate qualities which contribute to *formositas* is acknowledged, but she lacks those *je ne sais quoi's*: *venustas* and *mica salis*; Lesbia has all the separate qualities, and these indefinable qualities as well.

3 totum illud formosa 'that all-inclusive term "beautiful"'. *formosa* is quoted here from line 1, and is grammatically unaffected by the rest of the sentence.

4 mica salis 'a spark of style', perhaps; *sal* here is not confined to wit, though wit may be one of the elements of it.

5 pulcerrima the more usual *pulcherrima* is an instance of the overcorrection of which Arrius [Cat. 84 (86)] and others were guilty. Cicero, *Orat.* 160 says:

> Quin ego ipse, cum scirem ita maiores locutos ut nusquam nisi in vocali aspiratione uterentur, loquebar sic ut *pulcros, Cetegos, triumpos, Cartaginem* dicerem; aliquando, idque sero, convicio aurium cum extorta mihi veritas esset, usum loquendi populo concessi, scientiam mihi reservavi.

16 (CATULLUS 43) *Salve, nec minimo puella naso*

Metre: Hendecasyllabic (Phalaecean)

Addressed to Ameana, mistress of Mamurra, a henchman of Caesar, these lines, like Cat. 86 (15), are a compliment to Lesbia's beauty. But in this instance the catalogue of qualities is not complimentary to the woman addressed, and the reader assumes that every fault in Ameana balances a virtue in Lesbia.

1 **nec ... naso** cf Cat. 41, line 3, *ista turpiculo puella naso*.

5 This same line occurs also in Cat. 41, line 4. Mamurra was a notorious spendthrift, frequently attacked by Catullus for his personal faults and for his attachment to Caesar and Pompey (cf Cat. 29, 57, 94, 105, 113–15).

6 **ten** = *te-ne*. **provincia** i.e. Cisalpine Gaul. Had Catullus' involvement with Lesbia become a subject of gossip at home?

8 **insapiens et infacetum** the devastating series of negatives in lines 1–4 is capped by this final condemnatory pair of adjectives.

17 (CATULLUS 92) *Lesbia mi dicit semper male nec tacet umquam*

Metre: Elegiac

Catullus, analysing his own symptoms, applies this analysis to Lesbia's behaviour, and is sure her love is as fierce as his.

3 **mea** are we to understand *signa*, 'symptoms'? Fordyce (note *ad loc.*), after Kroll, rejects this suggestion, but offers nothing concrete in its place.

18 (CATULLUS 70) *Nulli se dicit mulier mea nubere malle*
Metre: Elegiac

One of a series of poems in which Catullus analyses Lesbia's words and promises [cf Cat. 72 (23), 83, 92 (17), 109 (21)].

1 **mulier** Catullus speaks of Lesbia as his *mulier* in several of these pieces. Does it suggest difference in attitude from *puella* used in other poems?

2 **Iuppiter** Lesbia's extravagance of statement in preferring Catullus to the King of gods and men is hinted at again in Cat. 72 (23), line 2. *nec prae me velle tenere Iovem*.

19 (CATULLUS 8) *Miser Catulle, desinas ineptire*

Metre: Choliambic or Scazons

Catullus' address to himself on the occasion of a falling-out with Lesbia – probably not the final break. One side of his nature calls for a complete rupture of relations, the other fondly recalls the joys of the past.

1 **ineptire** to one of Catullus' circle, behaviour such as this verb suggests is almost unforgivable; cf Cat. 12 (29), line 4; 17 (79), line 2.

3 **fulsere...soles** cf Cat. 5 (13), lines 4 ff.

5 **amata...nulla** cf Cat. 87 (20), lines 1 f.

9 **inpotens** this word probably carries double force here: 'don't live weakly submitting to Lesbia's will and whim', and 'don't live a life of unbridled passion'.

14 **nulla** colloquial usage for *non*; cf Cat. 17 (79), line 20.

E. Fraenkel, 'Two poems of Catullus', in *JRS* 51 (1961) 51–3.

Structure: There are several possible ways of analysing the structure of this poem; the following plan, while a little more complex than some that have been suggested, does not seem unreasonable. The poem would seem to fall into five parts, as follows:

  1–2 face facts
  3–8 fond recollections of past happiness
  9–13 but it's all changed now; be firm
  14–18 Lesbia will be sorry when she realizes all happiness is past
  19 be firm

Parts 1, 3, 5, expressing Catullus' present determination to break off the affair, and parts 2 and 4, which either directly or indirectly recall past joys (*iocosa*, 'fun and games'), alternate and intertwine; the various parts are clearly marked by key-words – *quondam* (line 3), *nunc iam* (line 9), *at* (line 14), *at* (line 19). His resolve is always in danger of weakening before the memory of what he's giving up; the series of questions, directed seemingly to Lesbia but actually to himself (lines 15–18), become increasingly nostalgic, almost maudlin, until *cui labella mordebis?* with its sentimental diminutive, brings him to a realization of how close he is to surrendering to his memories, and he restates his determination more strongly than before (line 19).

What reminiscences of previous poems do you find here?

20 (CATULLUS 87) *Nulla potest mulier tantum se dicere amatam*

Metre: Elegiac

Yet another statement of Catullus' emotional dilemma, the double-nature of his love for Lesbia, his physical longing and his deep hope for some more permanent relationship beyond the sensual.

1 ff. **amatam ... amata est ... fuit** note the perfect tenses.

3 **fides** cf Cat. 76 (26), line 3.
foedere cf Cat. 76 (26), line 3; 109 (21), line 6. For a discussion of Catullus' language in this and similar poems, see introduction to Cat. 76 (26).

4 **in amore tuo** 'in my love for you'.
ex parte ... mea perhaps technical language implying partnership in *foedus*. He emphasizes the one-sidedness of the relationship.

The structure is two simple statements:
1–2 his *amor* surpassed all other love, in the physical sense;
3–4 his loyalty (*fides*) had no match in history.

21 (CATULLUS 109) *Iucundum, mea vita, mihi proponis amorem*

Metre: Elegiac
Catullus is dissatisfied with Lesbia's view of their relationship, as he has been in several previous poems: *iocosa* (cf Cat. 8 (19), line 6), endlessly repeated, seem all she has to offer; but Catullus yearns for something deeper and more lasting, which he once again tries to define.

5 **tota ... vita** ablative of duration of time.

6 Catullus' tentative statement of what he wants their relationship to be is more thoroughly stated in other poems; cf Cat. 76 (26).
amicitia: i.e. more than a merely physical relationship; *aeternum*: life-long, not limited to youth, as sexual desire normally is; *sancta* attempts to lift the relationship to a new and higher plane; *foedus* gives it a formality, almost a legal status. On his language, see introduction to Cat. 76 (26).

Structure: 1–2 Lesbia's promise
3–4 his prayer that her promise – limited as it is – is genuinely meant
5–6 what he would hope their love might become

Analyse Catullus' language of love as it has appeared in the Lesbia-poems. Can you see any change in his vocabulary of love between the earlier and later poems? Does the study of his language contribute to the understanding of the progress of the affair?

22 (CATULLUS 73) *Desine de quoquam quicquam bene velle mereri*

Metre: Elegiac

Catullus laments the treachery of a friend; whether the poem belongs to the Lesbia-cycle is not absolutely certain. It may be addressed, like Cat. 77, to M. Caelius Rufus.

1 ff. **quoquam quicquam ... aliquem** this series of indefinite words seems to emphasize the extravagance of Catullus' despair, as does the sweeping *omnia sunt ingrata* and *nihil* (line 3). The three impersonal verbs in line 4 set up a kind of barrier to the world and friends, in contrast with the elaborate elisions of line 6, with their suggestion of close and intimate union.

2 **pium** *pietas* is the quality above all others which Catullus values in friendship; in his effort to define his view of his relationship with Lesbia, it is stressed, cf Cat. 76 (26), lines 2, 26.

6 **unicum amicum** 'only friend'; cf Catullus 100, line 6, *unica amicitia*, 'uncommon friendship'.

Structure: 1–2 Catullus' despair of finding personal loyalty
3–4 generalization
5–6 based on personal experience

23 (CATULLUS 72) *Dicebas quondam solum te nosse Catullum*

Metre: Elegiac

Catullus attempts in this and in a number of other poems to analyse the nature of Lesbia's attraction for him. In Cat. 109 (21), which is perhaps earlier than the present poem in date of composition, he defines it as a *foedus*, as *aeterna*, as a *sancta amicitia*. Here he compares it to the love a father has for his children. But Lesbia's approach is a purely sensual one; on this level she can still appeal though she has destroyed all purer affection.

1 **nosse** cf the phrase 'carnal knowledge' in English law.

2 **Iovem** cf Cat. 70 (18), line 2.

3 **dilexi** to be distinguished from *uror* (line 5) and *amare* (line 8), as the comparisons which follow show.

5 cognovi clearly intended to pick up the *nosse* of line 1, but his knowledge is that he is not alone in receiving her favours.

7 qui potis est, sc. *fieri* 'how is it possible?' *qui* is the old instrumental of the interrogative; *potis* and *pote* are used both personally and impersonally in Catullus; here *potis* is impersonal.

iniuria Lesbia's faithlessness serves to fire his sexual desires, while it destroys his purer affection (*bene velle*).

As in many other poems of Catullus, the structure is clearly outlined by the series of adverbs of time: *quondam . . . tum . . . nunc*. Lines 1–4 contrast Lesbia's view of their affair with his own, lines 5–8 the division within Catullus' own soul.

24 (CATULLUS 75) *Huc est mens deducta tua mea, Lesbia, culpa*

Metre: Elegiac

The emotional dilemma of Cat. 72 (23) is presented again, but the dichotomy in Catullus' emotional attitude is even more drastic than before.

1. **huc** 'to this point'.

deducta perhaps the imagery comes from the service (*officium*) a client performed for his patron: the morning *salutatio* and the escort (*deductio*) to the forum.

culpa cf *iniuria*, Cat. 72 (23), line 7.

2 officio suo ablative of cause or means.

3 iam nec . . . queat respect is now gone forever, no matter what reformation Lesbia may effect; at the same time nothing Lesbia can do will quench the physical fascination she possesses for him.

fias probably a true passive here; while he is quite prepared for anything Lesbia may do, her moral reformation will not be of her own doing.

4 amare cf Cat. 72 (23), line 8.

25 (CATULLUS 85) *Odi et amo. Quare id faciam, fortasse requiris*

Metre: Elegiac

The briefest statement of Catullus' dilemma, that lust (*amo*) without genuine affection (*bene volo*) is the cause of his mental torment.

1 **Odi** here the opposite, not of *amo*, but of *bene volo*, as Copley (*op. cit.*, p. 35) justly points out; cf Cat. 73 (22); 75 (24).

2 **excrucior** see note on Cat. 76 (26), line 10.

26 (CATULLUS 76) *Siqua recordanti benefacta priora voluptas*

Metre: Elegiac

A much more complex and analytical debate with himself than Cat. 8 (19); his view of his side at least of their relationship has changed and developed far beyond the fond memory of the *iocosa* of that poem. The effort to discover language in which to define his feelings for Lesbia reaches its climax in this poem: *sancta fides, pietas, foedus*, all of which occur elsewhere but are nowhere combined in a single statement, are buttressed by words and expressions which are attributes of *amicitia*: e.g. *benefacta, bene dicere, bene facere* (lines 6–7). But Lesbia has made no return (*ex hoc ingrato . . . amore ingratae . . . menti*). Now he must liberate himself from the physical desire he still feels for her, a passion which he goes on to describe, almost with disgust, as a foul disease, the source of his self-torture (*excrucies*, line 10).

The language in which he describes his purer feelings for her may owe something to the political vocabulary of his own time; in the largely private political alliances of the time, allies were called *amici* (cf Horace, *Odes* II 1 (6), lines 3 f.: *gravis . . . amicitias*, where the so-called First Triumvirate of Caesar, Pompey and Crassus is in question); such alliances were regarded as sacred bonds (*foedera*), cf Cicero, *Fam.* 5. 8. 5 (addressed to Crassus):

has litteras velim existimes *foederis* habituras esse vim, non epistulae, meque ea, quae tibi promitto ac recipio, *sanctissime* esse observaturum diligentissimeque esse facturum.

See also L. R. Taylor, *Party Politics in the Age of Caesar*, University of California Press, Berkeley (1949), chap. 1 *passim*.

3 **sanctam . . . fidem** his word was made holy by the oath which accompanied it. Cf Cat. 87 (20), line 3.

5 **in longa aetate** this phrase serves to magnify and enlarge the manifold *benefacta* he has performed; even a long life will not exhaust the memory of them.

9 **perierunt credita** all his investments of *benefacta* have brought no return.

10 **excrucies** cf Cat. 85 (25), line 1. The torture, as Copley ('Emotional conflict and its significance in the Lesbia-poems of Catullus', in *AJP* 70 (1949), p. 36) says, is not the 'conventional lover's despair', but is the result of his feelings of guilt over the realization that his lust (*amare*), lacking respect (*bene velle*), is wrong.

12 **dis invitis** this is usually understood as a causal ablative (see Merrill, Fordyce, *et al., ad loc.*); but Copley (*op. cit.*, p. 39, note 38), puts up a good case for treating it concessively: the gods are unwilling that you cease to be *miser*; otherwise why should Catullus, in his prayer, ask the gods to look upon him in his pain and be merciful to him (lines 17-18), why should he go on to list the merits which may well win him their pity (lines 25-6)?

13 **subito** Catullus' weaker self makes a lame protest; his long debate, culminating in the present poem, suggests there was nothing 'sudden' about the course proposed.

14 **qua lubet** 'no matter how'.

15 **salus** the imagery of disease and health begins here and continues through the remainder of the poem.

pervincendum note the effect of this spondaic word at the end of a hexameter.

18 **extremam ... opem** 'brought aid at the last' (Fordyce). Some editors prefer *extrema ... in morte*, 'in the final struggles of death'.

20 f. **eripite ... subrepens** cf Cat. 77, lines 3 ff.

21 **torpor** cf Cat. 51 (10), lines 6 ff.

26 **pietate** cf line 2; explained by lines 3-4 and Cat. 72 (23), lines 3 f.

Structure: 1-8 Catullus endeavours once more to define his view of his relationship with Lesbia
9-16 but his view has not been shared by Lesbia; he is tortured by feelings of guilt; he must rid himself of the cause.
17-26 prayer to the gods to aid him.

Explore fully the imagery of disease and health in the latter part of the poem.

27 (CATULLUS 11) *Furi et Aureli, comites Catulli*

Metre: Sapphic
Catullus opened the affair with Lesbia with a poem in Sapphics –

Cat. 51 (10); he breaks it off with his only other surviving poem in this metre.

1 **Furi et Aureli** this pair seem to have been the Rosenkrantz and Guildenstern of the circle in which Catullus moved. They had, it seems, betrayed his trust in the matter of the youth Juventius (see Cat. 15, 16, 21); now they seem to have come as emissaries from Lesbia to seek a reconciliation. But this attempt at *rapprochement* came after Cat. 76 (26) and his release from Lesbia's hold upon his passions.

1 ff. These lines almost certainly influenced Horace, *Odes* II 6, lines 1 ff.:

> Septimi, Gadis aditure mecum et
> Cantabrum indoctum iuga ferre nostra et
> Barbaras Syrtis, ubi Maura semper
>   Aestuat unda.

3 cf also Horace, *Odes* I 22 (41), lines 5 ff. *ut*, 'where'.

11, 12 **ulti/mos** balances *extremos* (line 2); Catullus has spanned the known world in these three stanzas; *horribile aequor*: the English channel.

15 f. The elaboration of the address to Furius and Aurelius is in startling contrast to the brutally unadorned conclusion – '*pauca . . . non bona dicta*'.

meae puellae perhaps Lesbia has so called herself in her message, in the hope of reminding Catullus of the feelings he felt at the first flush of the affair.

17 **vivat** not *vivamus* (Cat. 5 (13), line 1) any more.

19 **identidem** cf Cat. 51 (10), line 3.

21 **amorem** in the Catullian vocabulary of love [see Cat. 72 (23), 73 (22), 75 (24)], etc., even the purely physical longing, which possessed him after his purer love had gone, has now disappeared.

22 ff. The ending is quiet, mournful, after the brief, dreadful message.

culpa cf Cat. 75 (24), line 1.

23 **ultimi** our attention has been drawn from the ends of the world (*in extremos . . . Indos, ultimos Britannos*) to the edge of the meadow.

> *Structure:* 1–14 Furius and Aurelius, ready to endure dangers in strange and distant parts of the world with Catullus.

15-16 show your courage by carrying this brief message of rejection to Lesbia;

17-20 tell her she has made her choice: promiscuity rather than single-hearted devotion to Catullus;

21-24 his love is dead, destroyed by her and her behaviour.

The poems of the 'Lesbia-cycle' have been tentatively arranged in what seems to the editors a reasonable chronological order. Numerous other arrangements have been suggested. It might be a useful exercise to ask students to suggest and defend variations on this arrangement.

Do you believe there was a Lesbia? Could she have been, as some of the women to whom Horace addressed love poems clearly were, a fiction?

28 (CATULLUS 9) *Verani, omnibus e meis amicis*

Metre: Hendecasyllabic (Phalaecean)

Veranius is welcomed home from Spain where he has, presumably, been serving as a member of the *cohors* of the provincial governor, along with his and Catullus' friend Fabullus (see Cat. 12 (29), lines 15-16).

1 f. **omnibus... trecentis** 'of all my friends you are worth more to me than three hundred thousand others'; or *trecentis* may simply be taken with *amicis*, 'first of all my friends, all three hundred thousand of them'.

3 f. The news of Veranius' return seems to have come as a surprise to Catullus, who can hardly believe his ears or contain his joy.

8 **ut mos est tuus** a post in the *cohors* (suite or staff) of a governor could be an educational experience, serving as a kind of apprenticeship for the young man planning a political career. Veranius apparently served in this same kind of post before, as *mos... tuus* suggests, and was to serve once again (see Cat. 28, where Catullus sends his condolences to Veranius and Fabullus for the financial barrenness of their year with L. Calpurnius Piso Caesoninus in Macedonia, governor during 57-55 B.C.)

10 **quantum... beatiorum** equivalent to *omnium hominum beatiorum;* cf Cat. 3 (12), line 2.

R. Syme, 'Piso and Veranius in Catullus', *Classica et Mediaevalia* 17 (1956) 129-34.

COMMENTARY 133

29 (CATULLUS 12) *Marrucine Asini, manu sinistra*

Metre: Hendecasyllabic (Phalaecean)

2 **in ioco atque vino** cf Cat. 50 (2), line 6, *per iocum atque vinum*.

3 **lintea** linen-handkerchiefs also served as personal table-napkins. On other handkerchief-thieves see Martial VIII, 59; XII, 29.

4 **inepte** with *invenustus*, a strong and favourite word of condemnation with Catullus and, one assumes, his circle. Cf Cat. 25, line 8; 39 (81), line 16; he characterizes his own behaviour with the verb *ineptire* (Cat. 8 (19), line 1).

7 f. **vel ... velit** 'he'd be happy to pay a fortune even to have your thefts undone', or, perhaps, 'he'd be glad to pay a fortune even to purchase silence about your thefts' from the victims.

mutari has a commercial connotation; in exchange for his money, the best Pollio can expect is to have the scandal hushed up.

8 f. **leporum ... facetiarum** Pollio possessed the qualities Catullus valued so highly; cf Cat. 50 (2), lines 7 f.

differtus, 'stuffed'; the reading *disertus* presents problems of interpretation.

10 **hendecasyllabos** cf Cat. 36, line 5. Martial also frequently employed hendecasyllables for satiric purposes.

15 **miserunt** Veranius and Fabullus are assumed to have served at least twice together as *comites* on a governor's staff; the first occasion in Spain *c.* 60 B.C., the second time with L. Calpurnius Piso Caesoninus in Macedonia, 57–55 B.C. Catullus 9 (28), 12 (29), 13 (30) belong to the first tour of duty, Catullus 28 and 47 to the second.

30 (CATULLUS 13) *Cenabis bene, mi Fabulle, apud me*

Metre: Hendecasyllabic (Phalaecean)
Perhaps to be associated with the welcome home to Veranius, Cat. 9 (28). Young men returning from provincial posts were assumed to have 'made their pile' and, under lax governors, undoubtedly could; cf Cat. 10 (78).

5 **cachinnis** suggests a more vulgar and unrestrained expression than *risus*.

6 **venuste** again this quality which Catullus esteemed so highly in both men and women, cf Cat. 3 (12), line 2; 86 (15), line 3; even Sirmio shares this virtue (Cat. 31 (32), line 12).

9 **meros amores** 'unmixed affection'; a particularly appropriate adjective in a dinner invitation; *merus* is usually applied to *wine* unmixed with water; cf Cat. 27, line 7.

10 **seu quid... elegantiusve est** cf Cat. 22, lines 13 f.; 82, lines 2, 4.

11 **unguentum** perfumes commonly attended the *commissatio* or drinking party which followed the banquet proper.

meae puellae undoubtedly Lesbia; this seems to date the poem to the early stages of the affair.

12 **Veneres Cupidinesque** see note on Cat. 3 (12), line 1.

14 **totum... nasum** perhaps a joking hint that Fabullus' nose was rather special already? Cf Cat. 53 (85), where the whole point of the epigram seems to be the hit, in the final line, at Calvus' stature.

Analyse the imagery and tone of the invitational poem.

31 (CATULLUS 14) *Ni te plus oculis meis amarem*

Metre: Hendecasyllabic (Phalaecean)
As a Saturnalia gift, Calvus (*q.v.*) has sent Catullus a sampling of bad poets (*impii*, line 7), i.e. poets who did not accept the poetic creed of the *neoterici*. Catullus seizes the opportunity to launch an attack on the literary opposition.

1 **plus oculis meis** cf Cat. 3 (12), line 5; 82, lines 2, 4. Maecenas' parody of these opening lines is preserved in Suetonius, *Vita Horati*:

> ni te visceribus meis, Horati,
> plus iam diligo, tu tuum sodalem
> nimio vides strigosiorem ...

3 **odio Vatiniano** Catullus elsewhere [Cat. 53 (85), line 2] refers to Calvus' frequent prosecutions of Vatinius (*q.v.*).

6 **clienti** Catullus hints that Calvus had received this dreadful little gift from someone he had represented in the courts; hence a second-hand gift.

7 **tantum... impiorum** in what sense could such poets be labelled *impii*?

9 **litterator** not a literary man, but one who teaches the *litterae*, the a b c's.

10 **non est mi male** 'I'm not upset'; cf Cat. 38 (33), lines 1 f.

16 **mi = mihi. non abibit** 'you won't get away with it, my counterfeit friend'.

17 **si luxerit** perhaps Catullus suggests he may not survive to see the morrow. Elsewhere he pretends that bad literature affects him physically (Cat. 44 (82), lines 7 ff.).

18 **Caesios, Aquinos** 'Caesius, Aquinus and all their kind'.

19 **Suffenum** see Cat. 22 for a fuller treatment of this poetaster.

20 **remunerabor** cf *munus* (line 9).

22 **malum pedem** perhaps a double-entendre – 'your crippled foot' and 'your halting metre'.

A. W. Verrall, 'A metrical jest', in *Collected Studies in Greek and Latin Scholarship* (Cambridge, 1913) 249–67.

32 (CATULLUS 31) *Paene insularum, Sirmio, insularumque*

Metre: Choliambic
Catullus joyfully greets Sirmio on his return from his tour of duty in Bithynia.

2 **ocelle** as a term of affection, cf Cat. 50 (2), line 19. Catullus on several occasions calls someone or something 'dearer than his own eyes', e.g. Cat. 3 (12), line 5; 14 (31), line 1; 82, lines 2, 4.

3 **uterque Neptunus** i.e. Neptune's two departments, the waters of the seas and the inland lakes.

5 **Thuniam atque Bithunos** one suspects a technical, perhaps official, note in this unnecessary specification.

9 **larem** cf Cat. 9 (28), line 3, *domum ad tuos penates*.

12 **salve** Catullus greets Sirmio as he would a friend, cf Cat. 43 (16), line 1.
   venusta Sirmio possesses for Catullus this same highly esteemed quality.
   ero gaude the humanization of Sirmio continues.

13 **Lydiae** tradition, first reported by Herodotus (I 94. 6 f.), made the Etruscans, who settled the Po Valley, immigrants from Lydia. The waves, with this history, now share another experience with Catullus. The reference does not seem out of place, as some critics have complained.

> *Structure:* 1–6 joy and gratitude at beholding Sirmio again
> 7–11 reflections on the sources of this joy
> 12–14 calls upon Sirmio and Lacus Benacus to rejoice in return

This poem is 'emphatically not the simple song in praise of Sirmio that it is sometimes carelessly taken to be' (Quinn). Discover the elements which contribute to its complexity.

33 (CATULLUS 38) *Malest, Cornifici, tuo Catullo*

Metre: Hendecasyllabic (Phalaecean)
Catullus, suffering from some personal bereavement (perhaps his brother's death?), complains that his friend and fellow neoteric, Q. Cornificius, has not sent him words of consolation.

6 **sic meos amores?** 'is this the way you treat my affection for you?'

8 **lacrimis Simonideis** cf Horace *Odes* II 1 (6), lines 37 f. Quintilian, speaking of the dirges (*threnoi*) of Simonides, says (*Inst. Or.* X 1. 64):

> praecipua tamen eius in commovenda miseratione virtus, ut quidam in hac eum parte omnibus eius operis auctoribus praeferant.

34 (CATULLUS 46) *Iam ver egelidos refert tepores*

Metre: Hendecasyllabic (Phalaecean)
This poem was written on the eve of Catullus' leaving Bithynia, after his year as a member of the *cohors* or personal staff of C. Memmius, probably in the spring of 56 B.C.

1 **egelidos ... tepores** literally, 'the warmth with the chill taken out'.

4 **Phrygii ... campi** cf Cat. 31 (32), lines 5–6: *Bithunos ... campos*.

COMMENTARY

6 claras Asiae ... urbes the posting to the *cohors* of a provincial governor gave men a chance to see the world; cf Cat. 9 (28), lines 6–7. Catullus probably visited, on his return voyage, such famous sites as Ephesus and Rhodes. Cicero travelled to Rhodes on his return from Cilicia in 50 B.C. *puerorum causa* (*Att.* 6. 7. 2), i.e. for the sake of his son Marcus and his nephew Quintus.

volemus cf Cat. 4 (77), line 5, where the yacht also 'flies'.

11 diversae ... viae *diversus* emphasizes the difference of direction in which their separate paths lie, *variae* their difference in character. In spite of the eagerness which one feels throughout the rest of the poem, this final line has a sense of strain and effort, of regret at separation. Paul Goodman, *The Structure of Literature*: Chicago, 1954, pp. 184–92.

Structure: 1–6 divides into two sections:
    1–3 describes spring's arrival
    4–6 addressed to the poet himself, expresses the urge which spring arouses, the urge to be on his way.
    7–11 also falls into two parts:
    7–8 the poet's mental state, excitement and impatience
    9–11 addressed to his friends, spring's coming means the departure of his friends.

35 (HORACE, *Odes* I 3) *Sic te diva potens Cypri*

Metre: Second Asclepiadean

Horace addresses the ship in which Vergil is crossing to Greece. He offers a tirade against travel by sea and hopes that Vergil's crossing may be uneventful.

1 sic 'so', i.e. 'on condition that' the subsequent prayer be fulfilled.

diva potens Cypri Venus, protectress of sailors. Cyprus, where Venus stepped ashore after her marine birth, was a major cult centre where Phoenician, Greek, and Roman elements combined. *Cypri* genitive case, with *potens*.

2 fratres Helenae the Dioscuri, Castor and Pollux, finally elevated to the rank of the constellation, Gemini (Twins). St Elmo's Fire, an electrical phenomenon occasionally seen on ships' yards during storms, was thought to indicate the presence of the brothers, and promised safety.

Cf Catullus 4 (77), line 27 *Odes* III 29, lines 63–4.

3 **ventorumque ... pater** Aeolus (lit. shifting) instigated a storm in Verg. *Aen.* 1, lines 52–80.

4 **Iapyga** Greek accusative singular.

5, 6 **creditum/debes Vergilium** banking imagery. Vergil has been 'deposited' or 'entrusted' for 'remittance' in Greece (*reddas*, 7). Vergil died at Brundisium in 19 B.C. on his return from a voyage to Greece.

6 **finibus Atticis** dative plural, with *debes* and *reddas*.

8 **dimidium** cf *Odes* II 17, line 5: *te meae partem animae* used of Maecenas.

9 **robur et aes triplex** the words apply more aptly to the ship's fabric and armament (and strongbox) than to the sailor, but Horace obtains a striking contrast and clever antithesis by the juxtaposition *fragilem ... truci* (10).

12 **primus** 'pioneer, in days of old' cf Verg. *Aen.* 1, line 1: *Troiae qui primus ab oris*.

13 **decertantem** cf *Odes* I 1 (4), line 15: *luctantem Icariis fluctibus Africum*.

14 **tristis** 'depressing, rainy'. Used with Hyades, the Rain Constellation.

15 **quo** abl. of comparison.

20 **Acroceraunia** in apposition with *scopulos*.

24 **transiliunt** implies rash trespassing. Cf Remus' bound over Romulus' wall.

25 **omnia** the four elements: water (Horace's pioneer navigator), fire (Promethus, son of Iapetus), air (Daedalus), earth (Hercules who adventured into the Underworld).

31 **incubuit** 'lay upon, fell upon' cf Verg. *Aen.* 1, line 89: *ponto nox incubat atra*.

    cohors 'retinue'. Diseases and afflictions were the 'dowry' of Pandora, the first woman on earth.

33 **leti corripuit gradum** Horace imagined death as a persistent follower able to adopt a faster rate of marching when the situation demands a 'quick march'. Cf line 17, *mortis ... gradum*.

36 **Herculeus labor** Hercules made the descent to the Underworld (1) to capture the three-headed watchdog Cerberus, and (2) to deliver his friend Theseus.

COMMENTARY 139

37 **nil ... ardui est** 'nothing is too steep', i.e. 'difficult'.

J. P. Elder, 'Horace, Carm. 1, 3', in *AJP* 83 (1952) 140–58.
Notice the various words Horace uses to express 'sea'. Can you find general or particular reasons for the variations? The tenor of the poem is markedly reactionary and set against progress.
How do you explain Horace's stand against experiment and change? The structure of the ode is readily discerned: lines 1–8; 9–16; 17–24; 25–33; 34–40. Comment critically on the thought progression, use of link words, persistent imagery, etc. Comment on Horace's use of mythological figures to caution against restless enterprise (27–36).
Locate examples of athletic and military imagery in the ode. What purpose is served by their use?

Epode 10

Propempticon to an Enemy, the Poetaster Maevius,
En Route to Greece
Appendix to no. 35 (*Odes* I 3)

Mala soluta navis exit alite,
    ferens olentem Maevium:
ut horridis utrumque verberes latus,
    Auster, memento fluctibus.
niger rudentis Eurus inverso mari   5
    fractosque remos differat;
insurgat Aquilo, quantus altis montibus
    frangit trementis ilices;
nec sidus atra nocte amicum appareat,
    qua tristis Orion cadit;   10
quietiore nec feratur aequore
    quam Graia victorum manus,
cum Pallas usto vertit iram ab Ilio
    in impiam Aiacis ratem!
o quantus instat navitis sudor tuis   15
    tibique pallor luteus
et illa non virilis eiulatio,
    preces et aversum ad Iovem,
Ionius udo cum remugiens sinus
    Noto carinam ruperit!   20

>   opima quodsi praeda curvo litore
>   porrecta mergos iuverit,
>   libidinosus immolabitur caper
>   et agna Tempestatibus.

36 (HORACE, *Odes* I 5) *Quis multa gracilis te puer in rosa*

Metre: Fourth Asclepiadean

1 **gracilis ... puer** Horace's physique was stocky and rotund (cf *Epist.* I 4, line 15; 15, line 24; 20, line 24) and his sensitivity to his girth may account for his epithet attached to a younger subject. Some have identified the *puer* and the bore (*Sat.* I 9) with the elegist Propertius, member of Maecenas' circle, and many years Horace's junior (50–16 B.C.).

multa ... in rosa Sybaritic decadence was partly exemplified by their extravagant use of roses in pillows and mattresses. One should probably imagine a rose-garden as setting, with an artificial grotto, a Hellenistic extravagance which was featured in Roman town and country mansions.

2 **perfusus** another uncomplimentary epithet (cf *uvida*, 14), and the first statement of the water imagery which permeates the ode.

urget implies rather active courting.

3 **Pyrrha** a Graecism, suggesting a Titian-haired girl (flame-coloured, blonde). Her identity escapes detection, though, if Propertius is the *gracilis puer*, Pyrrha may be identified with 'blonde' Cynthia.

sub 'under cover of'.

4 **religas** 'bind or comb back, tie up', a contemporary hair style amply illustrated by contemporary portrait sculpture.

5 **simplex munditiis** Milton's version 'plain in thy neatness' or 'in simple elegance'. The epithet *simplex* is certainly not in accord with her emerging character which is marked by duplicity.

   fidem, sc. *mutatam.* 'faithlessness'. Cf Cat. 76 (26), line 3; 87 (20), line 3.

9 **aurea** 'golden', 'pure gold' with connotations of excellence.

10 **vacuam** 'free, fancy-free'.

COMMENTARY 141

13 ff. **me tabula sacer** ... Horace's experience with love, but not with Pyrrha, provides the poem's cadenza. Sailors rescued from shipwreck customarily dedicated an *ex voto*, a personal article or a terracotta tablet recording or picturing the event, to the saviour. Horace, shipwrecked on love's cruel sea, has renounced his past passion by a comparable votive offering for release from disaster.

15–16 **potenti ... maris deo** the marine divinity must be Neptune (cf Poseidon Asphaleios – Protector of Sailors).

K. Quinn, 'Horace as a love poet', *Arion* II 3 (1963) 59–77.
The poem is almost entirely one continuous metaphor identifying Pyrrha with the inconstant sea, birthplace of Venus. Examine the poem carefully to see how Horace sustains the marine imagery. How effective are the contrasts which are suggested throughout?

37 (HORACE, *Odes* I 8) *Lydia, dic per omnes*

Metre: Greater Sapphic

1 Lydia and Sybaris are typical poetic Greek names chosen to symbolize luxury and decadence.

4 **campum**, i.e. Campus Martius, see *Index Nominum*.

6 **Gallica** an excellent breed imported from Gaul.

6, 7 **lupatis ... frenis** 'with wolftooth bit'.

8 **flavum Tiberim** the muddy, silt-laden Tiber was Rome's nearest swimming area, and was much favored by the Roman youth then as today. Ostia's beaches were many miles distant. Cf Cicero, *Pro Caelio* 36, on the subject of Clodia's Tiber-side villa where the Roman youth bathed.
olivum olive oil was used by the athletes to lubricate their bodies before wrestling and before any exposure to the sun, and also for massage after the bath.

9 **sanguine viperino** a deadly poison, cf *Epode* 3, line 6.

14 **dicunt**, sc. *latuisse*
filium ... Thetidis The sea nymph Thetis disguised her son Achilles in female clothing and concealed him at the court of Lycomedes on Scyros. Ulysses and Ajax discovered him by a ruse,

and Achilles joined the expedition against Troy which resulted in his premature death.

What purpose is served by the mythical allusion attached to Horace's complaint?

38 (HORACE, *Odes* I 13) *Cum tu, Lydia, Telephi*

Metre: Second Asclepiadean
Horace is a prey to jealousy and grieves over his unrequited love. Blest is the tie that truly binds, unbroken to the end of life.

1 **Telephi** The original Telephus was the legendary son of Hercules and Auge, exposed, like Romulus and Remus, and suckled by a fawn. Finally discovered and recognized by his heroic father, Telephus became the founder of Pergamum, which later became capital of the wealthy kingdom of the Attalids ceded to Rome in 133 B.C. Horace uses the proper name to evoke romantic, wealthy associations. The repetition of the name in line 2 emphasizes Lydia's infatuation. For Lydia, cf *Odes* I 8, (37).

5 **tum nec mens** possibly a reminiscence of Catullus 51 (10), lines 5–11.

6 **certa sede** 'in a settled state'.

10 **immodicae** lit. 'unmeasured' a transferred epithet from *mero*; here 'abandoned, reckless.'

14 **non ... speres** potential subjunctive, almost a prohibition.

15 **oscula** 'lips,' a rare usage.

16 **quinta parte** 'quintessence,' no doubt a recollection of Pythagorean doctrine (*quinta essentia*), an element of the highest nature which pervades and unifies the canonical four (earth, air, water, fire).

20 In an age when divorce was easy and common, sepulchral epigrams, as here, single out lasting and harmonious marriages for eulogistic comment.

Examine the poem critically with attention to the metaphorical usages. Does the poem have unity?

COMMENTARY

39 (HORACE, *Odes* I 17) *Velox amoenum saepe Lucretilem*

Metre: Alcaic
Horace extends an invitation to Tyndaris to visit him and to enjoy the delights of his Sabine farm.

1 Faunus' presence, though unseen, has been frequent and always efficacious. Cf *usque* (4), *utcumque* (10).

2 **mutat**... 'takes (Sabine) Lucretilis in exchange for (Arcadian) Lycaeus'.

3 **capellis** dative. cf Vergil, *Ecl.* 7, 47; *Georgics* 3, 155.

6 **deviae** 'wayward'.

7 **olentis** 'malodorous'.

9 **Martialis** 'Mars' favourites' because the Founding Twins, sons of Mars and Rhea Silvia, were nursed by a she-wolf and discovered in the Cave of the Lupercal.

10 The preceding poem, *Odes* I 16 (88) in the same metre, is cast in the form of a *palinode* or recantation, and may be addressed to the same Tyndaris, though unspecified. One is reminded of the Greek lyric poet Stesichorus (sixth century B.C.), who slandered the heroine (or goddess) Helen in one of his poems, was blinded for his impiety, and only regained his sight after he had published his apology or recantation in verse. Horace's invitation might appropriately follow upon a poem of reconciliation. So Horace invites a second Helen to 'retreat' with him to Licenza.

11 **cubantis** here 'low-lying', 'reclining'; a suggestive word implying that relaxation on the Sabine Farm extends even to nature.

12 **lēvia** 'smooth-worn'.

13 **di me tuentur** Horace was convinced that the poet's divinely inspired craft insulated him from harm and disaster.

14 **cordi est** 'is dear', 'is pleasing'. *hic, hic* (17), and *hic* (21) indicate emphatic and demonstrative gestures, the complement to his pride of ownership.

14 ff. The idyllic superabundance is all the more remarkable by reason of the rich ambiguities: *ruris honorum*, with *cornu* or *opulenta*; *ad plenum*, with *manabit* or *benigno* ... *cornu*, abl. of separation with *manabit*, or instrumental ablative with *opulenta*.

18 **fide Teia** 'upon the lyre of Teos', or lit. 'on the string of Teos'. Cf fiddle. Anacreon, dislocated from his Asia Minor home at Teos by the Persian expansion, was that city's most famous lyric poet (c. 560–490 B.C.).

19 **laborantis in uno**, sc. *viro* 'struggling, contesting, or love-sick over one man', i.e. Ulysses. 'Weaving and labouring' may be implied also, and the ambiguity may extend to the loom of Penelope and the witchcraft of Circe.

20 **Penelopen vitreamque Circen** the repertoire will embrace Penelope's marital virtue and Ulysses' fidelity, along with the glamour of extra-marital adventure (Ulysses with the witch Circe), both appropriate themes for a second Helen, whose predecessor was at first faithful to Menelaus, but faithless when Paris appeared in Sparta. *vitream*: 'seagreen, glassy', because Circe was a marine goddess, and ancient glass is often green in shade.

22 **sub umbra** 'under a shady bower,' a *fête-champêtre* in Horace's garden. Cf *Odes* I 5 (36), line 3: *grato ... sub antro*.

23 **confundet ... proelia** 'combine blows, join battles'. Poetic for *miscere*, or *committere*, with added notion of confusion and uproar. The ambiguity deriving from the mixing of wine and water is surreptitious.

24 **proelia** completes the suspended meaning of *confundet*, 'brawls, bouts'.

25 **Cyrus** another poetic name. *male dispari*: 'no match at all for him'.

L. A. MacKay, 'Odes I 16 and 17: *O matre pulchra* ... *Velox amoenum*', in *AJP* 83 (1962) 298–300.

This idyllic poem is charged throughout with playful irony and affectionate humour. Where can these be detected? Analyse the poem for evidence of structural symmetry. What use does Horace make of the animal kingdom? Comment on the surprising passion and violence in the riotous last stanza.

40 (HORACE, *Odes* I 20) *Vile potabis modicis Sabinum*

Metre: Sapphic

Horace replies to a letter from Maecenas announcing his forthcoming visit to the poet's farm, his former property.

1 **vile potabis ...** Horace emphasizes the modesty of his domestic life, on the Sabine farm. *Vin ordinaire* is the staple beverage in the country.

COMMENTARY

2 **Graeca ... testa** probably alludes to South Italic ware purchased for the special vintage season.

3 **conditum levi** 'stored up and sealed' (*condo, lino*), with wax or gypsum.

3, 4 **datus ... plausus** Maecenas' recovery from a dangerous illness in 30 B.C. occasioned thunderous applause when he appeared in the theatre (of Pompey?) cf *Odes* II 17, lines 25–6. The Theatre of Pompey, Rome's first permanent stone theatre, in the Campus Martius, was close enough to the Mons Vaticanus and the west bank of the Tiber to produce an echo.

5 **care Maecenas** cf *Odes* II 20 (7), line 7: *dilecte Maecenas*.

eques Maecenas stubbornly refused to enter the political arena; his withdrawal was in keeping with his Epicurean sympathies.

paterni fluminis Tiber, or Etruscan Thybris, because Maecenas was born in Etruscan Arretium, and was descended from Etruscan kings (cf *Odes* I 1, (4) line 1).

6 ff. **iocosa ... imago** 'merry echo'. Cf *Odes* I 12, lines 3–4.

9 **domitam** poetic, for *pressam*.

10 **tu bibes** 'you may drink at your own home', a concessive use of the future. The pronoun is distinctly preferable to the alternative reading, *tum*, which makes little sense.

11 **temperant** *vinum temperare*, 'to add water to wine' in due proportions.

What is the symbolic or poetic value of the allusions to wine throughout the brief poem?

41 (HORACE, *Odes* I 22) *Integer vitae scelerisque purus*

Metre: Sapphic

The poem is addressed to his friend Aristius Fuscus, poet, wit, and grammarian. The genuine feeling at the outset gives way to a mock-heroic tone as Horace identifies himself with the upright man and describes his encounter with the wolf.

5 **aestuosas** may either refer to the 'seething, boiling' sandbanks, or the 'burning, sweltering' desert heat. Cf Vergil, *Aen.* 5, line 51. Cat. 7 (14), line 5.

7 **fabulosus** 'exotic, romantic'. Romans heard tales of gigantic snakes and gold-gathering ants along the Indus tributary. For Ethiopia and India, cf Horace, *Sat.* II 8, line 14.

8 **lambit** the river seems to be personified as serpent or lion, or other exotic creature. Bernini's 'Fountain of the Rivers' in the Piazza Navona in Rome provides a perfect illustration of the lion suggestion. R. J. Getty suggested that Hydaspes, and the other exotic associations, are injected to tease Aristius Fuscus whose cognomen 'dusky' has Eastern associations (*CP* 47 (1952) p. 106).

9 **namque me** Horace's experience provides an emphatic precedent to prove the philosophical maxim (Q.E.D.).

10 **Lalagen** an onomatopoeic fictitious name, 'chatterbox' (cf Greek, *lalagein*, to prattle).

11 Cf Cat. 31 (32), line 7: *O quid solutis est beatius curis*?

13–14 **militaris Daunias** Daunia (Apulia), Horace's native province in Italy, the domain of Daunus, was renowned for its military exploits.

15 **Iubae tellus** Mauretania and Numidia.

16 **arida nutrix** 'parched, dry nurse': the bizarre epithet is transferred from *tellus*.

17 **pigris ... campis** 'lifeless plains', 'frozen stretches', cf Lucan *Phars.* 4, line 50.

19–20 **malusque Iuppiter** 'gloomy sky'.
urget 'is heavy, overcast'.

21 **sub curru,** sc. of Helios, the sun god.

> H. Levy, '*Gallica quae dicitur explicatio*', in *CJ* 56 (1960–1) 117–22. The poetic structure is neatly articulated:
> A. 1–4 Solemn rhetorical opening: virtue is man's best protection.
> B. 5–8 Uninhabitable parts of the world: North Africa (Syrtes), Caucasus (cold), India (Hydaspes' monsters).
> C. 9–16 The encounter with the wolf in the Sabine forest, more terrible than anything in Apulia (Daunus) or North Africa (Iubae).
> D. 17–24 Uninhabitable zones of the world: cold, rain and heat.
> E. 25–26 Love, and love songs, with Lalage as theme (10), are Horace's best protection anywhere.

Examine the 'solemn' passages, striking imagery, and sonorous phrases for hints of parody and playfulness. How serious is the poem?

Horace draws some of his effective vocabulary and phrases from Catullus' two Sapphic poems [51 (10), and 11 (27)]. Examine both poems to see what Horace adopted and try to determine the 'creative' element in his borrowings.
What is the cumulative effect of the geographical imagery?

42 (HORACE, *Odes* I 23) *Vitas inuleo me similis, Chloe*

Metre: Fourth Asclepiadean

1 **Chloe** a poetic Greek name meaning literally 'green shoot, fresh young thing'.

2 **pavidam** a regular epithet of deer, 'startled, shivering'.

3 **non sine vano** litotes, to accentuate her timidity.

4 **silvae** trisyllabic.

9 **atqui** used to introduce the abrupt denial.

10 **frangere** inf. of purpose.

M. Owen Lee, 'Horace, Carm. 1, 23: simile and metaphor', in *CP* 60 (1965) 185–6.

The ode contains a reminiscence of Anacreon (frag. 52). The elaborate style, the complicated metre, and the somewhat artificial vocabulary (e.g. *veris inhorruit adventus*) lends a quaint, almost miniaturistic element to the ode. References to the mother frame the poem.

43 (HORACE, *Odes* I 24) *Quis desiderio sit pudor aut modus*

Metre: Third Asclepiadean

Horace addresses a threnody (lament) and eulogy to Vergil on the death of their mutual friend, Quintilius Varus, in 24 B.C. Horace mentions Varus in earlier and later contexts: *Odes* I 18, and *Ars Poetica* 438 ff.

1 **desiderio** cf Cat. 2 (11), line 5; 96 (47), line 3; *Odes* I 14 (68), line 18.

3 **Melpomene** 'Muse of my Lyrics.'
   pater Jupiter and Mnemosyne (memory) were parents of the Nine Muses.

5 **sopor** poetic for *somnus*. Cf Vergil, *Aen.* 10, lines 745 f. *oculos et ferreus urget/somnus.*

6 ff. Pudor, Fides, Veritas 'Honour, Good Faith, Truth' are characteristics of Quintilius' personality as a literary critic. Horace elsewhere (*Ars Poetica*, 438 ff.) celebrates Quintilius' honesty and candour as a critic.

10 **nulli** poetic for *nemini*.

11 **tu frustra pius ... poscis** *pius*, 'devoted, faithful' is Vergil's common epithet for Aeneas. *Frustra* modifies *poscis* and *pius*.

non ita creditum 'entrusted on no such terms'. Horace may be using the language of banking, the depositing of funds, usually in temples or shrines. One should recall that Horace served as a *scriba quaestorius* after the rout at Philippi.

13 Orpheus charmed beasts and trees with the power of his music. Cf *Odes* I 12, lines 7–8, 11–12.

14 **moderere** the reference to Orpheus may be a delicate compliment to Vergil for his skilful treatment of the Orpheus–Aristaeus myth in *Georgic* 4.

fidem 'lyre', literally the string.

15 **vanae imagini** 'the unsubstantial likeness.'

16 **virga horrida** the caduceus or wand of Hermes Psychopompos, escort of the dead souls to Hades. Cf *Odes* I 10 (60), 17–20.

17 **fata** brachylogy for *portas fatorum*.

18 **nigro compulerit ... gregi** dative of direction, instead of *ad* with accusative.

The ode's structure is comparatively simple:

   1–4   Expression of grief.
   5–8   Recollections of Quintilius.
   9–18 Complaint on the injustice of things; addressed to Vergil. The finality of death.
   19–20 Resignation is the proper course.

Examine the poem for similarities of expression and mood with *Odes* I 3 (35). What evidence can you find of genuine remorse for Quintilius' death? Can you detect any common traits with Catullus' lament for his brother's death (48) or with his Consolation to Calvus on Quintilia's death (47)?

COMMENTARY 149

44 (HORACE, *Odes* I 29) *Icci, beatis nunc Arabum invides*

Metre: Alcaic

Iccius, whom Horace pictures as an ardent student of philosophy, has set aside his texts and joined the Roman prefect of Egypt in his invasion of Arabia (24 B.C.). Unfortunately for any hopes that Iccius had of winning wealth and slaves in the East, the expedition was a failure.

1 **Icci** emphatic position and sound with suggestion of consternation and reprimand.

Nunc in contrast with his earlier philosophical learnings.

beatis Arabum gazis hypallage for *gazis beatorum Arabum*. The wealth of Arabia (and Sheba) was proverbial (cf Psalms 72, 15), but the reports were grossly exaggerated.

4 **Medo** Parthian. Cf *Odes* I 2 (66) line 22. Iccius' imperial horizons were very wide; tokens of his success were to be a Parthian cupbearer and a concubine attendant.

6 **sponso necato** slain in combat, by Iccius (?).

7 **aula,** sc. *regia*.

9 **doctus** cf Herodotus 1, 136. Persian boys were taught to ride, shoot, and speak the truth.

tendere properly applies only to the bow, but cf Vergil *Aen.* 5, line 508: *telumque tetendit*.

10 **arduis ... montibus** instead of *ad arduos montes*. Note the juxtaposition *arduis pronos*. Cf *Odes* I 6 (5), line 9, *tenues grandia*.

13–14 **coemptos ... libros** Iccius had acquired a large private library.

14 **Socraticam domum** Plato and Xenophon, Aeschines and others.

15 **loricis Hiberis** Spanish steel was a superior product, competing only with Noricum (cf *Odes* I 16 (88), lines 9–10).

16 **tendis** cf line 9.

What can be divined about Horace's attitude towards aggressive imperialism and the instinct for conquest from this ode? Examine *Odes* I 1 (4), lines 23–5 for additional evidence.

Iccius appears to have been an aggressive, flamboyant personality. Does Horace treat his actions and pretensions seriously?

45 (HORACE, *Odes* II 7) *O saepe mecum tempus in ultimum*

Metre: Alcaic
Horace rejoices over the restoration of Pompeius to home and citizenship. Once his partner in war and revelry, present with Horace at Philippi, Pompeius has reason to be thankful to the gods and to Octavian for his pardon.

1. **saepe** Brutus and Cassius campaigned for two years (43–42 B.C.) before the decisive battle at Philippi.

2 **deducte...duce** word play. Cf *fregi...fracta* (7, 11).

3 **quis** Octavian pardoned Antonian partisans after the 'ceasefire' at Actium.
redonavit Horatian coinage. **Quiritem** 'as citizen', with full rights and privileges.
Octavian's clemency in 29 B.C. was designed to forestall further civil war, to ensure the nation's survival, and to help integrate the new society.

10 **relicta parmula** Horace confesses to desperate action in the retreat of the Liberators after the second engagement at Philippi. But the shield is probably fictitious. On the brink of disaster, Horace simply chose to save his skin. Archilochus, Alcaeus, and Anacreon all admit to similar defection and Horace probably adopts the poetic and somewhat comical vogue for a poet's consternation in a losing engagement. Pompeius shared the same hasty retreat.
non bene litotes, 'ingloriously, unheroically'.

11, 12 **et minaces...mento** Horace's version of the Homeric formula (cf *Iliad* 2, 418 f.).
turpe adjective, with *solum*, but also adverbial.

13 **Mercurius** the poet's protector (cf *Odes* I 10 (60), line 6; II 17, line 29) intervened and lifted Horace from the battlefield in a cloud of invisibility. Horace expands his lucky escape to epic dimensions (cf Homer, *Iliad* 3, 380 ff. Aphrodite's rescue of Paris; Vergil, *Aen.* 1, 411 ff., Aeneas safeguarded by Venus; Horace *Odes* I 10 (60), lines 13–16, Priam protected by Mercury).

15 The tidal imagery may suggest that Pompeius joined the rebellious admiral Sextus Pompeius, finally defeated by Agrippa in 36 B.C. Compare these two stanzas (9–16) with the sketch evoked by Pollio's history of the Civil Wars (*Odes* II 1 (6), lines 17–24).

COMMENTARY 151

18 **latus,** i.e. *membra*.

25 **Venus** winning throw of the dice, with four different faces of the four dies showing. Cf *Odes* I 4 (49), line 18: *regna vini sortiere talis*.

26 **dicet** 'appoint'. *non sanius:* litotes.

28 **furere** cf *Odes* IV 12 (46), line 28: *dulce est desipere in loco*.

For an extended discussion of the ode's structure, see N. E. Collinge, *The Structure of Horace's Odes*, pp. 130–49 *passim*. Both Horace and Pompeius owe their renewed friendship to different agencies: Mercury and Octavian respectively.

Is the prevailing tone serious or humorous? The ode finds a natural continuity through Horace's use of link-words, repetitions, synonyms and associations. Examine the ode carefully to detect the clever interlocking word scheme.

46 (HORACE, *Odes* IV 12) *Iam veris comites, quae mare temperant*

Metre: Third Asclepiadean

An invitation to Vergil to attend a springtime celebration to which each will contribute. The ode is almost certainly addressed to the poet Vergil, and was perhaps withheld from the original publication in 23 B.C. because of its similarity to other poems in the collection.

1 **veris comites** in apposition with *animae Thraciae*. Cf Cat. 46 (34), lines 1–4.

2 **animae Thraciae** Homer (*Iliad* 9, 5) depicts Zephyrus as originating in Thrace.

animae, for *venti,* is found only here in Horace.

6 **infelix avis** the swallow's arrival is described in terms of the Tereus–Procne legend. Cf Cat. 65 (3), lines 13–14.

8 **regum libidines** generalizing plurals; Tereus' behaviour was characteristic of ancient kings and tyrants.

9 **dicunt** cf *Odes* III 4 (71), line 1: *dic age tibia*; and I 6 (5), line 5. The stanza which follows is almost a vignette of a Vergilian pastoral (*Eclogues*), perhaps deliberately so.

11 **deum** Pan or Faunus, patron of Arcadian shepherds (cf *Odes* I 17 (39), line 2).

nigri colles dark evergreens on the slopes of Arcady.

14 **pressum Calibus** cf *Odes* I 20 (40), line 9: *prelo domitam Caleno*.

15 **iuvenum nobilium** the youthful patrons are anonymous.

17 **parvus onyx** a small vial, made of onyx.

18 **Sulpiciis horreis** warehouses along the Tiber, at the foot of the Mons Aventinus, built by the Sulpicii in Republican times. They are often referred to as the Horreae Galbae. Cf Nash, *Pictorial Dictionary of Ancient Rome*, vol. I, pp. 481–4.

19 **amara curarum** 'bitter cares' cf *Odes* II 1 (6), line 23: *cuncta terrarum*. Neuter plural adjective, substantive use, followed by a 'possessive' genitive.

23 **tingere** colloquial, humorous usage.

26 **nigrorum ignium** the flames of the funeral pyre and the ashes of the deceased are implied.

27 **consiliis** 'with your plans', i.e., to amass further wealth, or 'with your code of life', i.e. the Stoic ethic.

28 **in loco** 'at the proper time', cf *Odes* II 7 (45), line 27: *recepto/ dulce mihi furere est amico*.

C. M. Bowra, 'Horace, *Odes* IV 12', in *CR* 42 (1928) 165–7.
The structure of the ode is bipartite: 1–12; 13–28.

- A. 1–4   Spring's advent: Zephyrs, meadows, torrents.
-    5–8   The swallow's arrival; Procne-Itys-Tereus
-    9–12 Shepherds' songs: sheep, Faunus.
- B. 13–24 Invitation to Vergil: Conditional on mutual offerings, Vergil, perfume; Horace, wine.
-    25–28 Vergil is to lay aside the pressure of affairs, the desire for gain, his normal code (Stoic?) in favor of (Epicurean?) relaxation.

Compare the thought, expression, and tone of Horace, *Odes* IV 12 (46) and Catullus 13 (30) the invitation to Fabullus.

47 (CATULLUS 96) *Si quicquam mutis gratum acceptumve sepulcris*

Metre: Elegiac Couplet

Catullus' letter of condolence to Calvus after receiving his poet-friend's threnody on the premature death of his wife Quintilia. Propertius also alludes to Calvus' elegy (II 34, lines 89–90):

> *Haec etiam docti confessa est pagina Calvi*
> *cum caneret miserae funera Quintiliae.*

COMMENTARY 153

Ovid suggests that Calvus had been guilty of infidelity to Quintilia:

> *Par fuit exigui similisque licentia Calvi*
> *detexit variis qui sua furta modis.*
> (*Tristia* 2, lines 431–2)

Catullus may actually be using Calvus' words – *veteres amores, missas amicitias* – when he recalls Quintilia's love, once treated lightly, now much regretted (cf *Odes* I 14 (68), lines 17–18, though in a different context: *nuper . . . taedium, nunc desiderium curaque non levis*).

1 **Si quicquam** . . . The death of Cicero's daughter Tullia was the occasion for a comparable condolence from Sulpicius (*Fam.* 4, 5, 6: *si qui etiam inferis sensus est, qui illius in te amor pietasque in omnis suos, hoc certe illa te facere non vult*).
mutis cf Catullus 101 (48), line 4: *mutam . . . cinerem.*

3 **desiderio** 'longing, heartache'. Cf *Odes* I 14 (68), line 18; Catullus 2 (11), line 5.

4 **missas** 'surrendered, voluntarily abandoned'. Cf. Catullus 66, line 29.

5 **certe** lends emphasis to the apodosis of the condition.

5, 6 **tanto . . . quantum** adjectival use correlative to the adverbial.

E. Fraenkel, 'Catulls Trostgedicht für Calvus', in *WS* 69 (1956) 278–88.

Notice the intricate unity obtained by the use of structural link words: 2, *dolore*; 3, *desiderio*; 3, *amores*; 4, *amicitias*; and the final link between *dolori* (5) and *amore* (6). Calvus' *amor* has revealed itself in his *dolor* and *desiderium*.

Compare the structure and content of Catullus 96 (47) and 76 (26), lines 1–6.

48 (CATULLUS 101) *Multas per gentes et multa per aequora vectus*

Metre: Elegiac Couplet
The death of Catullus' brother in the province of Asia was deeply lamented (cf Catullus 65 (3), lines 5–14; 68, lines 19–26, and 91–100). From the adjacent province of Bithynia Catullus probably visited the tomb in the Troad *c.* 57 B.C. The sepulchral epigram, by definition inscribed on the tomb, was developed as a literary form by Simonides, whose masterpieces on the war dead at Marathon, Thermopylae, Salamis, etc., were justly famous in antiquity. Catullus

adapts this literary form to compose an intimate and heartbreaking elegy on his brother's death.

1 **vectus** transported, by land and sea.

2 **advenio** present, with force of perfect tense.
ad purposive, 'to make this offering'.
inferias the funeral offerings *Dis Manibus*, 'to the spirits of the departed', at the tomb usually took the form of milk, honey, wine, a wreath of flowers, or a lock of hair.

3 **donarem** *vectus advenio* suggests secondary sequence.

4 **mutam ... cinerem** cf Catullus 96 (47), line 1: *mutis sepulcris*.
nequiquam pathetic usage.

5 **quandoquidem** Cf Catullus 64, line 218; Vergil *Ecl.* 3, line 55; Lucretius *DRN* 2, line 980.

6 **indigne** by its prematurity. Cf Vergil, *Aen.* 6, line 163: *indigna morte peremptum*. The scansion indicates whether *indigne* is vocative or adverbial.
frater adempte mihi cf Catullus 68, 20, and 92.

7 **nunc interea** and the imperative *accipe* (9) stress the change in thought and direction. Cf Catullus 14 (31), line 21: *hinc interea valete, abite*.
haec the offerings.

9 **multum manantia fletu** note 'drenched with copious tears' usage again in connection with his brother's death in 65 (3), line 6.

10 **ave atque vale** the thrice calling upon the name – here *frater* – is poignantly embodied in Vergil, *Aeneid* 6, 505–6:

> *tunc egomet tumulum Rhoeteo litore inanem*
> *constitui et magna manis ter voce vocavi.*

Cf Vergil, *Aen.* 11, line 97 (on the death of Pallas): *salve aeternum mihi, maxime Palla,/aeternumque vale*.

The apparently simple language conceals a clever complexity of form. Trace the thought-pattern of the elegy with careful attention to Catullus' technique which provides a mournful, almost 'liturgical' accompaniment to the elegy by means of alliteration and anaphora.

49 (HORACE, *Odes* I 4) *Solvitur acris hiems grata vice veris et Favoni*

Metre: Fourth Archilochian

The ode expresses a central tenet of Horace's philosophy – the

COMMENTARY 155

modest enjoyment of the present hour. The joys of life are fleeting and should be enjoyed when available. Rich and poor alike must leave this earth for a realm of endless exile.

1 **solvitur** suggests the Spring 'break-up'.
Favonius the 'favoring' West wind, sometimes called Zephyrus, signals the advent of Spring.

2 **machinae** 'roller and tackle' used in launching. Cf Caesar, *B.C.* II 10 (*phalangae*, 'rollers'). A carbonized windlass with rope attached has been found intact in the excavations of Herculaneum.

6 **iunctae** 'hand in hand with'.

7 **gravis** 'heavy, ponderous'. The epithet might also have been applied to the heavy-footed limping god of the forge.

8 **ardens** a pun or deliberate ambiguity on the reflected glow of the hearths and the kindled heart of the god who resumes his interrupted task of fashioning Jupiter's thunderbolts. *visit*: some editors prefer *urit* 'kindles', 'lights up', which is tautological with *ardens*. *Visit* provides better balance with *ducit* (5). Both parties resume their favourite pastime and profession.

9 **nunc decet** notice the rapid presentation of scenes and activities: *neque iam* (3), *iam* (5), *nunc* (9), *nunc* (11), halted abruptly by *pallida mors* (13).
 nitidum caput impedire myrto prelude to a party or celebration (cf *Odes* I 38 (90), lines 5–6). *impedire*, 'to wreath' is poetic usage for *cingere* or *vincire*.

10 **solutae** cf *solvitur* (1) and contrast with *impedire* (9).

11 **Fauno decet immolare** the admonition, enlarging on the earlier *nunc decet* (9), provides the dramatic date and setting for the ode, the Festival of Faunus on the Ides (13th) of February. Faunus (root, *fav-*; cf Favonius) is the protecting deity of flocks, herds, agriculture, and fruits (cf *Odes* III 18).

13 **pallida Mors** The Arcadian scene disintegrates with a vision of man's mortality. The alliteration and the violent impartial character of death's arrival signal the allegorical message.
 aequo pulsat pede 'pounds with impartial foot', is doubly effective. The measured tread after *alterno...pede* (7) and the imperative kick at the door heighten the melodramatic scene. *pauperum tabernas* (13) and *regum turris* (14) are perhaps best assigned to a single edifice: the lowly and the mighty share the same roof and fate. The large apartment blocks (*insulae*) at Ostia and at Rome shed

light on the Roman city life. *Tabernae* denote shops on the ground level with accommodation for the shopkeeper in a *cenaculum* ('garret,' small dining room) above the shop; *turris* may denote an independent multi-storeyed mansion, or, more likely, the top-storey housing for the wealthy, penthouse apartments with gardens and luxurious appointments on the third or fourth floor of apartment buildings. Some of the city apartments of a less durable fabric housed the poorer citizenry on the topmost storey (cf Juvenal, *Satires* 3, 193–211).

14 **regumque** applies to the social and financial élite, 'the rich', and has no royal significance.

beate 'wealthy' or perhaps, ironically, 'blessed, favoured'. Cf lines 13–14; and Catullus 51 (10), lines 15–16:

> *otium et reges prius et beatas*
> *perdidit urbes.*

Catullus reveals similar alliteration and word use.

15 **vitae summa brevis** the metaphor derives from book-keeping or banking. Gildersleeve suggested 'life's brief sum forbids us to open (a) long (account with) hope.' Cf *Odes* I 9 (50), lines 14–15.

16 **iam premet nox** *iam* underlines the urgency and swift passage of time and events; *premet* implies the crushing weight of death's darkness and the grave.

fabulaeque Manes the epithet may be interpreted to mean 'fictitious,' 'mythical', 'mere subjects of talk'. *Manes* (the Departed Spirits) recalls the tomb inscription *D(is) M(anibus)*, suggested perhaps by the grim contrast between *premet* and the customary formula, *sit terra tibi levis* (S.T.T.L.). Horace elsewhere provides grim spectacles of Hades, comparable to Vergil's Underworld in *Aeneid* 6. But Horace (and Cicero) was spiritually unimpressed. Cf *Odes* II 13, lines 21–40; II 14 (55), lines 17–20; Cicero, *De. Nat. Deor.* 2, 5.

17 **exilis** 'poor, cheerless, unsubstantial'.

quo simul mearis i.e., *et simul atque eo meaveris*. The poem becomes personal all of a sudden.

18 **regna vini** 'mastery, sovereignty of the wine-mixing'. The *arbiter bibendi* determined the ratio of water and wine at banquets and symposia.

talis a throw of the knucklebones (*astragaloi*) determined the master of the revel. The highest and best throw, when each of the four dice was different, was called Venus' throw (cf *Odes* II 7 (45) line 25).

COMMENTARY

19, 20 **Calet iuventus/ ... virgines tepebunt** Horace associates springtime and warmth with youth and love.

19 **Lycidan** the youth's name and the situation appear to have no immediate context or past significance for Sestius. The final quiet lines simply emphasize the quick passage of youth and the necessity for proper enjoyment of life as symbolized by love. The passage also balances the love 'motif' registered earlier by the association of *Venus* (5) and *Vulcanus ardens* (8).

C. L. Babcock, 'The role of Faunus in Horace Carm. II, 4', in *TAPA* 92 (1961) 13–19. W. Barr, 'Horace, *Odes* I, 4', in *CR* n.s. 12 (1962) 5–11.

The ode divides into two main sections: A – Spring (*ver*) 1–12; and B – Human Mortality (*mors*) 13–20.

Section A: Spring's Advent: a Bright Panorama.

1–4 Men and beasts resume their employments: seafaring (fishermen and sailors), pasturing (shepherds) and ploughing (*colonus*).

5–8 The Gods resume their pleasures and enjoyments.

5–6 Venus, the Nymphs and Graces, resume their dancing beneath the low-lying moon.

7–8 Vulcan and the Cyclops rekindle their volcanic forges.

9–12 Men prepare for pleasure, and for sacrifice.

Section B: Death's Advent and the Lesson: a Dark Panorama.

13–17 Death visits rich and poor; long-range hopes are thwarted; oppressive night, the Departed Spirits, and cramped quarters replace spacious living.

17–20 Death cancels Life's pleasures (*regna vini*) and love (*Lycidas*). The two sections, A and B, vary considerably in expression. Section A is laden with concrete imagery and everyday allusions. Section B is more economical with imagery and expression, and the familiar sights and sounds are abruptly altered; a cheerless pessimism replaces the former optimistic fervour.

Verbal links help immensely to unify the poem: e.g.

1 *solvitur*; 10 *solutae*; 20 *tepebunt*.

3 *neque iam*; 5 *iam*; 9 *nunc*; 16 *iam*; 20 *nunc omnis et mox*.
Verbal and image antitheses are equally effective unifying devices:

1 *acris*; 1 *grata*. 6 *iunctae*; 10 *solutae*.

5, 6 *Venus, iunctaeque Nymphis Gratiae.* 7, 8 *gravis Cyclopum Vulcanus ardens.*

9 *viridi nitidum caput impedire;* 10 *in umbrosis lucis.*

12 *agna; haedo.*

13 *pauperum tabernas;* 14 *regumque turris;* 17 *domus exilis.*

15 *brevis; longam.* 15 *nos;* 16 *te.*

29 *iuventus;* 20 *virgines.*

The verbal imagery is copious and concrete; ceaseless change and progress, cyclic (Nature) and final (Man), are imbedded in the Ode. Examine the lines for language of movement.

How does Horace's choice of metre contribute to the total effect of the poem? Be particularly attentive to line-endings.

Observe any remarkable instances of alliteration and internal rhyme.

Horace combines myth (5–8, 13–16), personal religion (9–12), and 'philosophic' denial of immortality (17–20) in his study of Man's transitory life.

What is the relevance of the mythical material to the final message of the Ode?

50 (HORACE, *Odes* I 9) *Vides ut alta stet nive candidum*

Metre: Alcaic

Horace's ode contains an oft-repeated piece of advice: enjoy the present since the future lies not in our hands. Nothing can call back the dead.

1 **Vides ut alta ...** Alcaeus provides the metre and the inspiration for the opening lines (cf Alcaeus, frag. 90. Diehl). There is a problem of visibility from Rome (or from Tibur). Soracte is approximately 24 miles north of Rome and rarely snow-capped (2,270 feet). These factors, combined with the unlikely scenery and hearth fire, support an allegorical rather than a literal interpretation of the ode. *Stet:* 'stands out' cf Vergil, *Aen.* 6, line 300: *stant lumina flamma.*

3 **laborantes** 'straining' under a load of snow.

4 **constiterint** 'have frozen to a halt'.

5 **dissolve** cf *Odes* I 4 (49), line 1: *solvitur acris hiems.*
 foco the fireplace contradicts the summer-time tryst (18–24).

COMMENTARY

6 **large reponens** may derive from Varro, *Sesquiulixes*.

7 **deprome** either 'bring down from the *apotheca*, the wine storage cupboard or shelf' or 'draw' from the *diota* or *amphora* to fill the mixing bowl (*crater*).

9 **simul**, sc. *ac* or *atque*.
  permitte divis cf *Odes* I 11 (51), lines 1–2; the start of a didactic excursus (9–12).

10 **stravere** 'have laid low' or 'laid to rest'.
  aequore fervido perhaps an oxymoron, with *aequor* suggesting the level sea and *fervidus* commonly applied to something warm or seething.

11 **deproeliantis** cf *Odes* I 3 (35), line 13: *decertantem*.
  nec cupressi associated with death and funeral pyres and cemeteries. Cf *Odes* II 14 (55), lines 22–4; *Epode* 5, line 18.

13 **fuge** equivalent to *noli*. Cf *Odes* II 4, line 22.

14, 15 **lucro/appone** phraseology used of financial entries in a ledger. Recall that Horace served as Treasury Clerk in the Temple of Saturn after Philippi.
  For similar usage cf *Odes* I 4 (49), line 15; II 5, line 15.

15, 16 **dulces amores sperne** cf *Odes* I 4 (49), lines 19–20.

17 **donec virenti canities abest** here the nature-symbolism emerges sharply and suggestively, the antithesis between nature's recurrent 'greenness' and 'youth', and winter's hoar-frost and white-haired old age.

18 **Campus et areae** The Campus Martius, under development by Augustus and particularly by Agrippa, was liberally provided with porticoes, baths, public gardens and public squares or piazzas.

20 **composita hora** 'at the trysting hour', 'at the hour appointed'.

21–4 the train of thought diminishes rapidly to a 'pen-and-ink' sketch of a lover's rendezvous. The passage is intricate. Horace makes *latentis proditor* his main phrase and subject, and translation should proceed accordingly, 'that betrays the hiding girl', in apposition to *gratus . . . risus ab intimo angulo*.
  pignus perhaps a bracelet, or ring.
  male 'weakly', a faint resistance.

M. G. Shields, '*Odes* I 9, A Study in imaginative unity', *Phoenix* 12 (1958) 166–73. G. J. Sullivan, 'Horace, *Odes* I 9', in *AJP* 84 (1963) 290–4.

Structure and thought-progression are intricate and artistic. The ode appears to fall into two equal parts: *Section A:* 1-12; and *Section B:* 13-24 [cf *Odes* I 4 (49)], but the two sections progress differently:

> *Section A:*   A formal strophic design.
> *Strophe* 1-4   the winter landscape; outdoors scene – cold, strain, frozen rivers. Evergreen branches bend under the weight of snow, and mountain streams are frozen to a halt.
> *Antistrophe* 5-8   Winter precautions: indoors scene – warmth, relaxation, flowing wine.
> *Epode* 9-12   The winter storm: divine intervention; final rest. winds and sea: battling and restless; winds and trees: restless.

Up to this point there have been few allegorical allusions, if any. But several usages may have disquieted the reader: *silvae laborantes* (3), *stravere* (10), *fervido* (10), *deproeliantis* (11).

Section B: Informal design; but steady progression through a philosophical aside (9) to the allegorical keywords (*virenti canities*, 17), and to the delights of youth and love in Rome in summer (18-24).

> 13-18   The Epicurean commonplace, with an appeal to enjoy life's pleasures (*dulces amores ... choreas*) while the green years of life are free from hoar frost. The nature imagery is deliberately symbolic and forces a review and reinterpretation of *Section A*.
> 18-24   a summertime idyll; at nightfall young lovers meet and struggle playfully in Rome's sports centre, the Campus Martius. The unity of the poem is basically allegorical; the progress of the seasons and human existence are parallel, and the nature symbolism is pervasive and instructive.

Examine Section A (1-12) to discover the nexus of antitheses, all applicable to the basic allegory (green-youth, white-old age) made explicit at 17 (*virenti canities*). What are the distinctly Epicurean sentiments in the 'didactic' excursus (9-18)?

Odes I 4 (49) and I 9 (50) are complementary and antithetic at the same time. Both are concerned with Nature and Human Existence, but the Soracte Ode [I 9 (50)] is more pointed and admoni-

COMMENTARY

tory. Which poem do you prefer? Find reasons for your preference. 'Technically the poem is asymmetrical, psychologically it is perfect' (Tracy). Do you regard the thought-pattern as coherent and true to life?
Look for striking instances of Horace's use of alliteration, and of perspective, both of distance and proximity.
How do they affect the meaning and impact of the ode? What does the Alcaic metre contribute to the ode?

51 (HORACE, *Odes* I 11) *Tu ne quaesieris, scire nefas, quem mihi, quem tibi*

Metre: Fifth Asclepiadean
Horace counsels Leuconoe to abandon astrology in favour of calm acceptance of the inevitable. The astrologers, whom the Romans called *mathematici*, found a prosperous living in telling the fortunes of all classes of people, from poets to potentates. They were repeatedly expelled by the government, but always returned. Horace himself seems to have been susceptible to their practice.

1 **ne quaesieris** *ne*, with perfect subjunctive, is a more polite form than *noli* with the infinitive. The expression is probably colloquial.

2 **Leuconoe** like Thaliarchus [*Odes* I 9 (50), line 8] the girl's name is probably an Horatian coinage, perhaps a descriptive name – 'simple-minded, clear-minded' which is appropriate to the injunction at the close – *quam minimum credula postero* – *sapias vina liques*. Pindar describes folly as *leukai phrenes* ('white wits') (*Pythian* 4, 109), and Horace may derive his name from Pindar.
nec *neve*, or *neu*, is normal usage.

3 **numeros** an allusion to the mathematical, astrological calculations of the Chaldaean astrologers (*mathematici*). Cf *Odes* II 17.

4 **hiemes** the passage of years is marked by the successive winters.

5 **debilitat** 'lames, cripples', a striking metaphorical use.
oppositis... pumicibus Verrall, alarmed by the inversion, for the sea should properly wear down the rocks and not *vice versa*, argued for identification with the 'aggressive' breakwater of the Agrippan *Portus Julius* confronting the Bay of Puteoli. But a non-literal interpretation seems equally valid: that the winter should cripple the sea with rocky remnants of a volcanic flow is striking and is in accord with the nature symbolism elsewhere in the ode.

6 **sapias** 'show some commonsense'.

liques (*liquo, – are*), refers to the practice of pouring new wine through a filter-cloth or bronze strainer (*colum*; cf colander) to free it from sediment.

spatio brevi absolute 'since life's span is short'; or perhaps dative 'prune back to a short life'.

7 **spem longam** cf *Odes* I 4 (49), line 15: *spem . . . longam*.

reseces horticultural allusion referring to the pruning of vines to promote better fertility and growth.

7–8 **fugerit invida/aetas** cf *Odes* I 14 (68), lines 1–2: *fugaces . . . labuntur anni*.

8 **carpe diem** continues the horticultural association: 'pluck the day, pluck the fruit (or flower) of the day', i.e. 'enjoy the day'.

postero, sc. *diei*.

R. E. Grimm, 'Horace's *carpe diem*', in *CJ* 58 (1962–3) 313–18. M. Owen Lee, 'Horace, *Odes* I 11', *Arion* III 4 (1964) 117–24.

Examine the relationship between the Soracte Ode [*Odes* I 9 (50)] and the Leuconoe Ode [*Odes* I 11 (51)]. Notice the similarity of theme, of admonition, and figurative language. What is the function of wine in both poems?

Examine *Odes* I 11 (51) for effective use of metre and of polysyllabic words.

52 (HORACE, *Odes* I 34) *Parcus deorum cultor et infrequens*

Metre: Alcaic

Horace comments on his inconsistency in philosophy and religion. Though earlier an avowed Epicurean, the phenomenon of lightning in a clear sky upsets his casual attitude towards religion. He muses on the power of Jupiter, the uncertain destinies of mankind, and the wanton malice exhibited in the divine direction of human affairs.

2 **insanientis** 'senseless, mad, raving'. The rhyming jingle *insanientis . . . dum sapientiae* may introduce a note of mockery.

4, 5 Horace's life was an aimless voyage until the thunderclap forced him to seek safer and more familiar waters for life's passage.

5 **namque** Horace provides an illustration (cf *Odes* I 22 (41), line 9: Namque me silva lupus . . .).

COMMENTARY 163

6–9 Lucretius and Epicurus accounted for thunder materialistically, as the atomic clash of clouds. But Horace's clear sky undermined the Epicurean belief or thesis and seemed therefore to invalidate the whole philosophy. Horace 'piously' resorts to the ancient mythological tradition, sanctified in men's minds, regarding thunder and lightning, and ascribes the phenomenon to *Dies-piter*. Jupiter in his archaic guise as sky was regularly ominous. Cf Vergil, *Georg.* 1, line 487; *Aen.* 7, line 141.

9, 10 Observe the chiastic structure:

quo bruta tellus ⎯⎯⎯⎯⎯⎯⎯⎯⎯⎯ *vaga flumina*
quo Styx ⎯⎯⎯⎯⎯⎯⎯⎯⎯⎯ *invisi horrida Taenari*

The repercussions are terrific on earth and beneath it, as they are, by implication, on Horace.

11 Atlanteusque finis the Atlas range in N.W. Africa, the western limit of the world.

14 apicem used of the conical cap (*pileus*) of the *Flamen Dialis* (Priest of Jupiter), or the tiara of Oriental potentates (cf *Odes* III 21 (63), line 20: *regum apices*). A revolution in Parthia in 30 B.C. resulted in the transfer of power from Phraates to Tiridates.

15 fortuna probably to be equated with the sculptural type of Hellenistic Tyche (Fortune), a seated figure, usually contemplating the city which she protects, with special attributes (sea-creatures, grain, turreted crown, etc.) about her. Horace here seems to equate Jupiter and Fortune as manifestations of one divine governance.

Note that Horace's Ode to Fortune (of Antium) follows immediately after I 34 (52).

stridore acuto probably to be associated with Jupiter's eagle (cf 14, *rapax*). Cf Vergil, *Aen.* 1, line 397: *stridentibus alis*.

What is the pattern of thought-structure in the ode? The choice lies between the diminuendo-type, from personal application to gentle reflections, and the crescendo-type, from momentous event to still more momentous reflections.

How do you interpret the last stanza? as a token of faith, fear of divine intervention (like the thunderbolt), or as critical of the acceptance of divine government of human affairs?

Does the ode testify to a religious conversion in Horace? What factors in the ode influence your decision? It is worthwhile to realize that opinions vary as widely as these:

Heinze: 'the poem is meant to be taken absolutely seriously as a confession of a religious conversion' and

Dr. Johnson, as reported by Boswell: 'Sir, he was not in earnest: this was merely poetical' and

Campbell: 'This ode announces in part allusively, but in effect, unmistakably, his conversion from Epicureanism to Stoicism'.

53 (HORACE, *Odes* II 3) *Aequam memento rebus in arduis*

Metre: Alcaic

Horace advises Dellius to temper his joy and sorrow with the thought of death, and to gather life's roses while he may. Everyone, rich and poor, is doomed to Charon's skiff and everlasting exile.

1 **aequam ... arduis** the verbal antithesis suggests a level head on a steep path, and moderation in adversity. Dellius had shown admirable sense of balance and political aplomb (cf Messalla's damning phrase: *desultor bellorum civilium*). The Augustan Age calls for less prodigious feats than Dellius' 'circus-rider' talents, and a more even tenor of life.

2 **in bonis,** sc. *rebus,* 'in times of prosperity'.

2, 3 **mentem ... temperatam** cf *Odes* III 4 (71), line 66: *vim temperatam,* with political implications.

6 **in remoto gramine** cf *Odes* I 17 (39), line 17: *in reducta valle.*

8 **interiore nota** Horace calls for a 'reserve' wine, kept in the rear of the storage area for a special occasion. *Nota* applies to the tag or label attached to the wine-jar, with the consular year marked to record the vintage season. Cf *Odes* III 8, line 12: *consule Tullo; Odes* III 21 (63), line 1: *consule Manlio.*

9 **pinus ingens albaque populus** notice the antithesis between the dark pine and the light-leaved poplar, the one bulky and spreading, the other rising to a slender peak, but both merge to provide a welcome shade.

13 **nimium brevis** the pathetic epithet marks the rose as symbol of life's beauty and brevity. The mention of the rose completes the portrait of the *fête-champêtre.*

15, 16 The Parcae are unwelcome guests, and introduce gloom into the happy event. Mention of the Fates assists the transition to the remaining stanzas of the ode which become increasingly sombre after the brightness of the picnic.

17 **coemptis saltibus** a reference, probably, to Dellius' material gains from his political 'acrobatics'. Grazing lands were often monopolized by capitalist ranchers to enlarge their *latifundia*, particularly in Calabria and Lucania.

17, 18 **domo/villaque** town and country house.

19, 20 **exstructis in altum/divitiis** immediately after the mention of the country house Horace alludes to piled up wealth (cf 17: *coemptis saltibus*) in terms which he usually reserves for villas which are built out into the sea (cf *Odes* III 1 (70), lines 33–6). Hoarded riches and encroachment on the sea both prompt Horace's outcry against extreme or selfish forms of materialism.

20 **potietur heres** cf. *Odes* IV 7 (57), lines 19–20, and notes. For the sentiment, that Dellius 'cannot take it with him' cf *Odes* II 14 (55), lines 21–8.

23 **sub divo moreris** suggests the limited span of a poor man under the open sky [cf *Odes* I 18, line 13: *sub divum*; *Odes* I 1 (4), line 25: *sub Iove frigido*].

24 **nil miserantis** cf *Odes* II 14 (55), line 6: *illacrimabilem*; and *Odes* I 24, (43), line 17: *non lenis precibus* (of Mercury).

25 **omnes eodem cogimur** implies cattle or sheep driven to the stalls or folds at nightfall. Cf Mercury Psychopompos (*Odes* I 24, (43), line 18: *nigro compulerit Mercurius gregi*). *eodem*, adverb.

25, 26 **omnium/versatur urna**... the image derives from the ancient method of taking lots. *Sortes* (chances) were placed in an urn, then mixed and tossed in such a way that one lot would fly out and consign a man to his fate. Cf *Odes* III 1 (70), line 16: *omne capax movet urna nomen*: Vergil, *Aen.* 6, line 432: *quaesitor Minos urnam movet*.

26–8 Note the duplication, for tragic emphasis: *serius ocius* (26), *exitura* (27), *impositura* (28), both of which may recall the epithet *moriture* (4) applied to Dellius at the outset.

28 **exsilium** a minatory allusion designed to shock Dellius into political and philosophical acquiescence in the Augustan settlement.
 cumbae, sc. *Charonis*. Vergil gives the classic description: *Aen.* 6, line 303.

The structure of the ode is obvious. Section A (1–16): General Admonition, Appeal to Nature:

 1–8 General and particular, *Memento Mori*.

 9–16 Particular, with generalizations, Appeal to Experience.

Section B: (17-28): Particular Admonition: renunciations associated with Death. The structural unity is secured and enhanced by clever verbal links and associated and contrasted thoughts and expressions: e.g., *aequam . . . rebus in arduis* (1); *moriture* (4), *vixeris* (5). Trace other instances in the poem.

Examine the ode for dramatic or rhetorical placing of key words to emphasize a major point and to dramatize the incident.

Note instances of alliteration, anaphora and assonance in the ode. Does the Alcaic metre contribute anything to the total impression? Do the requisite word-elisions make any artistic contribution?

Compare the natural imagery and party-sequence in stanzas 2, 3 and 4 with similar material in *Odes* I 9 (50), and I, 11 (51). Notice any similarities and account for any different symbolic emphases in *Odes* II 3 (53).

54 (HORACE, *Odes* II 10) *Rectius vives, Licini, neque altum*

Metre: Sapphic

A lesson in philosophy and a series of vignettes addressed to Lucius Licinius Murena, a relative of Maecenas. Horace had expressed the same idea earlier: 'There is a just measure in everything. There are fixed limits on either side of which right cannot find a resting-place.' (*Satires* I 1).

1 **rectius** part of the vocabulary of moral philosophy. Watch for other philosophical usages in the ode.

altum ambiguous, applicable to the 'deep' sea and Licinius' 'lofty' ambitions.

2, 3 **urgendo . . . premendo** anaphora. Both imply abnormal strain and risk at sea, and in the course of life.

5 **auream . . . mediocritatem** define the meaning carefully by etymology.

6 **diligit** 'loves, cherishes'. Some editors read *deligit*, 'chooses'.

6, 7 **caret** anaphora and asyndeton to emphasize the contrast.

7 **invidenda** cf *Odes* III 1 (70), line 45: *invidendis postibus*. Housing imagery recurs in stanzas 2 and 3. Somewhere between the squalid hut (6-7), and the pretentious mansion (7-8, 10-11) there lies the Golden Mean, probably the Sabine Farm. For the contrast cf *Odes* I 4 (49), lines 13-14: *pauperum tabernas . . . regumque turres*.

8 sobrius *sobrietas* is the Latin equivalent for the Greek *sophrosune*, temperance, moderation, or literally, safe-mindedness. Cf *Odes* II 3 (53), lines 2–3: *mentem . . . temperatam*.

9–11 ingens, celsae, summos triple emphasis on height, recalling the skyscraper *insulae* (apartment blocks) of Rome, and the palaces on the Palatine and Esquiline Hills.

14 alteram . . . praeparatam a philosophical commonplace. Cf Seneca, *De Vita Beata* 8: *Sapiens in utrumque paratus artifex vitae*; and Vergil, *Aen*. 2, line 61: *in utrumque paratus*.

15 reducit, i.e. from year to year.

16, 17 Jupiter appears as a celestial lictor or marshal of the seasons.

17 si male, sc. *est*.

23 contrahes a sailing metaphor.
sapienter 'philosophically'.
nimium secundo, i.e. following too fast, hence excessively favourable.

The structure of the ode is uncomplicated, and based on a symmetrical design of ideas:

A. 1–4 Nautical allusions: the storm; counsel against venturing into deep water;
B. 5–12 House imagery: hovel and mansion (5–8)
Natural and House Imagery: pines, towers, mountain peaks (9–12)
Counsel against heights.
C. 13–20 Seasonal and divine extremes in peace and war. Apollo as lyrist as well as destroyer (archer).
D. 21–24 Nautical allusions: the storm; a strategy to weather life's extremes:
The Golden Mean: *animosus* → *sapienter* ← *fortis*

Show, by means of argument or diagram (cf *supra*) the extremes which Horace uses in his philosophical diatribe. For example:

EXTREME   MEAN   EXTREME
altum semper urgendo/rectitudo/nimium premendo litus

What principle do you think motivated Horace to select the realistic details which feature in the Ode? How do these details assist the point and symmetry of the Ode which oscillates between allegory and reality?

How does Horace combine his two major themes, the need for moderate behaviour and the inevitable but transitory nature of adversity, so as to bolster his final counsel to Murena?

Examine the *Odes* to Pyrrha [I, 5 (36)], to Plancus [I, 7 (67)], and to Dellius [II, 3 (53)], for similar thought and language. How do you account for their similarity to *Odes* II 10 (54)?

How much irony can you detect in the poem? Does it add to the unity of the ode?

55 (HORACE, *Odes* II 14). *Eheu fugaces, Postume, Postume*

Metre: Alcaic

The days of wine and roses are few and brief; the years fly fast and nothing can delay the approach of death. Everyone must come finally to dark Cocytus, leaving behind everything which is held most dear.

1 **Postume, Postume** pathetic repetition. Cf *Odes* III 3, line 18: *Ilion, Ilion*; IV 4, line 70: *occidit, occidit*.

2 **labuntur** the first use of the pervasive water imagery which serves to symbolize passing time. Cf Ovid, *Fasti* 6, line 771: *tempora labuntur tacitisque senescimus annis*. Water-clocks were common in Greco-Roman society, particularly in the court system. (Lucretius uses the same metaphor for the secret erosion of time: 1, line 313.)

pietas probably a Vergilian reminiscence. Cf *Odes* I 24 (43), line 11; IV 7 (57), line 24.

6 **places** conative force.

illacrimabilem 'whose tears never flow, pitiless'.

8, 9 **tristi/compescit unda** cf Vergil, *Georg.* 4, lines 479–80: *tardaque palus inamabilis unda/alligat et novies Styx interfusa coercet*: *Aen.* 6, lines 438–9: *tristisque palus inamabilis undae/alligat et novies Styx interfusa coercet*.

10 **quicumque... vescimur** βροτῶν οἳ ἀρούρης καρπὸν ἔδουσιν the Latin version of Homer's phrase for Mankind: *Iliad* 6, line 142.

11 **enaviganda** Horatian coinage, implying passage 'to the farthest shore'.

reges Horace's usual term for the *rich*, the nabobs, wealthy leaders of society, contrasted with *coloni*, 'tenant farmers'.

14 Observe the interlocking word arrangement, and the sound-effect of the first two words.

15–16 Autumn, though *pomifer* [*Odes* IV 7 (57), line 11] and productive, was also deadly to men (cf *Sat* II 6, line 19: *Autumnus gravis, Libitinae quaestus acerbae*). The season of the Sirocco (Auster, and

Notus) blowing from the Sahara, is still noxious in Sicily and Italy as far north as Rome.

18 errans 'meandering', but with latent suggestions of behaviour, with *infame* (19).

20 Aeolides a patronymic 'son of Aeolus'. Aeolus, father of shifting treacherous winds, appropriate sire for the arch-rogue of Greek mythology, Sisyphus, and forefather of the wily Ulysses.

laboris genitive of the penalty (poetic use); normally genitive of the charge follows verbs of condemning.

21-4 cf Lucretius 3, lines 894-9, for equally sympathetic awareness of death's tragedy in the family circle. Notice the sharp contrast between *visendus* (17) and *linquenda* (21). Gray's *Elegy in a Country Churchyard* is markedly indebted to the Lucretian passage.

22, 23 The allusion to gardening and tree-raising reflects an Italian fondness for arboriculture.

23 invisas cupressos hateful because the cypress frequently marked the grave or mausoleum precinct. Cypresses were planted on the great mounds heaped over the Mausoleum of Augustus, and of Hadrian (cf Nash, *Pictorial Dictionary of Ancient Rome*, II, p. 39; Robathan, *The Monuments of Ancient Rome*, pp. 148-9). Cf Horace, *Epodes* 5, line 18: *funebris*; and Vergil, *Aen.* 6, line 216: *feralis*. The dark evergreen, sacred to Pluto, also sent down deep roots which might be thought to follow their master to Hades (24, *sequetur*). There is probably an implicit contrast between the evergreen tree, and the *brevem dominum* (24) who planted the tree originally.

24 dominum normally denotes a *possessor* (landholder) in perpetuity, as opposed to the tenant or leaseholder (*colonus*). Brevis implies short-term ownership, or a short lease on life.

25-8 The poem's solemnity is shattered with the sketch of the heir. The spendthrift's debauchery contrasts startlingly with the cautious regimen of the testator (*quas colis*, 22). Postumus' profligate heir, the male scion of the family, wins Horace's support as *dignior* (25) because he enjoys the present and has no miserly tendencies (cf *Sat.* II 3, lines 122-3). The Caecuban which he consumed with Hogarthian abandon is a libation poured to life.

27 tinguet pavimentum implies careless handling of the hoarded wine spilled onto the marble or mosaic floor of the triclinium. Cicero describes similar behaviour by Mark Antony and his associates: *Philippic* 2, 41, 104-5: *natabant pavimenta vino, madebant parietes*.

28 **pontificum** . . . cf *Saliaribus dapibus* [*Odes* I 37 (69), lines 2–4]. The pontifical feasts were proverbial for their sumptuous nature, particularly those of the priests of Mars.

The structure of the ode is obvious:

    Section A: 1–16   The inevitability of Death.
                      1–4 Devotion to the gods is no deterrent to age and death.
                      5–8 Offerings, on any scale, are ineffective.
                      9–12 Status is no protection; all are equal in the face of Death.
                    13–16 Precautions and safety measures are ultimately in vain.
    Section B: 17–28   Triadic statement: Generalizations on Life and Death.
                    17–20 The underworld.
                    21–24 Life's joys and occupations forsaken.
                    25–28 The dissolute heir enjoys the present, with reckless abandon.

Examine the ode for significant instances of alliteration, rhyme anaphora, and word-links.

Water imagery plays a large role in the unity and message of the ode. Analyse the poem with this in mind, and determine the musical, symbolic, and structural effects of its use.

Notice the shift from second personal singular to first person plural at verse 9. Can you account for this change; what effect does it have on the reader?

Contrast the tone of *Odes* I 13 (38) and I 14 (68). Though the poems have much in common, there is a distinct difference in tone.

Compare *Odes* II 14 (55) with II 3 (53). The general tenor is similar, and the structural and other effects are closely comparable.

Examine the poem for impressive use of sound, and rhyme patterns.

Does the Alcaic stanza lend itself to poems on an 'elegiac theme'? Would the Sapphic stanza have served as well?

This ode is a collection of Epicurean commonplaces and folk wisdom. How does Horace elevate these familiar sentiments to the level of high poetry?

56 (HORACE, *Odes* II 16) *Otium divos rogat in patenti*

Metre: Sapphic

Horace writes on peace of mind in its widest meaning, freedom from care and trouble and peril – a blessing which the war-weary

COMMENTARY

Roman world of Horace's day longed for desperately. The ode proceeds by an effective series of contrasts from the sailor at sea to joy and contentment in the present.

1 **otium** note the emphatic repetition. There is no single meaning for *otium*, for it has associations with storm (1), war (5), the troubled mind (11) and political ambition (17). Probably closest is 'peace of mind, tranquillity', with suggestions of the Epicurean *ataraxy* 'imperturbability', freedom from care and trouble, product of political disengagement, and the renunciation of religious fears and immoderate desire.

Seneca (*De Brevitate Vitae*, 5) says of Augustus: *omnis eius sermo ad hoc semper revolutus est ut speraret otium.* Cf Vergil, *Ecl.* 1, line 6: *deus nobis haec otia fecit.*

3 **condidit** 'hide away, bury'. Cf Vergil, *Aen.* 6, line 271: *ubi caelum condidit umbra.*

5 **bello furiosa** possibly concessive, 'though war-mad'. Thrace was *terra Mavortia* (Vergil, *Aen.* 3, line 13).

7 **purpura** scarlet garments, fit for the wealthy oligarchy.

ve-nale for division of word, and enjambement, cf *Odes* I 2 (66), line 19: *u-xorius amnis.*

10 **summovet** 'brush aside, remove', used technically of a lictor's action in clearing a path through a crowd for the magistrate he attends.

miseros tumultus/mentis continues the same metaphor 'disturbances of the mind'.

12 **volantis** like a flock of unwelcome sparrows in the house, possibly bats. Cf Vergil, *Aen.* 12, lines 473–7 (of Juturna, sister of Turnus).

13 **vivitur** impersonal passive use.

14 **mensa tenui** 'on the frugal table'.

17 Three rhetorical questions succeed one another in rapid order.

19 **mutamus,** sc. *patria* (ablative). The accusative, *terras*, with *mutamus*, expresses what is received in exchange. Cf *Odes* I 17 (39), line 2.

20 Travel is a manifestation of restlessness among the wealthy, but no cure for their anxiety. Cf Horace, *Epist.* I 11, line 27: *caelum non animum mutant qui trans mare currunt*; *Satires* II 7, lines 112–16; Lucretius 3, lines 1060–70; Seneca, *De Tranquillitate Animi*, 2; *Dial.* 9, 2, 14).

se quoque fugit cf *Odes* III 1 (70), lines 39–40; Lucretius 2, lines 47–53.

21 **aeratas... navis** warships with bronze prows.

22 **Cura...** cf almost identical words in *Odes* III 1 (70), lines 39–40. Both *naves* and *equites* have suggestions of speed, emphasized by the repeated use of *ocior*, and by the mention of stags and winds.

26, 27 **lento... risu** with a 'calm, tranquil, philosophic smile'.
oderit jussive subjunctive, with *curare*; cf *temperet*.

31 **negarit** future perfect, *negaverit*.

34 **tollit hinnitum** 'whinnies'. A hypermetric line (cf 7–8 though with enjambment).

35 **equa** the mare was preferred for racing. Cf Vergil, *Georg.* 1, line 59.

38 **tenuem** 'subtle, delicate' as a term of literary criticism. Cf Horace, *Epist.* II 1, line 225.
Camenae, the native Latin word (cf *carmen*), equivalent to *Musa*.

39 **Parca non mendax** possibly a play on words, *Parca* (cf *parco, -ere*) had been *sparing* or thrifty or economical in her gifts to Horace (cf *parva* 37, *tenuem*, 38). But *non mendax* may simply mean 'unerring'. (Cf *Carm. Saec.*, line 25: *vosque veraces cecinisse Parcae*; and Persius, 5, line 48: *Parca tenax veri*.)

39–40 **malignum... vulgus** the envious crowd begrudges Horace his high social position as the intimate of Maecenas, and friend of Augustus. Cf *Odes* III 1 (70), lines 1–2, and elsewhere.

K. Latte, 'Eine Ode des Horaz', *Philologus* 89 (1935) 294–304.
V. Pöschl, 'Die Curastrophe der Otiumode des Horaz', *Hermes* 84 (1956) 74–90.

The repeated use of *otium* at the start of the ode may derive from Catullus 51 (10). But there is a fundamental difference in the definition of *otium*. Catullus suggests 'having nothing to do, spare time, idleness' with the associated idea that idleness (and opulence) breeds degeneracy among people, rulers, and nations. Horace chooses the same Sapphic metre, but evaluates *otium* in a totally different manner. Assuming that the principal theme of the ode is Epicurean 'ataraxy' or 'tranquillity' how does Horace define and illustrate the doctrine?

What is the effect of the Catullian echo?

Show how Horace uses balanced pictures and contrasts to unify his poem and to make his points more concretely and meaningfully.

How do you interpret the final stanza? What light does stanza 4 shed on its meaning?

COMMENTARY 173

57 (HORACE, *Odes* IV 7) *Diffugere nives, redeunt iam gramina campis*
Metre: First Archilochian
A spring song addressed to Torquatus. The alternation of seasons is a reminder of life's brevity. Although the seasons come and go there is no return after death for mankind. So there is wisdom in the enjoyment of the passing hour since there is no appeal from the tribunal of Minos.

1 The inexorable passage of Time is suggested in *diffugere* [cf *Odes* I 11 (51), lines 7–8: *fugerit invida/aetas*; *Odes* II 14 (55), lines 1–2: *fugaces... labuntur anni*]. Notice the chiastic arrangement.

2 **comae** 'foliage', linked with *gramina*, emphasizes the greenness of youth's springtime. Cf *Odes* I 9 (50), line 17: *virenti canities*; I 21 (61), line 5; IV 3 (9), line 11.

3 **mutat vices** 'undergoes regular process of change'.

5 Cf *Odes* I 4 (49), lines 5–6.

7 **monet annus** the cycle of the revolving year cautions man to distrust arguments for immortality.

7, 8 **almum quae rapit hora diem** emphasizes the cruel haste of Time.

9 **ver proterit aestas** *proterit* underlines the speedy passage of the seasons: one pursues another, with intent to destroy [cf *Odes* II 18, line 15: *truditur dies die*; III 5 (72), line 34: *et Marte Poenos proteret altero*].

11 **effuderit** suggests the cornucopia (cf Vergil, *Georg.* 2, line 460).

12 **bruma recurrit iners** again Horace emphasizes the rapidity of the seasonal changes. For *bruma*, cf *Odes* II 6, lines 17–18: *ver ubi longum tepidasque praebet/Iuppiter brumas*. *Iners*, ironically juxtaposed to the active suggestions in *recurrit*, associates the year's end (*bruma*) with the end of man's lifespan.

13 **damna tamen... lunae** the metaphor is financial and commercial. The constellations recover their short-term losses in heaven; but man's cycle lacks nature's continuity and recuperative powers. For the metaphor cf *Odes* I 4 (49), line 15: I 9 (50), lines 14–15.

14 **decidimus** suggests 'descent' into the abyss of Hades; cf *Epist.* I 6, line 27; II 1, line 36; Ovid, *Met.* 10, line 18.

15 **pater Aeneas** some editors read *pius*, but either could derive from Vergil's *Aeneid* where they figure equally as the hero's epithet. *Pius* seems more effective in this setting (cf 24, *pietas*; *Odes* I, 24 (43), line 11).

Tullus dives Livy records the fame and prosperity of Tullus Hostilius (Livy 1, 31).

Ancus a model of consecrated goodness (cf Lucr. 3, line 1025 = Ennius *Ann.* 149 (Vahlen) *lumina sis* (= *suis*) *oculis etiam bonus Ancus reliquit.*)

16 **pulvis** in the cinerary urns, lodged in the family mausoleum or *columbarium* (dovecot niches).

17 A recurrence of the financial imagery. Cf *Odes* I 9 (50), lines 14–15.

19 **cuncta ... heredis** Horace may think of the rapacious fortune-hunter familiar to Roman law courts and the comic stage and in satirical writing. The decline in the birth-rate among the wealthier families created a situation where parasites and fortune-hunters flourished. Cf *Odes* II 3 (53), line 20; III 24, lines 61–2.

19, 20 **amico ... animo** 'your own dear soul'. Cf Greek adjective *philos* ('own, personal, dear') and contrast *manus avidas*.

20, 21 **dederis ... occideris** the final *-is* is long which is unusua in the future perfect; the variation probably derives from the analogy of the perfect subjunctive.

21 **cum semel occideris** cf Catullus 5 (13), lines 4–6.

21–2 **splendida Minos/fecerit arbitria** some editors regard *splendida* as a transferred epithet, but the epithet 'stately, august' is quite appropriate also to the Supreme Court decisions of Minos.

23–4 Horace lists Torquatus' distinctions: **genus** (Manilii), **facundia** (lawyer), **pietas** (faithfulness to family, state, and gods). Cf *Odes* II 14 (55), line 2.

25 Horace closes with a mythological parallel to generalize the foregoing statement.

25–6 The goddess Diana was powerless to save her chaste worshipper Hippolytus from death (cf Euripides, *Hippolytus*), but comforted his dying and released him from prolonged agony.

27–8 Theseus could not free his beloved Pirithous from Hades' imprisonment (cf *Odes* III 4 (71), line 80). Pirithous' punishment, shared by Theseus until his release by Hercules, resulted from his desire to abduct Proserpina, wife of Pluto. Theseus' love for Pirithous could not win his deliverance (cf Orpheus and Eurydice). For possible equation of Pirithous with Mark Antony, see *Odes* III 4 (71), lines 79–80 (notes).

COMMENTARY 175

R. R. Dyer, '*Diffugere nives*: Horace and the Augustan Spring', *G & R* n.s. 12 (1965) 79-84.

The possibility exists that *Odes* IV 7 (57) may have been written at about the same time as I, 4 (49) but was withheld from the first publication of the *Odes* in 23 B.C. Certainly there are indications of Horace's indebtedness to Vergil and to Catullus. For Catullian elements cf *Odes* IV 7 (57) and Catullus 5 (13). The language and thought are similar but the messages are distinctly different.

A. E. Housman once called *Odes* IV 7 (57) 'the most perfect poem in the Latin language'. But there are many similarities between IV 7 (57) and I, 4 (49). The nature symbolism is closely parallel, and both are equally subtle and compressed. Compare *Odes* I 4 (49) and IV 7 (57) with regard to basic theme, structural pattern, thought-progression and points of detail. Notice particularly in both odes the careful balance between Greek and Roman figures and scenes.

Discuss Fraenkel's comment: 'It is perhaps only a slight exaggeration to say that in i. 4 the thought of death is in the background of the poem, but in iv. 7 in its centre.'

58 (CATULLUS 34) *Dianae sumus in fide*

Metre: Glyconics and a Pherecratic

A hymn to Diana, probably not intended for any special occasion nor to be sung, though the conventional choir of boys and girls is maintained. Whether the poem is to be divided between the two groups is doubtful, though stanzas 2 and 4 might, because of their content, be appropriate for the girls, while stanzas 3 and 5 deal with more masculine concerns; the opening and closing stanzas would quite properly be sung by the whole choir.

3 This line, omitted in the manuscripts, was restored by early editors.

11 Note the elision of the final syllable of *reconditorum*; a similar elision occurs at the end of line 21.

21-2 **quocumque... nomine** the ancient suppliant takes great care to ensure attention to his prayer by this 'escape clause'. A similar formula occurs in Greek (cf Plato, *Cratylus* 400e; Aesch. *Agam.* 160 ff.). Horace employs a similar formula in his hymn-parody, *Odes* III 21 (63), line 5.

What are the functions of Diana?
What use does Catullus make of assonance and rhyme?
Select the words which would seem to point to a conscious archaizing on Catullus' part.

59 (CATULLUS 62) *Vesper adest, iuvenes, consurgite; Vesper Olympo*

Metre: Dactylic Hexameter

An exercise in the epithalamium, or marriage hymn, not intended, it would seem, for a special occasion. The poem possesses elements of both Greek and Roman marriage practices; the setting, as indicated in the opening line, is Greek, while the absence of the bride at the beginning of the hymn is characteristic of the Roman practice. The Epithalamium, as the name suggests (*thalamos* was the bridal chamber), was normally sung outside the entrance to the bridal apartment; the *hymenaeus* was sung during the procession to the bridegroom's house. But the feast at the home of the bride's parents was also the occasion for song, and such is the setting Catullus has chosen here. The poem takes the form of a contest between the male and female guests, and the lines are distributed as follows:

Boys: lines 1–5; 11–19; 26–31; 33–8 (this stanza is mutilated at the beginning); 49–58; 59–66.
Girls: 6–10; 20–5; 32 (the remainder of this stanza is lost); 39–48.

Note the careful symmetry of the contest proper, which begins on line 20 and continues through line 58. The closing stanza (lines 59–66) is sung probably by the boys, who regard themselves as victors in the competition though it may have been intended for both boys and girls, and would represent a quick surrender by the latter.

1 **Olympo** either 'from Mount Olympus' or 'in the heavens'. The reference to Mt. Oeta (7) sets the scene in Thessaly.

2 **vix tandem** emphasizes the impatience of the men, already indicated by *exspectata diu*.

4 **iam veniet virgo** to join the bridegroom and begin the procession to her new home.

5 **Hymen...Hymenaee** note the variation in length of the initial syllables to accommodate the metre.

6 ff. The chorus of girls reacts, not to the appearance of the evening star, but to the activity among the boys; hence the uncertainty, at first (*nimirum, sic certe est, viden ut perniciter exsiluere*), then the certainty that they have correctly interpreted what the boys are up to.

9 **non temere** 'not just for the fun of it.'

12 ff. The boys suspect the girls of greater preparation and rehearsal for the occasion; the boys, again as usual, have put things off, and

been half-hearted in their preparation (15). The girls are out to win.

14 **quae ... laborant** a causal clause with the indicative, not uncommon in early Latin (see Woodcock, *A New Latin Syntax*, sec. 159).

tota ... mente this ablative with *mente* is the origin of a large family of adverbs in Romance languages; e.g. *tranquilla mente* (Lat.) gave *tranquillement* (French), *tranquilmente* (Italian). Cf *tacita ... mente* (37), *obstinata mente* (Cat. 8 (19), line 11).

20 ff. The contest proper begins.

21-3 The repetitions and rearrangements of phrases emphasize the tug-of-war, as it were, between mother and lover, the pretended reluctance of the bride, the struggle which precedes the 'capture', the shifting nature of the 'siege'. The question in line 24 is appropriate, then, to the preceding lines.

27 **qui ... firmes** 'bring to fulfilment'. Here the causal relative has the more usual subjunctive.

27-8 **desponsa ... pepigere** the marriage-contract has already been agreed to by the bridegroom and the bride's parents.

32 In the mutilated stanzas beginning here, the girls presumably continued their diatribe against Hesperus, who brings with him darkness, when acts of thievery, such as this, occur (cf Cat. 7 (14), lines 7-8: *aut quam sidera multa, cum tacet nox,/furtivos hominum vident amores*) while the boys defend Hesperus as the catcher of thieves; they play fast-and-loose with the fact that both the evening star and the morning star are the planet Venus, though both stars are not visible at the same time of the year.

36 **ficto ... questu** the boys recognize the element of play in the girls' pretended sense of horror and shock; cf the next line.

carpere the image is picked up in the girls' reply.

39 ff. Note the elaborate comparison of maidenhood to the delicate flower, protected (*saeptis secretus*) from the violence (*convulsus, carptu*) of the world outside.

45 **dum ... dum** following Quintilian (IX 3, 16), most editors regard only the first clause as subordinate; the second *dum* is then correlative ('as long as ... so long'). But both clauses may be taken as subordinate to *sic virgo* (*est*). The same statement applies to the balancing line 56.

49 ff. The imagery of marriage and widowhood (or bachelorhood) was commonly applied to the vine not trained to the tree; such words

as *marita, maritare, caelebs* occur in the agricultural writers and were taken up by the poets; cf *Odes* II 15, line 4, *platanusque caelebs*.

59 The bride appears at this point, and is addressed directly.

E. Fraenkel, 'Vesper adest', in *JRS* 45 (1955) 1–5.

60 (HORACE, *Odes* I 10) *Mercuri, facunde nepos Atlantis*

Metre: Sapphic
This hymn to Mercury offers simple praise, without prayer.

6 **curvae ... parentem** cf *fraterna ... lyra, Odes* I 21 (61), line 12.

9 ff. How does Horace, through the structure of this stanza, suggest the cunning (*callidum*), the sleight-of-hand of Mercury?

10 **puerum** legend attributed both the invention of the lyre and the theft of Apollo's cattle to Mercury's first day; cf Homeric *Hymn to Hermes*, lines 20 ff.

11 **voce** cf line 3; Apollo foolishly attempts to master Mercury with Mercury's own invention, eloquence.
dum terret 'while he was trying to scare'.

13 ff. Cf *Iliad* 24. 16 ff. Horace attributes his own 'departure' from Philippi to Mercury [*Odes* II 7 (45), lines 13 ff.]

17 ff. Cf *Odes* I 24 (43), lines 16 ff.
reponis the prefix *re-* may have a double force here; the souls of the *pii* are *restored* to Elysium, a restoration which is their *due*.

>*Structure:* 1–8   Mercury is praised as a civilizing force – patron of eloquence, wrestling, inventor of the lyre, patron of poets; as messenger of the gods; and finally as 'patron-saint' of thieves and master of the devious.
>9–12   an *exemplum* illustrates this last characteristic:
>(1) playfully
>13–16 (2) more seriously
>17–20 the serious overtones of the preceding stanza lead to a return to the listing of Mercury's powers: his role as *psychopompos*, shepherd of the souls of the dead to the underworld.

COMMENTARY

61 (HORACE, *Odes* I 21) *Dianam tenerae dicite virgines*

Metre: Fourth Asclepiadean

2 intonsum Apollo is regularly represented in art as youthful, unbearded, with long, flowing hair. Cf *Odes* IV 6 (65), line 26.

5 coma regularly of foliage; cf Catullus 4 (77), lines 11 and 12.

6 gelido ... Algido for Algidus, cf *algeo*, *algidus*; the mountain's name itself contains the idea of 'coolness'. Horace elsewhere [*Odes* III 23 (64), line 9] qualifies Algidus with *nivalis*.

7–8 nigris ... viridis the dark green of the firs and pines contrasted with the lighter green of the oaks and beeches. Cf *Odes* IV 4, line 58, *nigrae feraci frondis in Algido*.

11–12 Cf Horace, *Odes* I 10 (60), line 6.

insignem, sc. *Apollinem* or *deum*; *umerum*: an accusative of respect with *insignem*.

13 hic ... hic some editors would read *haec ... hic* here, to preserve the just distribution of praise and prayer to Diana and Apollo found throughout the rest of the poem; certainly Diana was as capable of bringing punishment in the form of sickness as Apollo.

14 principe Augustus in 27 B.C. adopted this title as the one which would best describe the special place he held in the new political dispensation. In *Res Gestae*, 34. 3, he defines this position as follows:

> *post id tempus* [i.e. Jan. 13, 27 B.C.] *auctoritate omnibus praestiti, potestatis autem nihilo amplius habui quam ceteri, qui mihi quoque in magistratu conlegae fuerunt.*

15 Persas Horace frequently uses *Persae* for *Parthi* [cf *Odes* I 2 (66), line 22; III 5 (72), line 4, etc.], and it is impossible to discover any principle at work in his usage, unless he regarded the Parthians as representing a danger as great to Rome as the Persians under Xerxes had been to the Greeks.

Whether this poem was produced for a special occasion has been often debated without any result. It seems too slight to have been written for performance at any event such as the dedication of the temple of Apollo in 28 B.C. (cf *Odes* I 31).

The hymn, in the final stanza, becomes a patriotic song (Fraenkel, *op. cit.*, 209–10). The special place which Apollo held in the Augustan pantheon may justify the apparent exclusion of Diana from the closing prayer.

Compare this poem with Catullus' hymn to Diana, Cat. 34 (58) for structure, language, etc.

62 (HORACE, *Odes* III 13) *O fons Bandusiae, splendidior vitro*

Metre: Fourth Asclepiadean

A hymn of praise – and self-praise – addressed to the Bandusian spring.

1 **fons Bandusiae** Horace may have transferred to the neighbourhood of his Sabine farm (*mod.* Licenza) a spring with which he was familiar in his hometown of Venusia. On Bandusia see Norman Douglas, *Old Calabria* (Peregrine Books, 1962), pp. 57–9; Gilbert Highet, *Poets in a Landscape*, pp. 150–1.

3 **cras ... haedo** the poem is set on the eve of the Fontanalia, when, according to Varro (*Ling. Lat.* 5), 'men throw wreaths into springs and garland wells'.

6 **frustra** Fraenkel (*op. cit.*, p. 203) points to the 'delicacy' of this word.

6–8 **gelidos ... rubro ... lascivi** the chill of death wipes out the life and wantonness of the victim.

9 ff. Note the **te ... tu ... tu,** characteristic of the ancient hymn.

13 **nobilium ... fontium** such springs as Hippocrene on Helicon, Castalia at Delphi, Arethusa at Syracuse.

15 f. **unde loquaces ... tuae** note the sound-effects.

loquaces simply 'prattling'? or, as Commager suggests (*op. cit.*, p. 324), do the waters 'speak' through Horace's poetry?

E. M. W. Tillyard, *Poetry Direct and Oblique*: London, 1934, pp. 206–8.

Structure: 1–8 promise of sacrifice
9–16 *laudatio* (with self-praise)

E. M. W. Tillyard comments, 'however fond Horace may have been of his fountain, he puts the poor unsuspecting thing very much to his own uses'. Discuss the use Horace makes of what seems, on the surface, a straightforward nature poem.

COMMENTARY

63 (HORACE, *Odes* III 21) *O nata mecum consule Manlio*

Metre: Alcaic
A hymn to a wine-jar, celebrating the powers of wine.

1 **consule Manlio** L. Manlius Torquatus was consul with L. Aurelius Cotta in 65 B.C.

4 **pia testa** cf the usual address to the deity in Horace's hymns.

5 **quocumque... nomine** though it probably has here a commercial application, this phrase was a common safeguard in ancient hymns; cf Cat. 34 (58), lines 21–2.

6 **servas** cf *Odes* I 35, line 29; I 3 (35), line 8.
bono die an 'auspicious' day.

7. **Corvino** see *Index Nominum*.

9 **madet** why is this an appropriate verb?
Socraticis... sermonibus dialogues like those of Plato, but not necessarily the Platonic dialogues; these provided the model for a large dialectical literature; see *Oxford Classical Dict.* under 'Dialogue, Greek'.

11 **prisci Catonis** certainly M. Porcius Cato Censor, the elder, a type of the strict, stern, rigid old Roman.

13 **lene tormentum** what figure of speech? *tormentum* instrument of torture, employed by courts to extract the truth: e.g. Cicero, *Pro Cluentio* 176, 'tormentis omnibus vehementissimis quaeritur'.

16 **Lyaeo** 'loosener' from cares; cf Liber (from Gk. λύω, 'to loose').

18 **addis... pauperi** cf *Odes* II 19, line 30; the horn is the symbol of strength and power.

21 **si laeta... Venus** not the *insanos amores* of line 3.

22 **segnesque... Gratiae** the Graces regularly are represented hand-in-hand (*nodum*); cf *Odes* I 4 (49), line 6; III 19, lines 16 f.; IV 7 (57), line 5.

23 **lucernae** the lamps are appropriately personified.

Structure: 1–12 (*a*) origin, qualities of wine (1–8)
            (*b*) power over even strict men (9–12)
       13–24 the power and company of wine (laudatio)

A few of the parallels between this ode and the hymn proper have been indicated; read the poem carefully and collect the expressions which may have both a religious and secular connotation.

64 (HORACE, *Odes* III 23) *Caelo supinas si tuleris manus*

Metre: Alcaic

Instructions to a young girl or farmer's wife ('Thrifty' is her name), on how to pray to the gods of her household, the Lares and Penates (*parvos deos*), in order that her farm may be protected from the familiar blights and hazards which beset the farmer. The simple ceremonies open (1-4) and close (15-20) the poem, framing the more elaborate and expensive offerings of the state-cults, proffered on the nation's behalf by the *pontifices* (9-14).

2 **nascente Luna** the beginning of the month is the appropriate time to get your accounts with the gods straight.

3-4 **horna...fruge** i.e. the first fruits of the year's harvest.

5 **pestilentem...Africum** the Sirocco, the hot, sultry wind from the Sahara.

7 **robiginem** the Roman farmers sacrificed to a god Robigo, whose province was to avert mildew.

8 Compare *Odes* II 14 (55), lines 15 f.: *per autumnos nocentem/corporibus metuemus Austrum.*

9 **nivali...Algido** cf *Odes* I 21 (61), line 6, *gelido...Algido.*

10 **devota** the uses to which the cattle were to be put were decided at birth; cf Verg. *Georg.* 3, lines 157-60:

> post partum cura in vitulos traducitur omnis,
> continuoque notas et nomina gentis inurunt,
> et quos aut pecori malint submittere habendo
> aut aris servare sacros aut scindere terram...

11 **Albanis** the priests possessed estates in the *ager Albanus*, assigned according to tradition in the times of the early kings (Dionysius, *Ant. Rom.* 3, 29).

14 **temptare** 'to assail'; such sacrifices on her part would be clearly excessive. Note the *multa...parvos* contrast.

16 **deos** to be taken with both *temptare* and *coronantem.*

COMMENTARY

17 immunis sometimes considered equivalent to *immunis scelerum*, but this would be introducing a completely new element into the poem. Page (*ad loc.*) treats it as equivalent to *sine munere*, 'without a gift' (*mola salsa* was not regarded as a gift, but the normal accompaniment of a sacrifice). Gow (*ad loc.*) considers the *munus* to mean 'office' and contrasts the public sacrifice of the state *pontifices* with the unofficial or private sacrifice of the individual.

19 aversos Penatis it was always safer to assume that the gods were hostile.

20 Pliny, *Hist. Nat.* Praef., *mola tantum salsa litant qui non tura habent.*

Mola salsa (meal mixed with salt) was the accompaniment of all expiatory sacrifices; for state sacrifices it was prepared by the Vestal Virgins, for the domestic cult by the wife and daughters of the family.

F. A. Sullivan, 'Horace's ode to rustic Phidyle', in *CP* 55 (1960) 109–13.

65 (HORACE, *Odes* IV 6) *Dive, quem proles Niobea magnae*

Metre: Sapphic

This poem was inspired by Horace's selection to compose the hymn for the celebration of the *Ludi Saeculares* in 17 B.C., his *Carmen Saeculare*; it is addressed first to Apollo as god of music, and then to the chorus of noble boys and girls who will sing his hymn.

4–20 These lines are a lengthy digression from the *laudatio* of Apollo. Such digressions were common hymnic practice, particularly with Pindar, to whose *Paean* VI this poem is indebted.

9–12 The simile of the hero's fall recalls Homer, *Il.* 5, line 560; 16, line 483.

14 male feriatos 'celebrating an ill-fated holiday', so unlike the present auspicious occasion – *saeculo festas referente luces* (line 42).

16, 19 falleret, ureret for *fefellisset, ussisset.*

21–4 Horace here, as elsewhere in this poem, works in themes from the *Carmen Saeculare*; Apollo, by destroying Achilles before Troy's end was due, was one of Rome's true founders; cf *CS* 37–44.

25 ff. Most manuscripts read *argutae* 'clear voiced'; but *Argivae*, also found, would strengthen the contrast with *Dauniae . . . Camenae* in a way which Horace uses elsewhere – e.g. *Odes* III 30 (8), line 13:

princeps Aeolium carmen ad Italos/deduxisse modos; and IV 3 (9), lines 12 and 23: ... *Aeolio carmine* ... *Romanae lyrae*.

29 f. **spiritum ... poetae** cf *Odes* II 16 (56), line 38; IV 3 (9), lines 21 ff.

33 **Deliae tutela deae** i.e. Diana. Cf Cat. 34 (58), *Diana sumus in fide*. Horace here, as elsewhere, gracefully introduces Diana, now as protectress of chastity, later as Noctiluca, favourer of crops, who hastens the passage of the seasons. Diana shares with Apollo the honour of the *Carmen Saeculare*, and both these aspects of her concern are woven into that hymn (*CS* 13-32).

35 **Lesbium ... pedem** the Sapphic metre.

meique pollicis ictum Fraenkel (*op. cit.*, pp. 403 f.) dismisses the suggestion that Horace may have trained the choir himself.

42 **saeculo** reckoned as one hundred and ten years; cf *CS* 21.

44 **vatis Horati** the only use by Horace in the *Odes* of his own name, although the same words appear as a variant for *vatis amici*, *Odes* II 6, line 24.

vatis this word was brought into new repute by Vergil and Horace; it here conveys a hint of a title, 'poet-laureate'; certainly this was the role Horace was playing when he composed the *Carmen Saeculare* and certain of the odes of Book IV.

G. L. Hendrickson, 'The so-called prelude to the *Carmen Saeculare*', in *CP* 48 (1953) 73-9.

Structure: Stanzas 1-7   praise of Apollo as one of the founders of Rome through his destruction of Achilles; prayer for his support of Horace's Italian muse.

Stanzas 8-11   addressed to chorus which was to sing his *Carmen Saeculare*. Having assured himself of the assistance of Apollo, he turns to the human instruments on whom he must rely, his chorus, and begs them to be attentive, faithful interpreters of his hymn; then he turns to one of the girls (perhaps she was restless and inattentive?) and promises her that, in years to come, she will be proud to recall this day and boast of the part she played.

How does Horace make the transition from Apollo, the god of destruction, and from purely Greek mythology, to the god's more peaceful role as patron of poetry and music?

66 (HORACE, *Odes* I 2) *Iam satis terris nivis atque dirae*

Metre: Sapphic

Horace addresses his ode to Augustus, appealing to him as protector and guardian of the Roman state. He refers to the portents which indicated divine wrath over the assassination of Caesar. The poet asks for deliverance from the agony of civil war, and appeals to heaven to assist the Romans to expiate their guilt: to Apollo, Venus, Mars, and Mercury, in the guise of Augustus. The ode concludes with a prayer for Augustus' long life and for his retributive measures against the Parthians.

1–2. The onomatopoeic use of the syllable *-is* reinforces the picture of the storm. Cf lines 21–4; *Odes* I 37 (69) lines 26–7; II 2, lines 13–16.

3 **iaculatus arces** 'striking the citadels'. *Arces* denotes the Capitoline Hill, seat of the Temple of the Capitoline Triad, and the Arx, with the Temple of Juno Moneta. Other sanctuaries included those of Jupiter Tonans, Jupiter Feretrius, and Terminus, god of boundaries. In Porphyrio's view the portents recalled those which ensued after Caesar's assassination (cf Vergil, *Georg.* 1, lines 466–88; Tibullus II 5, lines 71–8; Ovid, *Metam.* 15, lines 782–98; Dio Cassius 45, 17). But such an allusion would hardly be as fresh fifteen years or more later. The flood was not an event of 44 B.C. It is preferable perhaps to regard the aberrations and convulsions of nature as analogous to the upset of Civil War. The figurative use of military language is striking.

13 **flavum** 'sandy, tawny'.

14 **litore Etrusco** the right bank (*ripa Veientana*) of the Tiber; contrast 18–19, *sinistra . . . ripa*. But *litus Etruscum* may also mean the Tyrrhenian Sea (*Carm. Saec.* 38; *Epodes* 16, line 40).

15 **monumenta regis** the Regia, seat of the Rex Sacrorum, adjoined the Vestal cult-site. It was commonly ascribed to Numa, the priest-king of early Rome.

17–18 **nimium querenti/iactat ultorem** The syntax of *nimium* is ambiguous, somewhat comical if applied to Ilia and her relationship with Tiber, serious and critical if applied to the river god's excessive revenge. Augustus' Temple of Mars Ultor was a reminder of the revenge he took on Caesar's murderers.

19–20 **u-xorius** for the division cf *Odes* I 25, line 11; II 16 (56), line 7. For the usage cf Vergil, *Aen.* 4, line 266.

21 **cives acuisse ferrum**, sc. *inter se*, or *in se*.

23 **vitio** the crime of murder which Horace associates with civil war; cf 29, *scelus*; 47, *vitiis*.

24 **rara iuventus** 'the ranks of our youth thinned by the crimes of their fathers', i.e. depleted by the heavy losses in the Civil Wars.

28 **Vesta** was deaf to the appeals, because the Pontifex Maximus, Julius Caesar, had been assassinated. Ovid records Augustus' succession to Lepidus the triumvir, Pontifex Maximus since 43 B.C. (Ovid, *Fasti* 3, lines 421–5; 12 B.C.).

31 **nube candentis umeros amictus** *amictus*, active in meaning, a 'middle' use of the passive voice. Cf Homer, *Iliad* 15, line 308; Vergil, *Aen.* 8, line 720, *candentis limine Phoebi*.

33 **Erycina ridens** Homer's 'laughter-loving' Aphrodite in Greek literature is usually accompanied by Himeros (Longing) and Eros (Sexual Desire). Horace has her escorted by Iocus 'Mirth' and Cupido 'Desire'. Horace's Venus seems to resemble Lucretius' *Aeneadum genetrix*: in both poets she appears as goddess of growth and increase, and of peace.

36 **respicis** Cicero (*De Leg.* 2, 11) suggests the title of Fortuna Respiciens (sc. *ad opem ferendam*) for a Temple of Fortune.

auctor Mars appears not as War God but Father of the Roman race; the etymology of *auctor* (= *augeo* etc.) suggests 'increaser'. Cf the honorific title assumed by Octavian in 27 B.C. (Augustus).

39 **Mauri**: *certissima emendatio* is *Marsi*. Mars delights in the war cry and the bloodstained face of the Roman infantryman only when turned against a national enemy: civil war is an aberration. For the Marsian cf *Odes* II 20 (7), 18 as the embodiment of the tough Roman military man.

41 **iuvenem** Octavian (Augustus) is probably 40 years old. Cicero, at 43, calls himself *adulescens* at the time of his suppression of the Catilinarian conspiracy (63–62 B.C.). A man became *senex* at 45. Any man not yet *senex* must be *iuvenis*, i.e. young enough for military service.

COMMENTARY 187

42–3 **almae/filius Maiae** Mercury is not named. The adjective, applied properly to Maia, extends naturally also to her son, and is a characteristic which Horace seems to emphasize in his image of the god, and, presumably here, of Octavian. Cf *Odes* III 4 (71), line 42.

43 **patiens vocari** a Graecism. Note the contrast with Tiber (17–18: *nimium . . . iactat ultorem*).

44 **ultor** Octavian, at Philippi (42 B.C.) vowed a temple *pro ultione paterna*, finally completed in 2 B.C. (Suetonius, *Aug.* 10).

45 **serus in caelum** Octavian's illness in 29 B.C. may have prompted this prayer. Certainly many Romans must have regarded the event as hazardous for the future security of the state.

49–50 **hic magnos potius triumphos/hic ames dici pater . . .** Commager (*The Odes of Horace*, 175–94) argues that Horace may entreat or applaud Octavian's return to Rome to celebrate his triumphs. He suggests that *Odes* I 2 (66) might be regarded as a 'welcome home' comparable to Vergil's *Georgics*, read to Octavian on successive days at Atella in Campania, where Octavian relaxed en route to Rome after landing at Brundisium in the summer of 29 B.C. Horace is certainly indebted to Vergil, *Georg.* 1, lines 498–514 (501: *satis iam pridem*; 503: *iam pridem*). Cf Donatus–Suetonius, *Vita Vergili*, 27. The three triumphs which awaited Octavian's arrival were over the Pannonians and Dalmatians, Actium, and finally Alexandria.

pater, sc. *patriae*. The highest civilian honour was given first by the Senate to Cicero after the suppression of the Catilinarian revolt (cf *Odes* III 24, line 27; Juvenal 8, lines 243–4.)

51–2 Foreign war as a cure for civil strife was advocated by Isocrates in the shape of a crusade against Persia. Here only does Horace forthrightly countenance a belief in Octavian's divinity. He pictures him as a heaven-sent saviour, a Messiah, a redeemer from original sin (cf *Epode* 7; *Odes* III 25, line 19; Vergil, *Georg.* 1, lines 498–514).

S. Commager, 'Horace, *Carm.* 1, 2', in *AJP* 80 (1959), 37–55. G. Nussbaum, 'A postscript on Horace, *Carm.* I 2', in *AJP* 82 (1961), 406–17. L. A. MacKay, 'Horace, Augustus, and *Odes* I 2', in *AJP* 83 (1962), 168–77.

Why does Horace bring the archetypal story of Pyrrha and Deucalion and the Flood into the context of the political ode?

Examine the allegorical nature of the poem throughout. What purpose is served and what effect is gained?

Why does Horace finally select Hermes-Mercury for the epiphany, and for the saviour-god? Examine the respective claims of the other divinities cited. How appropriate are they to an equation with Octavian-Augustus?

What light does the Hymn to Mercury [*Odes* I 10 (60)] throw on the final stanzas?

Does the final warning detract from the panegyric? What are the tasks of the redeemer?

Can you detect Horace's views on vengeance and reprisals in Rome's recent political history?

Determine the structure of the poem, and the thought-progression from the solemn opening to the 'allegorical' saviour at the close of the ode.

Epode 7
Appendix to No. 81 (*Odes* I 2)

Quo, quo scelesti ruitis? aut cur dexteris
    aptantur enses conditi?
parumne campis atque Neptuno super
    fusum est Latini sanguinis,
non, ut superbas invidae Carthaginis   5
    Romanus arces ureret,
intactus aut Britannus ut descenderet
    Sacra catenatus via,
sed ut secundum vota Parthorum sua
    urbs haec periret dextera?   10
neque hic lupis mos nec fuit leonibus
    umquam nisi in dispar feris.
furorne caecus, an rapit vis acrior,
    an culpa? responsum date!
tacent et albus ora pallor inficit   15
    mentesque perculsae stupent.
sic est: acerba fata Romanos agunt
    scelusque fraternae necis,
ut immerentis fluxit in terram Remi
    sacer nepotibus cruor.   20

67 (HORACE, *Odes* I 7) *Laudabunt alii claram Rhodon aut Mytilenen*

Metre: Alcmanic

Plancus, probably L. Munatius L. f. Plancus, may have been serving abroad with Augustus in Spain (27–25 B.C.) when he received

COMMENTARY 189

Horace's advice. Pompeius Trogus (Just. 44, 5, 8) tells that the Gallaeci, a Spanish tribe opposed to Augustus, derived their descent from Teucer, a tradition perhaps known to the Roman commanders during the long campaign. Horace certainly compares Augustus' adventures in Spain to those of Hercules who contested there for the cattle of Geryon [cf *Odes* III 14 (74)].

Horace seems familiar with the Epicurean commonplace connected with Teucer's exile in Cicero, *Tusc.* V 108: 'Postremo ad omnes casus facillima ratio est eorum, qui ad voluptatem ea referunt, quae sequuntur in vita, ut, quocumque haec loco suppeditetur, ibi beati queant vivere. Itaque ad omnem rationem Teucri vox accommodari potest, "Patria est ubicumque est bene".'

1 **laudabunt** concessive rather than temporal. Cf Vergil, *Aen.* 6, line 847: *excudent alii spirantia mollius aera. claram:* 'glorious'. Cf Catullus 46 (34), line 6: *claras urbes Asiae.* Rhodes, Mytilene and Ephesus are *clarae urbes Asiae.* Rhodes and Ephesus contained two of the Seven Wonders of the World, the Colossus beside the harbour of Rhodes, and the Temple of Artemis (Diana) at Ephesus. Cicero praises Mytilene (*De Leg. Agr.* 2, 40) as: *urbs et natura ac situ et discriptione aedificiorum et pulchritudine in primis nobilis.*

2 **bimarisve** 'facing two seas', the Corinthian Gulf on the west, the Saronic Gulf on the east.

5 **sunt quibus** cf *Odes* I 1 (4), line 3: *sunt quos.*
intactae 'virgin'; cf Greek *Parthenos*, the Maiden Goddess of Athens.

6 **perpetuo** 'unbroken' song.

7 **undique decerptam olivam** i.e. material garnered from every conceivable source on the mythical and legendary background of Athens.

8 **plurimus** singular for plural.

9 **aptum ... Argos** cf Homer, *Iliad* 2, line 287, 'horse-raising Argos'.
ditisque Mycenas, 'rich in gold' (cf Homer, *Iliad* 8, line 180).

10 **patiens** suggests the rigorous Spartan training. Contrast *Larisae opima* (11).

12 **domus Albuneae resonantis** a Sibyl at Tibur (Tivoli) gave her name to a grove and a fountain (cf Vergil, *Aen.* 7, lines 81–4).

15 **albus** 'clear'.

17 **sapiens** 'like a philosopher'. Cf *Odes* I 11 (51), line 6: *sapias, vina liques*.

19 **molli** adjective, or, less likely, imperative. Cf *finire memento*.

20 **tenent... tenebit** notice the tenses carefully. *Tiburis tui*: Plancus was born at Tibur.

21 ff. The story of Teucer, used by Sophocles and Pacuvius, is also found in Cicero (*Tusc.* V 37, 108).

22 **cum fugeret** 'when he was starting on his exile'.

23 **populea** the poplar was sacred to Hercules; a sanctuary to Hercules Victor was erected by Sulla at Tibur (MacKendrick, *The Mute Stones Speak*, 134–6). Teucer, as an exile, wandering over the face of the earth, might reasonably be expected to sacrifice to Hercules (cf *Odes* III 3, line 9: *vagus Hercules*).

25 Cf Vergil, *Aen.* 1, line 198.

27 **duce et auspice** 'as guide and guardian'. Horace's usage recalls the formal *ductu et auspiciis*. A Roman military campaign was under the auspices of the Consul or Imperator, never under his personal conduct (cf Suetonius, *Aug.* 21).

28 **certus** 'unerring, sure' in prophecy; contrast *ambiguam* (29), a new Salamis to 'dispute' the older one.

30 **peioraque passi** cf Vergil, *Aen.* 1, line 199: *o passi graviora, dabit deus his quoque finem*.

E. L. Highbarger, 'The Pindaric style of Horace', in *TAPA* 66 (1935) 222–55. J. P. Elder, 'Horace, *Carm.* 1, 7', in *CP* 48 (1953) 1–8. F. R. Bliss, 'The Plancus Ode', in *TAPA* 91 (1960), 30–46.

Determine the structure and thought-progression of the ode.

Comment critically on the relationship between formal and informal elements in the Plancus Ode, and on the mythical parallel to Plancus' condition.

'The poem is not just a restatement of the familiar Horatian doctrine of contentment for its own sake, but a solemn warning, that discontent with one's lot is subversive, and rebellious against the just regime of Jupiter, who has before now punished rebellion.' (Silk). Discuss. What is the meaning of the poem?

Make a comparative or synoptic study of three political poems with travel and/or returns as common theme: *Odes* I 7 (67); III 14 (74); IV 5 (75). What is the function of wine in each of the three poems?

COMMENTARY

68 (HORACE, *Odes* I 14) *O navis, referent in mare te novi*
Metre: Fourth Asclepiadean
The poem is an allegory on the Ship of State and may have been called forth by some new threat of civil war.

1 referent ... novi Horace uses the same metaphor of civil war in *Odes* II 7 (45), lines 15 f.: *te rursus in bellum resorbens/Unde fretis tulit aestuosis*. The same implications exist here.

2 Palmer, *Hermathena* 60 (1942), p. 95, emends *fluctus* to *flatus* ('fresh blasts') to conform more closely with Alcaeus, where the winds make trouble for the ship, not the waves (cf Horace, *Epist.* I 18, lines 87–8).

fortiter occupa portum peremptory command to the helmsman and ship to make a brave effort to enter port.

4 nudum, sc. *sit. Nudum* and *saucius* (5) suggest a personification. The ship resembles an embattled and scarred veteran.

6 sine funibus 'without cables, or understraps' (cf Plat. *Rep.* 616 C; and *Acts* 27, 17). Ropes were passed around the hull to prevent the timbers from starting.

7 durare cf Vergil, *Aen.* 8, line 577: *durare laborem*, 'to stand the strain.'
carinae 'strakes' or 'hull'.

8 imperiosius cf *Odes* I 2 (66), lines 19–20: *nimium uxorius*, 'too much the husband'; here, 'too much the ruler, or tyrant, oppressive'.

10 non di sc. *sunt integri*: images of divinities which protected the ship, perhaps Castor and Pollux. Cf Catullus 4 (77), lines 22–7.

11 Pontica pinus cf *Odes* I 1 (4), line 13; Catullus 64, 1 (= of the ship Argo); Catullus 4 (77), 9–16. Pontic pine came from the southeast coast of the Black Sea, where the forests of Sinope were renowned for their ship-building timber (Strabo 12, 546).

12 nobilis genitive case, with *silvae*. Cf *Odes* III 13 (62) line 13: *fies nobilium tu quoque fontium*.

14 puppibus used of the entire ship. Cf Vergil, *Georgics* 3, line 362. For painted decoration on ancient ships cf Vergil, *Aen.* 5, line 663.

15–16 nisi ventis/debes ... cave 'unless you are doomed to be mocked by the winds, take care', otherwise exhortations to exercise caution are useless. *cave* occupies the emphatic position.

16–18 ludibrium; sollicitum ... taedium; desiderium curaque non levis the passionate language and the emotional overtones are more appropriate to love poetry. Cf Catullus 2 (11).

19 **nitentis** 'gleaming'. Appropriate to the glistening marble shores of Naxos and Paros, and the Cyclades generally. Cf *Odes* III 28, line 14: *fulgentes Cycladas*; Vergil, *Aen.* 3, line 126: *niveam Paron*.

C. W. Mendell, 'Horace, *Carm.* I 14', in *CP* 33 (1938) 145–56.
L. P. Wilkinson, 'The earliest odes of Horace', *Hermes* 84 (1956) 495–9.

The ode is usually accepted as allegorical. Quintilian's comment (*Inst. Orat* VIII 6, 44) has strengthened the view: 'The author names the ship for the state, the waves and tempests for the civil wars, and the harbour for peace and harmony': (*navem pro republica, fluctuum tempestates pro bellis civilibus, portum pro pace atque pro concordia dicit.*). In his use of the 'ship of state' image Horace evokes a pattern of poetical and political thought entirely familiar to his contemporaries. The image of the ship caught in a storm at sea derives from epic poetry (Homer, *Iliad* 15, lines 381–3), and from archaic poetry (Alcaeus frag 46A; Theognis, 671–82; Aeschylus, *Seven against Thebes* (*passim*); Archilochus fr. 56 (Diehl), Pindar, etc.).

Alcaeus' lyric (46A, Diehl) is Horace's most obvious model. The Lesbian poet spent his youth in opposing attempts at social reform in Mytilene, the island's capital.

Storm in the State

I cannot understand how the winds are set
against each other. Now from this side and now
from that the waves roll. We between them
run with the wind in our black ship driven,

hard pressed and laboring under the giant storm.
All round the mast-step washes the sea we shipped.
You can see through the sail already
where there are opening rents within it.

The forestays slacken....

Now jettison all cargo; ride out
best as we can in the pounding surf beat.

They say that, beaten hard by the running seas,
the ship herself no longer will fight against
the wildness of the waves, would rather
strike on the reefs underneath, and founder.

Richmond Lattimore, *Greek Lyrics* (Chicago, 1955).

COMMENTARY   193

The first century A.D. rhetorician, Heraclitus (*Allegoriae*, 5), comments helpfully: 'Who would not immediately conclude from the foregoing image concerning the sea that the fear was the fear of the sea felt by men who were sailing? But such is not the case. The subject is Myrsilus and a tyrannical conspiracy hatching against the Mytileneans'. Horace's poem has been called 'an armchair piece' in comparison with the Alcaic model. Do you agree?

The political context and date of Horace's ode are unknown and problematical. But important for any decision is the sharp contrast that Horace draws between *nuper* (17) and *nunc* (18), between his earlier attitude towards the political situation and his present view of the state. Perhaps on his return from Philippi (42 B.C.) the state had been a *sollicitum taedium*, 'a troubled source of annoyance'. Horace found escape and solace in poetry (cf *Odes* II 7 (45), lines 13–16; *Epist.* I 1, line 16; II 2, line 85). But presently (after Actium) the state became 'a yearning and an anxious care'. The ode probably dates from the years following Actium (September 31 B.C.) when the promise of peace after a century of civil war seemed close to realization, for then the least tremor of political unrest (suggested in the ode) would make thoughtful and experienced men despondent and fearful. Hints of political uprising would reawaken visions of stormier days which had left the State shattered and virtually defenceless against the inroads of successive despots and ambitious generals.

Examine the structure of the ode. Two thematic ideas intertwine throughout the ode and impart unity: *the perils* to which the ship is exposed, and *the resources* which the ship has for withstanding them. Everything is expressed objectively except towards the close (17–18) where Horace's estrangement from the political scene earlier is analogous to a lover's quarrel, not a lasting divorce or separation. Examine the lines in connection with Catullus 2 for similarities in thought and expression. What does Horace gain by these borrowed usages? Consider the suggestion that Horace may use the Fourth Asclepiadean metre for special effects which heighten the excitement and urgency of his message. Compare *Odes* I 5 (36) (to Pyrrha) for an earlier instance of a poem using the same metre, a poem which also finds its metaphorical point and unity in the marine metaphor.

69 (HORACE, *Odes* I 37) *Nunc est bibendum, nunc pede libero*

Metre: Alcaic

A victory song and joyful thanksgiving for the success at Actium, and the suicide of Cleopatra VII in August of 30 B.C. Antony's name is deliberately omitted as it was in the declaration of war: Octavian championed Rome and the West against an Egyptian, Eastern enemy, not against a Roman renegade who had once been his brother-in-law. Horace imitates Alcaeus' victory song over the death of Myrsilus, tyrant of Mytilene in the first two lines (Alcaeus, fr. 20).

Cf *Epodes* 1 and 9; Cassius Dio, 51, 6–15; Plutarch, *Antony*; Propertius, III 11, lines 29–58; IV 6, lines 63–8; Vergil *Aen.* 8, lines 675–713.

1 **pede libero** sounds the keynote of the celebration, the new freedom from war and anxiety; all restraint and caution are abandoned.

2 **Saliaribus** 'fit for the Salii' cf *Odes* II 14 (55), line 28.

3 **ornare pulvinar** the *supplicatio* took the form of a thanksgiving banquet (*lectisternium*) spread before the images of the gods which were laid on cushioned couches (*pulvinaria*).

4 **tempus erat** the *imperfect* tense is used to express surprise at the *present* discovery of a fact already existing. Cf *Odes* I 27, line 19 (Allen and Greenough, 471 d): 'Now is the proper time, finally'. Horace balances the public event (*supplicatio*) with the private festivities.

sodales 'drinking companions', 'accomplices'.

5 **antehac** disyllable.

Caecubum very special reserve stock. Cf *Epode* 9, line 1: *repostum Caecubum in festas dapes*.

6 **cellis** 'the wine cellars' for the oldest, choicest vintages.

Capitolio the symbol of Rome's rule [cf *Odes* III 30 (8), line 8; and *regiam* I 37 (69), line 25].

7 **regina** an odious word to Roman ears; *dementes ruinas*: transferred epithet. Cleopatra was subject to delusions of grandeur and intoxicated fantasies in the popular view (cf 12), and Horace reflects contemporary propaganda.

10 **virorum** i.e. *eunuchorum*. Cf *Epode* 9, line 13.

10–11 **impotens/sperare** 'wild enough to hope for'.

12 **ebria** 'drunk, intoxicated with good fortune'. The drunkenness which Horace attributes to Cleopatra is not supported by the literary tradition (except Plutarch, *Antony*, 29). The notorious drunkard, popularly identified with Dionysus-Bacchus, was Antony (cf Cicero, *Phil.* 2, 42, 63, 75, 104–5; Pliny, *Nat. Hist.* 14, 147–8; Vell. Pat. 2, 81, 4).

13 Antony's fleet was totally destroyed but he had provided for his own escape by lodging sails aboard his vessel (Plut. *Ant.*, 64).

COMMENTARY

Cleopatra's ships never engaged with the Roman fleet and escaped intact to Taenarum, a promontory in the Southern Peloponnesus, thence to Alexandria (Dio Cass. 51, 5).

14 **lymphatam** lit., 'nymph-struck, panic-stricken'. Cf Catullus, 64, lines 254f.: *lymphata mente furebant/euhoe bacchantes*. Cleopatra's carousals, like those of a Maenad or Bacchant, with Antony, and the heavy consumption of wine at the banquets made her an easy prey to panic and hallucinations. The nightmarish fantasies, reflected perhaps in the similes which follow (17–20), became a sober reality at Actium (*veros timores*).

16, 17 **ab Italia** poetic licence. Cleopatra's fleet avoided Italy and Octavian reached Alexandria in the autumn of 30 B.C. The battle at Actium occurred in September, 31 B.C.

16–17 **volantem/remis adurgens** the imagery of flight continues into v. 17. The epic association implied by the use of Haemonia (home of Achilles) suggests such airborne pursuers and destroyers as Perseus and Bellerophon, successful against Medusa and Chimaera, both *monstra* in the great tradition, and perverse and formidable opponents. The battle of Actium was conceived by some as a holy war, in a sense a crusade against the animal-headed gods of Egypt (cf Vergil, *Aen.* 8, lines 698–700).

20 **Haemoniae** poetic for Thessaly. The Thessalian plains were probably familiar to Horace from his service there with Brutus before Philippi (42 B.C.).

21 **monstrum** Horace may imply less opprobrium than awe or awareness of the complexity and contradiction in Cleopatra's character, a factor which emerges strongly at the close of the ode. The word may also conjure up sculptural versions of the Gigantomachy myth [cf *Odes* III 4 (71), lines 43–79] in the Pergamene Altar, the pediment of the Agrippan Pantheon, and the Augustan Temple of Jupiter Tonans.

fatale cf *Odes* III 3, line 19: *fatalis incestusque iudex* (of Paris):
generosius 'more nobly', sc. *quam in catenis*.

22–3 **nec...ensem** Plutarch, *Antony* 79 records that Cleopatra tried to stab herself on the arrival of Proculeius, Octavian's aide, but was prevented. She may then have conceived the plan to convey her fleet across the Isthmus of Suez and so escape down the Red Sea. The ships which had been transported across the Isthmus were destroyed by the Arabs of Petra (cf Plut. *Antony* 69).

24 **reparavit** 'exchanged' (cf *mutavit*) her *patria* for another, cf *Odes* I 31, line 12.

25 iacentem 'ruined', or 'lying in ruins'. Cf Dio Cass. 51, 11; Plut. *Antony*, 83; *serpentes*: for additional information see Plut. *Antony*, 86; Vergil *Aen.* 8, 697; Propertius 3, 11, lines 53 f.

28 combiberet 'drink to the full, drain to the dregs'. Cassius Dio casts doubt on the story of her suicide by the asp's poison (51, 14); Suetonius, *Augustus*, 17, shares the same doubts.

29 deliberata morte 'as she resolved to die'.

30 Liburnis dative. Cf *Epode* 1, line 1.

31 privata 'private citizen' as opposed to *regina*, 'stripped or deprived of her status'. Cf *redegit* (15). Cleopatra is imagined as reduced to civilian status, as 'unqueened'. Cf Plutarch, *Antony*, 86 for burial details.

deduci present infinitive passive, direct object of *invidens*, 'scorning'.

32 mulier triumpho *triumpho* is dative. The juxtaposition assigns the triumph to Cleopatra as well as to Octavian.

For the triumphs of Octavian see: *Res Gestae* 4, 3; Suetonius, *Augustus*, 17, 4; Dio Cassius, 51, 11, 3; Plutarch, *Antony*, 86, 4. Cleopatra dies with almost Stoic fortitude. Consider points of comparison between Cleopatra's death and the suicide of Cato Uticensis [*Odes* II 1 (6), lines 23–4; I 12, lines 35–6].

S. Commager, 'Horace, *Carm.* 1, 37', *Phoenix* 12 (1958) 47–57. J. V. Luce, 'Cleopatra as *Fatale Monstrum*', in *CQ* n.s. 13 (1963) 251–7.

Do the central images of the hawk and doves, hunter and hare, tend to glorify or diminish Octavian's triumph?

Examine the thought-sequence in the ode and account for the difference between the beginning and the end, from triumphal paean to an elegy or panegyric over Cleopatra's death.

Examine the poem for metaphorical and effective use of the imagery of drinking and intoxication.

Consider the argument that Horace exalts and magnifies Cleopatra to extol the victory of Octavian.

70 (HORACE, *Odes* III 1) *Odi profanum vulgus et arceo*

Metre: Alcaic

Horace addresses the youths and maidens who have not experienced the Civil Wars. After a solemn proclamation of his poetic

COMMENTARY

mission, Horace issues a warning against power, wealth, and luxury as goals for the average person.

1 **profanum** lit. 'outside the shrine'. Here, 'the uninitiated', men hostile to Horace's profession or unable to profit by his direction. The metaphor of the sacred mysteries of poetry is continued by *favete linguis* and *Musarum sacerdos*. Cf Vergil, *Aen.* 6, line 258: *procul, o procul este, profani*.

2 **favete linguis** 'observe a sacred silence'. Cf Vergil, *Aen.* 5, line 71: *ore favete*. Cf *Odes* III 30 (8), line 9: *cum tacita virgine pontifex* (see note *ad loc.*).

2–3 **carmina non prius/audita** Horace's claim to originality is based on content and tone rather than metre. Cf *Odes* II 20 (7), lines 1–3.

3 **sacerdos** cf Vergil, *Aen.* 6, line 662, *pii vates*; *Georg.* 2, line 475 f; *Musae, quarum sacra fero*.

4 **virginibus puerisque** Horace's songs are designed to instruct the rising generation. His *Carmen Saeculare* was written especially for performance by choirs of girls and boys [*Odes* IV 6 (65)].

5 **regum... proprios greges** *regum*, emphatic by position, marks a chiastic construction with *imperium est Jovis* (6). The use of *greges* suggests an oriental despot's rule over cattle-like subjects (cf *Odes* I 37 (69), lines 9–10: *contaminato cum grege turpium/morbo virorum*. The allegorical parallel of the Olympian victory over the Giants and Augustus' victory over the 'faction' whose domination deprived Romans of their liberty is pronounced. Cf Augustus, *Res Gestae* 1: annos undeviginti natus exercitum privato consilio et privata impensa comparavi, per quem rem publicam a dominatione factionis oppressam in libertatem vindicavi.

7 **clari Giganteo triumpho** cf *Odes* II 12, lines 6–9; II 19, lines 21–4. The Gigantomachy of *Odes* III 4 (71), lines 42–79, is a distinct parallel, and a warning against revolt.

9 **est ut** 'it is a fact that'; *ordinet* is used of viticulture, of vines planted in files or ranks.

11 **descendat** implies descent from a hilltop residence in Rome, or entry into the political 'arena', with intimations of combat.
Campum the Campus Martius was equipped with a voting precinct (Saepta Julia and Diribitorium) for popular elections. Cf Nash, *Pictorial Dictionary*, 2, 291–3.

13 **turba** used technically in connection with the morning *salutatio* and implying the reception committee (*clientes*) whose attendance on the Great Man was a mark of honour and distinction for ambitious Romans.

14 **Necessitas** cf *Odes* I 3 (35), lines 32–3: I 35, line 17; III 24, lines 5–8.

16 **omne capax movet urna nomen** the urn containing the lots was shaken until the lot emerged fortuitously. The rhythm of the line helps to convey the constant movement of the urn. Cf *Odes* II 3 (53), lines 21–8 where the context is Epicurean.

17 **destrictus ensis** a reference to the sword of Damocles which was suspended over him by a hair, symbolizing the insecurity of royal power. Cf Cicero, *Tusc.* 5, 61.

18 **Siculae dapes** Sicilian banquets were proverbially luxurious and bountiful.

20 **avium** many Roman villas maintained aviaries: cf Pliny *Nat. Hist.* 10, 7; 17, 6; Varro, *R.R.* 3, 5. Vergil introduces an ancient counterpart in connection with Evander's hut at Pallanteum (*Aeneid* 8, line 456).

21–2 **agrestium ... virorum** ambiguous syntax, to be construed either with *somnus* or *domus*.

25–8 Horace's portrait of the *mercator* illustrates the insatiable, indomitable desire for gain. Cf *Sat.* I 4, line 29; *Odes* I 1 (4), lines 15–18, I 31, lines 10–15, III 24 lines 35–41.

27 **Arcturi cadentis** the Bear, setting in October.

28 **impetus** a reference to storms.

Orientis Haedi the rising of the Kid, in early or mid-October, introduces a stormy season. Cf Vergil, *Aen.* 9, line 668: *pluvialibus Haedis*.

30 **mendax** 'deceitful' in that the fields do not produce the promised yield. Cf *Odes* III 16 line 30: *segetis certa fides meae*.

31 **torrentia** a period of drought accompanies the Dog Star's heat. Cf *Epode* 16, line 62.

33 **contracta ... aequora** Horace has a marked aversion for porticus-villas which extend into the sea. Cf *Odes* II 18 lines 17–22; III 24, lines 3–4. Vergil's only simile drawn from building

operations describes a comparable operation off the shores of Baiae, with prefabricated concrete blocks (*Aeneid* 9, lines 710–12).

34 molibus the massive concrete foundations.

35 caementa applied to the rough stones and rubble used to fill interstices in the foundations.
frequens redemptor 'many a contractor'.

37 Minae 'threatening shapes, bogeys'.

38 scandunt the unwelcome company joins the plutocrat aboard his yacht, to ruin the pleasure cruise.

39 aerata triremi the 'bronze-plated yacht' of the wealthy man, a pleasure craft perhaps comparable to the yachts recovered from Lake Nemi.

40 atra Cura cf *Odes* III 14 (74), lines 13 f.; IV 11, lines 35 f.

41 Phrygius lapis 'Phrygian marble', usually white with red and blue streaks, with the technical name 'pavonazetto' (lit. 'peacock-coloured'). The chief port of export was Synnada in Phrygia. Some of the Pantheon columns are constructed of this marble. Cf *Odes* II 18 line 3; Statius, *Silv.* I 5, line 36; Martial, *Epigr.* VI 42, line 13.

42 clarior 'more lustrous'; *purpurarum*: cf *Odes* II 18, line 8; II 16 (56), line 36.

44 Achaemenium 'Persian'. Cf *Odes* II 12, line 21: *Dives Achaemenes*.
costum 'unguent, hair oil'.

45 postibus Vergil, *Georg.* 2, line 463, describes the withdrawal of the clients from a rich man's levee: *varios inhiant pulchra testudine postes.* Cf Horace *Odes* IV 15 (76), line 8: *derepta Parthorum superbis/ postibus.*

46 novo ritu 'in the modern style', adverbial with *moliar*, and felt with *sublime* as well. *Moliar* points to the massive large-scale design. There is a marked contrast implied between the millionaire's mansion, high-ceilinged and luxuriously outfitted, and the simple atrium-style house favoured by Horace.

F. Solmsen, 'Horace's first Roman Ode', in *AJP* 68 (1947) 337–52. V. Pöschl, 'Die Einheit der ersten Römerode', in *HSCP* 63 (1958) 333–46.

According to Horace, what are the hallmarks and practices of wealthy Romans? Rank, wealth, and political power are all included in Horace's poetic sermon. What are the disadvantages associated with each?

Determine the structure and thought-progression of the ode.

'The political character and purpose of the ode is not obvious; it is more a philosophical than a political poem'. Discuss the ode from an ethical standpoint. Examine *Odes* III 1 (70) and III 6 (73) for a close relationship of theme, ideas, and argument. Which is more concerned with Rome's destiny?

71 (HORACE, *Odes* III 4) *Descende caelo et dic age tibia*

Metre: Alcaic

The fourth Roman Ode is, at the outset, an address to the Muses who watched over Horace's infancy in the woods of Mount Voltur, again after the rout at Philippi, and also saved him from a falling tree and shipwreck. Horace also commends Augustus for selecting men of peace as his advisers, and for admitting literary men to his court. The success of Augustus in his gigantic contests was due to the *consilium* of the Muses.

1 **descende caelo** Horace opens with a solemn invocation; the Muses live in heaven but favour special haunts on earth. Hesiod (*Theogony*, 80 ff.), whose lines may have provided inspiration for Horace, remarks 'Calliope is the most exalted of them (the Muses) for it is she who attends on the majesty of kings' (80). The vocal solo may be sung to flute accompaniment or strings (lyre). Cf *Odes* I 12, lines 1–2. *lyra vel acri/tibia*.

2 **longum melos** this is the longest of all the Horatian Odes.

3 **voce acuta** 'clear-sounding voice'. Horace suggests that the song may be unaccompanied, perhaps intoned; but the line may be simply an expansion of *tibia* (1).

4 **fidibus** the invention of Mercury (*Odes* I 10 (60), line 6).

5 **auditis** Horace speaks to his companions.

6 **audire et videor** sc. *mihi*. Cf *Odes* II 1 (6), line 21.

5, 6 **amabilis/insania** oxymoron; the divine madness (*mania*) was another name for inspiration (cf Plato, *Phaedrus*, 245).

9 **me** emphatic. Horace may recall stories of the infancy of Greek poets who enjoyed protection and favour or were singled out for privileged status, e.g., Stesichorus, on whose lips nightingales settled and sang; Pindar, whose lips were bathed with honey by bees; etc.

COMMENTARY

fabulosae the doves 'of story', Venus' birds which draw her chariot and carry ambrosia to Jupiter (Homer, *Odyssey* 12, lines 62-3). Venus' doves may have appeared in the foundation story of Horace's home town, Venusia.

10 **Apuliae** the text here is corrupt. Some emend and read: *limina Pulliae*, and regard Pullia as Horace's story-telling nurse, a pendant to Horace's schoolmaster in Rome, *plagosus Orbilius* (*Epist.* II, 1, line 71).

11 **fatigatum** construe with *ludo* and *somno*.

13 **mirum quod foret** a consecutive clause.

14 Notice how Horace provides a pen-sketch or characterization of the three sites.

17 **ut** with *mirum* (13): *atris*; 'deadly' cf *Odes* I 37 (69), line 27f.; II 3 (53), lines 16 f.

18 **premerer** 'I was covered'; *sacra*: to Apollo.

20 **non sine dis** Horace suggests that human inspiration was lacking.

21 **vester** emphatic, by repetition.

22 **tollor** an ambiguous usage which hints at transportation by ship, or soaring flight.

frigidum Praeneste (modern Palestrina) occupies a high and cool position, some 2500 feet above sea level. Cf Vergil, *Aen.* 7, line 682: *altum Praeneste*.

23 **supinum** 'sloping'.

24 **liquidae** Horace refers to the clear, cloudless atmosphere, and possibly also to the curative waters of Baiae.

27 **devota arbos** cf *Odes* II 13 and II 17, line 27. With *devota* supply *dis inferis* (cf *Epode* 16, line 9).

28 **Palinurus** Horace may have narrowly escaped shipwreck off this dangerous Lucanian headland on his return from Philippi. Horace attributes his escape from his three near disasters to divine intervention in each case: *Odes* II 17, line 28 (Faunus); III 8 (Bacchus); III 4 (71), line 27 (Muses).

32 **litoris Assyrii** of the Assyrian strand. Horace alludes to Mesopotamia.

viator contrast *navita* (30).

34 **Concanum** Horace transfers a Scythian custom to a Cantabrian (Spanish) tribe. Cf Vergil, *Georg.* 3, line 461.

36 **Scythicum amnem** the Tanais (Don) River. Horace compliments Augustus on his literary accomplishments and patronage.

37 **vos** the Muses. An instance of anaphora (cf *vester* 21).
  altum 'august' cf Vergil, *Aen.* 10, line 875 *altus Apollo*; id., 6, lines 9–10: *quibus altus Apollo/praesidet*.

38 **abdidit** 'retired'. 120,000 troops were demobilized after Actium (*Res Gestae* 15, 3). The manuscripts suggest either *reddidit*, or *addidit*: but both imply that existing colonies were enlarged by veteran settlements.

39 **quaerentem** implies a distaste for war, and a longing for peace.

40 **Pierio antro** Donatus–Suetonius (*Vita Vergili* 27) tells that Octavian, on his return from the East, recuperated for a while at Atella (29 B.C.). Vergil and Maecenas read the completed *Georgics* to Octavian over a four-day period.

Pierio antro may be Horace's figurative use to compliment Augustus' taste for literature and his inspired patronage of poets like Vergil and himself. Grottoes were often used for entertainment. Tacitus (*Annales* 5, 59) refers to Tiberius' retreat at Sperlonga (anc. Spelunca), a site only recently discovered and excavated. Horace refers to some quiet intellectual retreat rather than a specific cave and bower.

41 **lene consilium** Horace alludes to Octavian's moderate policy after Actium; *cōnsīlium* is trisyllabic here.

42 **gaudetis** the Muses have reason for rejoicing because their instruction is accepted; once again, Horace compliments Augustus, perhaps for heeding the poet's wisdom and counsel.

43 **Titanas** Horace's Gigantomachy, as usual, confuses Titans with Giants. He may have seen the Altar of Zeus at Pergamum (Asia Minor) where the Giants, symbolizing the Galatians, appear in a diversity of grotesque shapes.

45 Notice the series of antitheses *inertem – ventosum* (46); *urbes – regnaque tristia*; *divos – mortales turmas*. *Temperat*: used of inanimate nature, *regit*, used of sentient beings.

50 **fidens iuventus horrida bracchiis** Hecatoncheires (*Gyas centimanus*, 69) were sons of Uranus and Gaia (Heaven and Earth); usually they assist Zeus against the anarchic forces.

COMMENTARY

52 **Pelion** cf Vergil, *Georg.* 1, line 281.

54 **statu** 'posture' or 'stance'.

55 **truncis** instrumental ablative, with *iaculator*.

56 **Enceladus** a Titan, pinned beneath Mt. Etna. Cf Vergil, *Aen.* 3, lines 578–82.

57 **contra** with *possent*, and *ruentes*, and governing *sonantem*: the shaking of the aegis by Minerva causes panic; comparable action by Zeus, the only other party to wield the aegis, causes thunder (cf Vergil. *Aen.* 8, lines 435–8).

58 **avidus**, sc. *pugnae*.

61–4 the description of Apollo is inspired by Pindar, *Pythian* 1.

62 **tenet** 'resides', 'holds under his sway'. Horace suggests that Apollo lived six winter months at Patara in Lycia, and a summer in Delos.

65 The Pindaric moral of the myth: a *sententia*. Force, when used intelligently, receives divine help; *consilium* comes from the arts, music, and poetry.

    mole ruit sua a building metaphor, used of a collapsing house, cf *ruentes* (58).

69 **testis**, sc. *est*; cf. *scimus* (42), which introduces a well-known *exemplum*, part of the reader's knowledge.

73 **monstris...suis** the earthborn giants. The Mother *Terra* occasionally appears in art rising from the earth pleading for her children.

74 **partus** the Titans were hurled into Tartarus (Vergil, *Aen.* 6, line 580); Tityus was a Giant.

76 **impositam...Aetnen** a fate assigned to Enceladus, Typhoeus and Briareus.

    celer 'swift-consuming'.

77 **incontinentis** 'lustful'. Tityus attacked Latona, mother of Apollo and Diana; *iecur*, the seat of passion, was the vulture's target. Cf Vergil, *Aen.* 6, line 597.

79 **trecentae** used to represent a large number. Cf *Odes* II 14 (55), lines 5 and 26.

    amatorem ironical; some detect an allusion to Mark Antony, so perhaps 'adulterer'. Pirithous is introduced as an *exemplum* since he is not technically Titan or Giant.

R. Hornsby, 'Horace on art and politics', in *CJ* 58 (1962–3) 97–104.
Determine the structure and thought-progression of the ode.
Augustus is central to the ode. Are the political ideals on either side duly emphasized?
What are the powers of the Muses (or Music) as outlined and illustrated by Horace in this ode?
Compare *Odes* III 4 (71) and I 2 (66) for use of allegory.
'The ode is admonitory as well as eulogistic' (Commager). Discuss the tension between praise and admonition in the ode.
How far can one press the argument that Jupiter equates with Caesar Augustus and that there are analogies between the war of the Titans and Gods, and of Octavian and Cleopatra's host?
Compare *Odes* III 4 (71), lines 25–36, with Catullus 11 (27).

72 (HORACE, *Odes* III 5) *Caelo tonantem credidimus Iovem*

Metre: Alcaic

The fifth Roman Ode draws a parallel between Jupiter's rule in heaven and Augustus' rule on earth. The emperor's divinity will be recognized after he has added the Britons and Parthians to the empire. Regulus' behaviour at Carthage contrasts with the disgraceful actions of the Roman captives in Parthia.

1 **credidimus** 'we have come to believe [by experience]', perfect tense in apposition to future tense which ensues.

tonantem epithet, and cause of belief. Cf *Odes* I 34 (52), lines 5–12; Lucretius 5, lines 1188–93. Augustus dedicated a Temple of Jupiter Tonans on the Capitoline Hill in 22 B.C. The Temple reliefwork probably depicted the Battle of the Gods and Giants.

2 **praesens** 'on earth'. Cf *Odes* I 12, lines 57 f.

3, 4 **adiectis** (= *cum adiecerit*) **gravibus Persis** 'the dread Parthians' cf *Odes* I 2 (66), line 22.

5 **Crassi** consult *Index Nominum*.

6 **turpis** 'debased, degraded', requires an ablative of cause. Observe the chiastic arrangement between lines 5, and 6–7.

6–8 **hostium ... socerorum** 'of enemy fathers-in-law'.
pro curia inversique mores cf Cicero, *Cat.* I 1: *o tempora, o mores*.

8 **consenuit** more than twenty-five years had elapsed since the disaster of 53 B.C.

COMMENTARY

9 **sub rege** abhorrent to Roman republican sentiments; *Marsus, Apulus*; the best type of Roman soldier of Samnite or Lucanian extraction.

10 **anciliorum** 'the sacred shields'. During the reign of Numa a shield fell from heaven, a gift of Jupiter. Prophecy declared that the prosperity of Rome would depend on its preservation. Numa had eleven others made of the same design to guard against the theft of the original shield. The twelve *ancilia* were kept by the Salii, priests of Mars, in the War God's temple. Both the shields and the Vestal fire were therefore *pignora imperii* 'tokens of rule ; the toga was a symbol of the *nomen Romanum*.

13 **Regulus** see *Index Nominum*.

14 **condicionibus** dative, 'on terms of peace'.

15, 16 **exemplo trahentis/perniciem veniens in aevum** Manuscript reading emended by Canter to *trahenti. exemplo*: dative, a legal usage. Regulus, the valiant proconsul and lawyer, is pictured as arguing before the Curia against the adoption of the treaty with Carthage. For similar legalistic tone, see *condiciones* 'terms, stipulations . *trahere*: part of the legal vocabulary, 'to assign to a legal category' (cf *ad exemplum trahere*). *pernicies*: 'dangerous act, source of destruction'; Cicero calls Verres *pernicies provinciae Siciliae* (*Verr.* 1, 1, 2). *in aevum*: should be construed with *exemplo* rather than with *perniciem*, 'a precedent for time to come'. Translate: 'This the presaging mind of Regulus guarded against, for he refused the shameful terms, and branded this dangerous action a precedent for time to come, if the captive young men did not perish unpitied'.

18–21 **ego ... vidi, vidi ego** an eyewitness account to enhance the dramatic effect.

19 **adfixa** as thankoffering for victory.

21–2 Observe the correspondence between *retorta tergo bracchia libero* (22) and *qui lora restrictis lacertis/sensit iners* (35–6) : both describe the soldiers' reaction to captivity. *Civium* is emphatic: sc. *civium liberorum tergo*. The captured Romans, no longer *milites*, have forfeited their claim to be called soldiers and revert to their civilian status. Observe that Regulus himself is defined with the same scrupulous use of language when he makes his speech before the Senate (42: *ut capitis minor*); he interpreted his *deminutio capitis* literally, and with the proper legal restraint refused the kisses of his family after his years of imprisonment in Carthage.

23 **portas non clausas** 'gates wide open' (litotes), a mark of peacetime and national security.

25 **scilicet** underlines the ironic tone. Cf Livy 22, 59–60: the speech of T. Manlius Torquatus against ransoming the captives taken at Cannae (216 B.C.): *militibus utemini . . . nobis etiam promptioribus pro patria, quod beneficio vestro redempti atque in patriam restituti fuerimus . . . pretio redituri estis eo unde ignavia ac nequitia abiistis?*

27–32 Two allegorical parallels.

27 **damnum** 'add injury to shame'.

27, 28 For the parallel of the dyed wool cf Lucretius 6, lines 1074 f.: *purpureusque colos conchyli iungitur una/corpore cum lanae, dirimi qui non queat usquam.*

Medicata and *fuco* are technical terms in the dyeing trade.

31 The second comparison is with a stag, caught, then freed from the nets.

33 **perfidis se credidit hostibus** 'has thrown himself on the mercy of a deceitful enemy': grim sarcasm, equivalent to '*in fidem se dedit*, but *Punica fides* was notoriously untrustworthy.

35 **restrictis** cf *retorta tergo* (22).

38 **duello** 'war', an archaic form of *bello*, appropriate to the ancient history.

38–40 A passionate peroration.

40 **ruinis** instrumental ablative, with comparative.

41 **fertur** usually reserved to introduce a mythological parallel.

42 **capitis minor** 'as one deprived of civil rights', technical phraseology for a loss (*deminutio*) of civil rights, both personal and political.

46 **auctor** 'by his influence'.

48 **egregius exsul** a fine oxymoron; *exsul* is not used in the technical sense.

49 Cf Cicero, *De Off.* 3, 100: *neque vero tum ignorabat se ad crudelissimum hostem et ad exquisita supplicia proficisci.* Polybius (1, 31–4) and Diodorus Siculus (23, 12–15) are both ignorant of the story in their account of the Punic Wars, suggesting that the entire tale may be apocryphal.

COMMENTARY

53 **longa** 'lengthy, tedious'. Though captured in 255 B.C. at the Battle of Tunis, Regulus was executed in 251 B.C.
clientum poetic variant for *clientium*.

54 **diiudicata** implying a lawsuit which Regulus had handled as counsel or judge, possibly as arbitrator (*patronus*).

55 **Venafranos in agros** The holiday retreat to Tarentum and Venafrum is anachronistic for Regulus' time but appropriate for Horace's (cf *Odes* II 6, lines 11 and 16). However, the situation is timeless and the political geography is unimportant. The diminuendo ending is quiet and idyllic in contrast with the rhetorical emphasis and emotional character elsewhere in the ode.

H. T. Rowell, 'The free citizens in Horace, *Odes* III 5', in *Robinson Studies* II: (St. Louis, 1953), pp. 663-77.

. Examine *Odes* III 5 (72) as an example of the progressive design. Outline and comment on the structure and unity of the ode.

The 'causa Reguli' was a hackneyed theme in the schools of rhetoricians in Cicero's time (Cicero, *De. Off.* I 39). Consider the ode as a 'great oration against a tragic background'.

73 (HORACE, *Odes* III 6) *Delicta maiorum immeritus lues*

Metre: Alcaic
The last Roman Ode deals with the decline of religion, the moral vacuum of the closing decades of the Republic. The Parthians, Dacians, and Egyptians came close to destroying Rome as a result. The impurity within the Roman home is the gravest offence and is implicit in the decline of the nation.

1 **maiorum** the generation of the civil wars (88-31 B.C.).

2 **Romane** collective usage, in a general address. Cf Vergil, *Aen.* 6, line 851: *tu regere imperio populos, Romane, memento.* **refeceris:** cf Suetonius, *Aug.* 30: *Aedes sacras vetustate collapsas aut incendio absumptas refecit*; *Res Gestae* 4, 17; Vergil, *Aen.* 8, line 716.

5 **dis te minorem** cf *Odes* I 12, line 57; Cicero, *De Nat. Deor.* 3, 5.

6 **principium,** sc. est. *principium* is here trisyllabic. Cf *Odes* III 4 (71), line 41: *cōnsīlium*.

7 **neglecti** causal force.

8 **luctuosae** proleptic use.

9 **iam bis** probably the invasion of Crassus and the disaster at Carrhae (55–53 B.C.) and the repulse of Mark Antony by Phraates in 36 B.C.

10 **non auspicatos** the expedition of Crassus began with dire omens. Cf Cicero, *De Divin.* I 29; 2, 84.

12 **torquibus** decorations in the form of necklaces were awarded by the Parthian monarch for bravery or distinguished service.
exiguis 'paltry, poor', in a derogatory sense rather than 'simple finery'. The Parthian awards are inconsequential compared with the rich spoils taken from the defeated Romans.

13–14 **paene** with **delevit**.

14 **Dacus et Aethiops** barbaric auxiliaries who fought with Antony and Cleopatra at Actium. Cf Vergil, *Aen.* 8, lines 685–8.

17 ff. The corruption of domestic life and discipline and the general moral vacuum of the age exercised Horace frequently: Cf *Odes* III 24, lines 19–24; IV 5 (75), lines 21–4.
culpae 'vice' of unchastity, loose morals.

18 **genus** 'stock'.

21 **motus...Ionicos** 'Ionic (Asiatic) dances,' often mimetic, were designed to entertain diners and resembled modern cabaret performances. Roman moralists severely censured voluptuous dancing. Cf Sallust, *Cat.* 25.

22 **fingitur artibus** 'trained in the arts' (of seduction).

23 **iam nunc** contrast *mox* (25).

24 **de tenero ungui** either 'from the quick of her nails, in every nerve or fibre, from the depth of her being', a phrase used to express the impassioned dance steps and gestures, or, more likely, 'from her earliest childhood'. i.e. when her nails were soft like a young baby's.

29 **sed iussa coram non sine conscio** 'but summoned before witnesses, with the full complicity of her husband' (Gow). Cf Juvenal, 1, 56 ff., for the husband's connivance. *non sine conscio/marito*: litotes, 'not without her husband's knowing.'

30, 31 **institor** 'pedlar', often an agent for the proprietor of the shop (*taberna*), occasionally of servile status.
magister 'skipper, master of a vessel', usually someone who received wages for services on the trading vessel.

COMMENTARY

35 **ingentem** a poetic variant for the usual cognomen *Magnus*.

38 **Sabellis** the Osco-Sabellians were proverbial for their strict high principles and modest way of life. Cf Livy, 1, 18, 4: *quo genere nullum quondam incorruptius fuit* (of the Calabrian peasant).

41, 42 **ubi/mutaret** subjunctive of repeated action.

44 **agens abeunte** oxymoron.

46 **peior avis** 'worse than those of our ancestors.' Brachylogy for *aetate avorum peior*.

What reasons do you suppose induced Horace to close his great patriotic cycle with this ode?
'The absence of imagery does not mean a lack of real feeling' (Collinge). Discuss.
Examine the thought-structure of the ode.

74 (HORACE, *Odes* III 14) *Herculis ritu modo dictus, o plebs*

Metre: Sapphic
Written after the return of Augustus from his Spanish campaign against the Cantabrians, in 24 B.C. His illness over a period of several months at Tarraco (Tarragona) caused great anxiety at Rome. Cf *Odes* IV 2; IV 5 (75).

1 **Herculis ritu** Hercules was a favourite mythical prototype for Augustus, Cf *Odes* III 3, line 9; IV 5 (72), line 36; Vergil *Aen.* 6, line 801, *nec vero Alcides tantum telluris obivit* and 8, lines 201 f. Horace here refers especially to Hercules' adventures at Gades (Cadiz) in Spain where he fought with the triple-bodied herdsman Geryon. The Ara Maxima in the Forum Boarium commemorated the visit of Hercules to Evander's Pallanteum, subsequently Rome, and the ritual recalled the Spanish adventure along with others (cf Vergil. *Aen.* 8, lines 185-305.

plebs cf *Odes* II 2, line 18, for comparable use of *populus* and *plebs* as an embracing term for the citizenry.

2 **morte venalem** cf *Odes* II 16 (56), line 7, Vergil, *Aen.* 5, line 230: *vitamque volunt pro laude pacisci. petiisse . . . repetit*: word play.

5 **unico gaudens marito** Some edd. read *unice* (cf Catullus 29, line 11). Livia was the pattern of Roman matronal fidelity.

6 **operata** to be taken as a present participle, 'making sacrifice'. *prodeat*: sc. *in publicum*; *divis*: older manuscript prefer *sacris*, 'sacrifices, duly performed'.

7 **soror** Octavia, widow of Mark Antony, and mother of Marcellus by her first husband.

8 **supplice vitta** suggests that Horace has in mind a *supplicatio* rather than a triumph. Cf Vergil, *Aen.* 4, line 637: *ipsa pia tege tempora vitta*.

9–10 **virginum . . . puellae** refers to the young wives of the legionaries. Livia and Octavia are to have the assistance of matrons in the rites. The returned soldiers, with their young wives as spectators, are asked to observe a 'religious silence', to control their emotions.

11 **male ominatis** probably the original text. Some have preferred *male nominatis* and *inominatis* (Bentley) to cure the hiatus between a short and a long vowel with no natural break in the line.

13, 14 **atras . . . curas** the anxiety attendant on Augustus' illness [cf *Odes* III 1 (70), line 40].

15 **mori metuam** for similar sentiment cf *Odes* IV 15 (76), line 17.

17 Horace issues abrupt orders for a carousal [cf *Odes* II 3 (53), line 13].

18–20 An allusion to the Marsic or Social War (91–88 B.C.). *Qua*: adverbial, cf Vergil, *Aen.* 1, line 18: *si qua fata sinant* (sc. *via*). Spartacus is associated with the Servile War (73–71 B.C.).

18 **duelli** archaic for *belli*.

19 **Spartacum vagantem** 'the roving Spartacus'.

21 **argutae** 'clear-voiced, sweet-voiced' singer. Cf Thalia (*Odes* IV 6 (65), line 25).

22 **murreum** 'chestnut'.

23 **ianitorem** 'doorkeeper', the *ostiarius* of the music-girl Neaera's home.

25 **albescens** cf *Epist.* I 20, line 24: *praecanum*, 'prematurely grey'. Horace in his fortieth year was grey-haired.

27 **ferrem** imperfect (for *tulissem*) to express continuous action in the past.

28 **Planco** L. Munatius Plancus, consul in 42 B.C., the year of the Battle of Philippi. Cf *Odes* I 7 (67).

The structure of the ode divides into two major sections, with a transitional passage:

1–12 The civic welcome, a public thanksgiving, as if prescribed by public proclamation, in honour of Augustus' return from Spain.

13–16 Transitional passage: a private expression of relief, to match the earlier public thanksgiving, provides the first hint of a personal element in the ode and the private party forthcoming.

17–28 The private declaration of relief; a celebration is to be arranged, an invitation sent to Neaera, which may not get past her door; the time for truculence is past.

Try to account for the somewhat melancholy tone of the ode. Compare *Odes* III 14 (74) and II 7 (45).

75 (HORACE, *Odes* IV 5) *Divis orte bonis, optime Romulae*

Metre: Third Asclepiadean
Horace appeals to Augustus to return to Rome after his long absence in Gaul (16–13 B.C.). The ode affirms the fulfilment of the hopes expressed in *Odes* I 2 (66) and III 24, III 1–6 (70–3). The ode is characterized by a sense of tranquillity, peace, and repose.

1 **divis ... bonis** 'when the gods were kindly disposed'.

2 **custos** cf *Odes* IV 15 (76), line 17: *custode rerum Caesare*; but Jupiter, in *Odes* I 12, line 49, is *pater atque custos*.

4 **sancto concilio** 'the august Senate'. Cf Vergil, *Aen.* 1, line 426: *iura magistratusque legunt sanctumque senatum*.

5 **lucem,** sc. *tuam,* and cf *Sat.* I 7, line 24: *solem Asiae Brutum*.
it 'passes', cf *Odes* II 14 (55), line 5: *quotquot eunt dies*.
dux bone 'blessed leader'

9 **quem Notus invido** Horace imagines a young sailor in Egypt (Wickham) or perhaps Rhodes (Gow) detained by 'spiteful' winter winds between November and early March.

13 **ominibus** ablative of means. Her frequent consultation of omens indicates her impatience.

16 **quaerit** 'longs for' (cf *Odes* III 24, line 32).

17 **rura perambulat** grazing rather than ploughing cattle; a picturesque usage.

18 **Faustitas** *Fausta Felicitas* is represented on Roman coins with the cornucopia, token of Good Fortune and Plenty.

19 **pacatum** 'free from piracy'. Cf *Res Gestae* 25: *mare pacavi a praedonibus*; Suetonius, *Aug.* 98 (an incident at Puteoli = Pozzuoli) *vectores nautaeque de navi Alexandrina Augusto acclamarunt, per illum se vivere, per illum navigare, libertate atque fortunis per illum frui.*

volitant frequentative.

22 **mos et lex** for the combination cf *Odes* III 24, line 35: *quid leges sine moribus vanae proficiunt?*

edomuit 'totally stamped out, overcame thoroughly', a poetic exaggeration. Horace probably refers to the *Lex Julia de Adulteriis coercendis*, passed in 17 B.C.

24 **comes** Vengeance follows closely on the guilty; Poena no longer appears lame (*Odes* III 2, line 32).

26 **Germania** Horace refers to the *clades Lolliana* (16 B.C.) and the wars with the Sygambri.

horrida a reference to the forests and barbaric people.

parturit 'breeds in swarms' 'breeds in hordes'. Cf *Odes* I 7 (67), line 16: *neque parturit imbris/perpetuo.*

27 **ferae Hiberiae** Horace often alludes to the long resistance of the Concani in Spanish Cantabria. The tribe was finally subdued by Agrippa in 19 B.C. (*Epist.* I 12, line 27); cf *Odes* II 6, line 2; III 4 (71), line 34.

29 **condit ... diem** 'sees the sun set';

suis possessive, 'his own vineyards', which are no longer menaced by proscription (the misfortune of Vergil and Horace) and occupation.

30 **viduas** 'unwed' trees (elms, poplars).

ducit borrowed from the language of the Roman wedding, lit. 'leads in marriage'. Cf *Odes* II 15, line 4: *caelebs* 'bachelor' trees, lacking the clinging vine.

31 **alteris** 'at dessert' (cf *mensae secundae*). The Roman custom was to begin the second course by offering libations to the Lares; thereafter the guests might 'toast' one another.

32 **adhibet** 'invoke, invite their presence'.

34 **Laribus** the *Genius Augusti* was worshipped among the Lares. Cf *Odes* III 17, lines 14–15; Ovid, *Fasti* 5, line 145: *mille Lares geniumque ducis qui tradidit illos,/Urbs habet.*

35 **Castoris** one of the Lares (with Pollux); dependent on *numen memor*.

COMMENTARY 213

39 Cf *Odes* I 18, line 3; *Epist.* I 19, line 9.

40 **subest** 'sinks beneath'.

Structurally, the ode incorporates a double theme: (1) Eagerness for Augustus' return, and (2) the tonic effect of his presence.

1-4 Solemn invocation: Italy longs for Augustus' return.
5-8 Simile: the effect of the sun in Springtime, in contrast to Winter's storms.
9-16 The mother longs for her son's return.
17-24 The internal State of the Union: the benefits of Augustus' rule at home; commercial, social, and moral factors.
25-8 The external state of the Empire: Augustan Peace on the Imperial frontiers.
29-36 The Italian farmer: effects of the Augustan Peace on the agricultural economy: the vineyard, the dinner table; prayers of gratitude.
37-40 Solemn finale: Italy praises Augustus; universal gratitude.

Examine the ode for reminiscences of style and usage in the sacred hymns.
Compare *Odes* IV 5 (75) and III 14 (74).
What effects are obtained by the use of the Asclepiadean metre and asyndeton?
Discuss the function of wine in the ode, and the cumulative effect of the various words for distance, separation and length of time.
How do you explain the changes in tone within the ode, from solemn and grandiose, to simple, homely associations?

76 (HORACE, *Odes* IV 15) *Phoebus volentem proelia me loqui*

Metre: Alcaic

Horace celebrates the return of Augustus after his prolonged absence in the western provinces (16-13 B.C.). To commemorate his safe return the Senate decreed that an Altar of Augustan Peace should be erected in the Campus Martius near the Via Flaminia.
Res Gestae 12: Cum ex Hispania Galliaque, rebus in iis provinciis prospere gestis, Romam redi Ti. Nerone P. Quintilio consulibus, aram Pacis Augustae senatus pro reditu meo consacrandam censuit ad Campum Martium, in qua magistratus et sacerdotes et virgines Vestales anniversarium sacrificium facere iussit.

2 **increpuit** 'rebuked me with his lyre'. The image seems to derive from Vergil, *Ecl.* 6, lines 3–4: *cum canerem reges et proelia, Cynthius aurem/vellit et admonuit.*

5 ff. Notice the polysyndeton and anaphora (cf lines 19–24).

6 **signa** the standards captured from Crassus at Carrhae in 53 B.C. The long-sought standards were finally restored by Phraates to the future emperor Tiberius in 20 B.C. Cf *Odes* III 5 (72), line 5; III 6 (73), line 9. The relief on the breast-plate of the statue of Augustus of Prima Porta depicts the event.

nostro ... Iovi The recovered standards were deposited first in the Capitoline Temple of Jupiter, later in the Temple of Mars Ultor in the Forum Augusti (2 B.C.); cf *Res Gestae* 29: *signa militaria complura per alios duces amissa devictis hostibus recepi ex Hispania et Gallia et a Dalmateis. Parthos trium exercitum Romanorum spolia et signa reddere mihi supplicesque amicitiam populi Romani petere coegi. Ea autem signa in penetrali, quod est in templo Martis Ultoris, reposui.*

9 **Ianum Quirini** see *Index Nominum.* Augustus claimed to have closed the gates of Janus three times, in 29 B.C. after Actium, in 25 B.C. after the Cantabrian wars, and again between 9 and 1 B.C.

10 Horace refers to the *Leges Juliae de Adulteriis coercendis*, and *de Maritandis Ordinibus* (cf *Odes* III 24, line 29).

12 **artis** the 'virtues' of the old Roman way of life. Cf *Res Gestae* 8: *Legibus novis me auctore latis multa exempla maiorum exolescentia iam ex nostro saeculo reduxi et ipse multarum rerum exempla imitanda posteris tradidi.* The virtues which Augustus sought to revive were: *castitas, fides, fortitudo, frugalitas, iustitia, patientia, temperantia.* Cf *Odes* III 1–6 (70–3).

17 **custode** cf *Odes* IV 5 (75), lines 1–2: *optime Romulae/custos gentis*; and III 14 (74), line 15: *tenente/Caesare terras.*

18 **exiget** 'will expel'. Cf *Odes* II 13, line 31: *exactos tyrannos. otium* 'peace' cf II 16 (56), lines 1 and 5.

20 **miseras** proleptic use, 'to their sorrow'.

inimicat 'sets at variance, embroils'.

21 **qui ... bibunt** either the Vindelici (*Odes* IV 4, line 18) or the Daci (*Odes* III 6 (73), line 14).

22 **edicta ... Iulia** 'the Julian ordinances'; not to be taken literally, since edicts are technically *interpretations* of the law, though the phrase suggests the *leges Iuliae* of 18 B.C. which in effect constituted a new

COMMENTARY 215

code, for they provided for criminal law and legal procedures, as well as for moral reform.

25 profestis lucibus 'working days'.

29 more patrum patriotism was fired by recollection of exemplary deeds. Cf Cicero, *Tusc.* I 3: *solitos esse in epulis canere convivas ad tibicinem de clarorum hominum virtutibus.* (2nd cent. B.C.)

30 Lydis suggests either the 'classical' instrument, or soft Lydian music.

32 progeniem Veneris Aeneas, Julius Caesar, and Augustus. Cf *Carm. Saec.* 50, *clarus Anchisae Venerisque sanguis.*

H. Dahlmann, 'Die letzte Ode des Horaz', *Gymnasium* 65 (1958) 340–55.

77 (CATULLUS 4) *Phaselus ille, quem videtis, hospites*

Metre: Iambic trimeter

Catullus (*erum*, 19), in the presence of his friends, extols the yacht which brought him home from his provincial service in Bithynia. The itinerary is related in reverse: from Sirmio (Lake Garda) down the Po valley, across the Adriatic, around Greece, across the Aegean to Rhodes and through the Aegean Islands, the Propontis (Sea of Marmora), and so into the Euxine (Black Sea) to the point of embarkation in Bithynia, two hundred miles east of the Bosphorus on the south shore of the Black Sea. Editors generally regard the poem as fanciful, the life story of an imaginary ship, or as a poem addressed to a ship model, a votive offering to record Catullus' safe return from Bithynia. The actual *mise en scène* of the poem is probably a *recitatio* involving Catullus and his literary friends (*hospites*, line 1). The pattern of the poem is strongly reminiscent of the sepulchral and dedicatory epigrams found elsewhere. The poet recites the account of the yacht's birthplace (10–12), parentage and ancestry (13–17), travels (2–9; 18–21), and final journey (22–4). The poem closes somewhat ambiguously with suggestions of dedicatory (*senet*, 26) and sepulchral epigrams (*recondita quiete*, 25–6).

1 phaselus suggests a craft shaped like a bean-pod, a light sailing-vessel (Vergil, *Georg.* 4, lines 287–9; Juvenal 15, line 127) used in Egyptian waters and for cruises along the Campanian shoreline (Cic. *Att.* 1, 13, 1; 16, 1; Martial X, 30, line 18). Cf Horace, *Odes* III 2, line 28: *fragilemve mecum/solvat phaselon.*

2 **ait fuisse navium celerrimus** Greek usage, nominative and infinitive construction, instead of accusative and infinitive.

3 **impetum trabis** epic or tragic language.

neque nequisse double negative, to express positive idea. Cf line 6: *negat... negare*.

4 **palmula** diminutive use for *palma* elsewhere (Cat. 64, line 7).

6 **minacis** the Adriatic is proverbially stormy, and subject to sudden off-shore winds. Cf Horace, *Odes* I 33, line 15; III 3, line 5; III 9, lines 22 f.

7 **insulas Cycladas** dangerous waters. Cf Horace, *Odes* I 14 (68), lines 19 f.

8 **Rhodum nobilem** Rhodes was noted for its distinguished schools of philosophy and rhetoric, sculpture, religious sanctuaries (especially Lindos), and one of the Seven Wonders, the Colossus, which used to stand alongside the harbour.

8 f. **Thraciam** agrees with **Propontida.** Notice the symmetrical structure; *horridamque Thraciam Propontida*; *trucemve Ponticum sinum*.

9 **Propontida trucemve** a metrical irregularity, long *a* in *Propontida*, which is repeated in *impotentiā freta*.

11 **Cytorio in iugo** the range of hills above the Paphlagonian seaport of Cytorus. The entire south coast of Pontus was well forested and provided wood for the local shipbuilding and smelting [Horace, *Odes* I 14 (68), line 11; I 35, lines 7 f.].

12 **loquente coma** cf Vergil, *Ecl.* 8, line 22.

13 **Amastris** the capital town of Paphlagonia, part of the province of Bithynia. Cytorus was the neighbouring port, which provided boxwood to a large market (Strabo 544; Vergil, *Georg.* 2, line 437).

14 ff. **tibi... tuo** Amastris (where the ship was launched) and Mount Cytorus (the source of the timbers).

18 **impotentia** 'raging'. Cf Horace, *Odes* III 30 (8), line 3.

20 ff. **Iuppiter** a reference to Jupiter as wind god (cf Greek, Zeus Ourios).

utrumque... in pedem the stern wind falls on the square sail directly so that both sheets (*pedes*) which brace the lower corners grow taut simultaneously.

22 **litoralibus deis** sea deities like Glaucus, Melicertes (Vergil, *Georg.* 1, lines 436–7), Panopea, Palaemon (Statius, *Silv.* V 3, line

2), or Neptune, Venus Marina (Greek, Euploia), the Dioscuri (Cat. 68, line 65), for all had temples along the shore, objects of sailors' vows and benefactions (Venus: Horace, *Odes* I 5 (36), lines 13 ff.; I 3 (35), lines 1–2; IV 11, line 15).

23 **sibi** dative of agent, with the perfect participle passive.

mari novissimo 'the last sea', Adriatic or Pontus, depending on the interpretation.

24 **limpidum** 'clear'.

26 **senet** archaism for *senescit*.

dedicat the yacht dedicates herself to the Dioscuri (Sons of Zeus), protectors of mariners, who dispelled storms, and manifested themselves in the shape of the electrical phenomenon known as St Elmo's Fire or as bright stars (*lucida sidera*, *Odes* I 3 (35), line 1), sure guides during storms. (Cf Catullus 68, line 65; *Odes* I 12, line 25; IV 8, line 31; *Epode* 17, line 42.) Castor is the predominant partner in the address, and in the Aedes Castoris in the Forum Romanum. (Cic. *Verr.* 1, 129.)

Consult bibliography in Fordyce, *Catullus*, p. 99. H. J. Mette, 'Catull *Carm.* 4', in *RhM* 105 (1962) 153–7. M. J. C. Putnam, 'Catullus' Journey', in *CP* 57 (1962) 10–18. R. Hornsby, 'The Craft of Catullus', in *AJP* 84 (1963) 256–65.

The *Appendix Vergiliana* contains a parody on Sabinus, the former mule-driver.

Catalepton 10

Sabinus ille, quem videtis, hospites,
ait fuisse mulio celerrimus
neque ullius volantis impetum cisi
nequisse praeterire, sive Mantuam
opus foret volare sive Brixiam.   5
et hoc negat Tryphonis aemuli domum
negare nobilem insulamve Caeruli,
ubi iste post Sabinus ante Quinctio
bidente dicit attodisse forcipe
comata colla, ne Cytorio iugo   10
premente dura vulnus ederet iuba.
Cremona frigida et lutosa Gallia,
tibi haec fuisse et esse cognitissima

ait Sabinus: ultima ex origine
tua stetisse dicit in voragine, 15
tua in palude deposisse sarcinas,
et inde tot per orbitosa milia
iugum tulisse, laeva sive dextera
strigare mula sive utrumque coeperat,

*

neque ulla vota semitalibus deis 20
sibi esse facta, praeter hoc novissimum,
paterna lora proximumque pectinem.
sed haec prius fuere: nunc eburnea
sedetque sede seque dedicat tibi,
gemelle Castor et gemelle Castoris. 25

Catalepton 10 (Vergil?)

1 **Sabinus** cognomen.

2 **mulio** 'muleteer', 'mule-driver'.

3 **cisi** *cisium* 'gig', a Gallic conveyance. *Oxford Classical Dictionary*, 'For rapid journeys the carriage most frequently used was the two-wheeled *cisium* or *essedum*, which attained considerable speeds.'

4, 5 **Mantua ... Brixia** both Mantua and Brixia (Brescia) are located in Vergil's home territory of Cisalpine Gaul.

7 **insulamve** 'building block', Trypho and Caerulus are probably Greek freedmen, now property-owners.

8 **Quinctio** nominative.

9 **attodisse** perfect infinitive, *attondeo* 'clip, cut'.
   bidente ... forcipe 'with two-bladed shears'.

11 **iuba** 'mane'.

12 **lutosa** 'muddy'. Cf Cat. 17 (79), line 9: *ire praecipitem in lutum;* 11, *lividissima ... vorago;* 25, *in gravi caeno*. Colonia (mod. Cologna?) and Cremona were liable to cold wet periods common in Cisalpine Gaul.

14 **ultima ex origine**, i.e. *a puero*.

16 **palude** 'marsh'.
   deposisse contracted form of *deposuisse*.
   sarcinas 'packs'.

COMMENTARY

17 **et inde,** sc. Cremona; *orbitosa* 'rutted, rutty'.

18 **iugum tulisse** 'have worn the yoke, have borne the pressure of the yoke'.

19 **strigare** 'falter, flag'.

20 **semitalibus deis** 'to the gods of the by-ways'.

22 **lora** 'reins'.
pectinem 'curry-comb'.

23, 4 **eburnea... sede** 'in his ivory chair', the *sella curulis*, reserved for magistrates in Rome and in municipal towns and colonies like Cremona. Sabinus apparently became a duumvir of the colony.

25 **gemelle Castor** a temple of Castor was located about twelve miles east of Cremona (cf Tac. *Hist.* 2, 24; Suetonius, *Otho* 9). How successful is the parody?

R. E. H. Westendorp Boerma, *P. Vergili Maronis Catalepton* (Pars Altera) (Assen, 1963) 28–48. R. Syme, 'Sabinus the Muleteer', *Latomus* 17 (1958) 73–80. R. E. H. Westendorp Boerma, 'Virgil's debt to Catullus', *Acta Classica* (1958) 51–63.

78 (CATULLUS 10) *Varus me meus ad suos amores*

Metre: Hendecasyllabic (Phalaecean)
Catullus visits Varus after his return from Bithynia where he had failed to make the fortune he had anticipated. He tells a story of how he had his bluff called after boasting that he had brought back 'eight strapping fellows' to carry his litter.

2 **visum** *visere* frequently occurs in connection with visits to the sick (cf Lucretius 6, line 1238). The appearance of Serapis (26) may support the belief that Varus' girl friend is masquerading as an invalid.

3 **repente** 'at first sight'.

4 **non... illepidum neque invenustum** both words, and their opposites, are hallmarks of Catullian sophisticated society (cf Cat. 36, line 17).

6 f. **quid esset iam Bithynia** conversational asyndeton.

8 A sad commentary on the character of Roman provincial administration in this area.

9 f. **ipsis** the staff.

10 **cohorti** formerly the governor's bodyguard, but by this date the company of friends and adventurers attached to the provincial governor. Maintained at public expense, they frequently found ways and means to acquire sizable sums of money. Occasionally, as here, the *comites* numbered poets and writers, and the *cohors* was as much literary coterie as governor's staff. Memmius patronized Catullus and Varus; Messalla maintained a similar group in the East (Tibullus I 3, line 2); and Horace cites a literary group associated with Tiberius in the East in 20 B.C. (*Epistles* I 3, line 6: *studiosa cohors*).

11 **caput unctius** hair sleek with ointments, token of luxury and wealth, and prelude to a celebration, a *festa*.

13 **faceret pili** cf Cat. 5 (13), line 3.

14 f. **quod illic natum** the local product was the litter-bearer. In Republican times the *lectica* (covered litter) was used only in the country, and on short trips. Women used it to such an excess in the city that Julius Caesar was forced to limit its use (Suetonius, *Julius* 45, 1).

17 **facerem** 'pass myself off as', 'make myself appear as'.

18 **non mihi tam fuit maligne ut**... Colloquial, 'things haven't gone so badly for me that...'.

20 **rectos** 'straight-backed', 'upstanding'.

21 **at** used to introduce a confidential side remark.

23 **in collo... collocare** a Plautine jingle.

24 **hic** 'thereupon'.

26 **commoda** shortened ă in the imperative; probably colloquial pronunciation.

26 f. **ad Serapim deferri** the Hellenistic cult of Serapis reached Italy from Egypt *c.* 105 B.C., first at Puteoli, the cosmopolitan seaport in Campania, later at Rome and Ostia. The Roman sanctuary to Isis and Serapis was located in the Campus Martius, and lay between the Saepta Julia on the west and the Porticus Divorum and round Temple of Minerva Chalcidica on the east.

27 **mane** short ĕ: 'hold on there, not so fast, wait for me'.

28 **quod** introduces an adverbial clause.

29 **fugit me ratio** colloquial: i.e. 'I did not think'.

29 f. The erratic syntax emphasises the confusion and embarrassment; so also the inversion of the *nomen* and *cognomen*. The repeated use of *is* probably derives from Roman comedy.

32 tam bene quam mihi pararim *si* is omitted, after *tamquam*, an ellipse.

33 insulsa male . . . vivis colloquial usage in an uncomplimentary phrase. *vivis* is a substitute for *es*.

79 (CATULLUS 17) *O Colonia, quae cupis ponte ludere longo*

Metre: Priapean

Catullus expresses contempt for a fellow-countryman who neglected his pretty young wife. He confesses a strong desire to hurl him from the town's new bridge. The place defies identification. Some identify it with the modern Cologna Veneta, a small town some twenty miles east of Verona where the Ponte di Catullo today bridges the river Gua. But there is no evidence of colonial status for the town in Catullus' time, or for *any town* in the vicinity.

1 ludere 'to celebrate a religious ceremony, festival'; the *ludus* may be connected with rites attached to the bridging of streams.

ponte longo 'along the bridge'.

2 salire paratum habes the infinitive replaces the noun; lit. 'you have dancing in readiness'.

3 axulis diminutive for *axis*, 'board, lath, plank'. The diminutive, *ponticuli* ('bridglet'), implies that the structure is worthless.

redivivis 'second-hand, resurrected materials'.

4 supinus eat a colloquial expression: 'fall flat'.

5 sic 'on this one condition'; expressed by the following imperative.

6 Salisubsali either genitive of *Salisubsalus*, or *-ius*, the divinity (Mars?) to whom the dances were consecrated; or the name of the dancers. The form recalls the Salii, 'the leaping priests' of Mars.

7 maximi . . . risus descriptive genitive.

8 municipem a fellow-townsman (Veronese).

volo short final o (cf Cat. 10 (78), line 26).

9 per caputque pedesque 'head over heels'.

10 verum . . . ut defining use 'in fact let it be where' (for *ut*, cf Cat. 11 (27), line 3).

totius short i.

12 **instar** cf Vergil, *Aen.* 2, line 15: *instar montis equum*, 'a horse as large as a mountain'.

13 **tremula** 'rocking'.

15 **et puella** emphatic repetition, 'and what is more'. Cf Vergil, *Aen.* 2, line 49: *timeo Danaos et dona ferentes*, 'I fear the Greeks and still more when they bring gifts.'
 tenellulo a double diminutive.
 delicatior 'more wilful'. Augustus' remark is illuminating: *duas se habere filias delicatas quas necesse haberet ferre* (Macrob. 2, 5, 4). 'that he had two spoiled daughters whom he had to endure', i.e., Rome and Julia.

17 **ludere** 'flirt'.

18 f. **alnus ... securi** a scene from the Ligurian highlands.

19 **fossa** a canal, irrigation ditch, or waterway designed to expedite the floating of logs to the shipbuilding factories (cf Strabo 4, 202).
 suppernata 'hamstrung' by the Ligurian axe.

20 **nulla sit** 'as if it did not exist at all'.

21 **talis iste meus stupor** the abstract noun is used for the person; the abstract noun is used for the concrete: 'that numbskull of mine'.

24 **si pote,** sc. *est* 'on the chance that he can'. Cf Cat. 45 (83), line 5.

25 **supinum** ambiguous: 'spineless', 'on his back'.

26 **soleam** a leather sock or slipper with metal plates on the sole fastened by thongs about the fetlock to assist the animal over difficult spots.

 N. Rudd, 'The Structure of Catullus 17', in *TAPA* 90 (1959) 238–42.
 Read the poem aloud several times to sense the dance metre, reminiscent of peasants' folk dances. The poem is full of humour and ribaldry. Comment on the thought-progression, and examine the possibility of imaginative links between the husband and the bridge, and the wife and Colonia.

80 (CATULLUS 26) *Furi, villula vestra non ad Austri*

 Metre: Hendecasyllabic (Phalaecean)
 The point of this short poem depends on the ambiguity contained in *opposita* (2), either 'facing' or 'pledged' (cf English lean and lien).

The joke comes in the last two verses where the overdraft (financial) and windy draught confound the poet and Furius.

1 **vestra** the little country place of Furius. Some edd. read *nostra* and have Catullus ridicule his own financial troubles. Catullus may have been told the benefits of the villa's location and so deflates the boastings with mention of a different kind of exposure, a mortgage which acts like a Sirocco.

2 **opposita** cf *pignori opponere*, 'to mortgage, pledge'.

4 **milia quindecim et ducentos** hardly a sizable mortgage. A good town house rented for 30,000 sesterces; Caelius rented an apartment in a Roman *insula* (apartment block) for 10,000 sesterces (Cicero, *Pro Caelio* 17). However poets are proverbially impoverished.

5 **horribilem atque pestilentem** cf Horace, *Odes* III 23 (64), line 5 (referring to the Sirocco), *nec pestilentem sentiat Africum/fecunda vitis*.

81 (CATULLUS 39) *Egnatius, quod candidos habet dentes*

Metre: Choliambic

Egnatius, a native Spaniard, came to Rome and incurred the enmity of Catullus on two counts: because he became Clodia's lover, and because he smiled on every occasion to show off his teeth. Elsewhere (37, lines 18-20) Egnatius is described as long-haired and bearded, the cynosure of women.

2 **renidet usque quaque (via)** 'is constantly smiling wherever he goes'.

2 f. **rei ... subsellium** the wooden benches appointed for the prosecutor and defendant faced each other in the court room. Egnatius has been engaged as *advocatus* to defend the accused, but grins inopportunely.

5 **lugetur** impersonal passive 'an occasion for mourning'.

7 **morbum** 'weakness', cf Cat. 76 (26), line 25.

9 **bone** ironical, somewhat disparaging use.

10 **urbanus** 'from the City' (Rome).

11 **pinguis Umber aut obesus Etruscus** Some edd. read *parcus*, 'thrifty, stingy', but the physical connotation seems more apt; the

Umbrians were known for easy living; the Etruscans, judging by sculptural representations on sarcophagus lids, and tomb wall-paintings, tended to be stout. (Cf Vergil, *Georg.* 2, line 193: *pinguis Tyrrhenus*.)

12 **ater atque dentatus** 'dark complexioned with a fine set of teeth'.

13 **meos** 'my own people,' Catullus' Transpadanes.
   ut attingam 'to touch upon'.

17 **nunc** 'as matters stand'.

82 (CATULLUS 44) *O funde noster, seu Sabine, seu Tiburs*

Metre: Choliambic

Publius Sestius concocts superb dinners but bad speeches. He had invited Catullus to dinner and at the same time requested a critique of his speech against Antius, a candidate for office. Catullus read his host's speech and caught a cold so that he had to retreat to his villa to recuperate and thereby forfeited his dinner invitation.

The point of the poem is probably double-edged: first, there is a pun contained in *frigus* (line 20) for Sestius' speech was so 'frigid, bombastic, affected and precious' that Catullus caught a cold (lines 13 and 19); second, the poem may allude humorously to the *Lex Antia*, proposed by Gaius Antius Restio shortly after 78 B.C. The details of the sumptuary law are wanting, but one clause certainly restricted the freedom of magistrates in office or designate, and of candidates for office (*petitores*), to accept dinner invitations. The measure was apparently designed to curb political intrigue no less than conspicuous consumption on the part of wealthy *Optimates*. However, although the legislation was directed against *sumptuosas . . . cenas* (line 9), it did permit the unrestricted use of vegetables (e.g. *urtica*, line 15).

1 **funde** the farm and the buildings.

2 f. Catullus' property, on the borderline of fashionable Tibur (Tivoli) and rustic Sabine country, plain farmland and orchards, probably formed part of a new property development.
   autumant early Latin, 'assert, maintain'.

2, 3 **non est cordi** 'who do not desire'.

4 **quovis . . . pignore . . . contendunt** 'are set to maintain with any stake'.

COMMENTARY

6 **fui libenter** colloquial usage.
suburbana on the limits of Tivoli, not in the country.

10 **dum** temporal meaning with *volo*, causal with *appeto*.

11 **petitorem** 'candidate for office'. Cf Horace, *Odes* III 1 (70), lines 10–11: *descendat in Campum petitor*.

12 **veneni** 'poisonous style'. Cf Cat. 14 (31), line 19: *omnia venena* (used of verses).

13 **hic** 'thereupon'.
gravedo 'the common cold'. Celsus 4, 5, 2, describes the customary symptoms: '*nares claudit, vocem obtundit, tussim siccam movet . . . haec autem et brevia, et, si neglecta sunt, longa esse consuerunt*.
frequens, quassare medical language. Cf Suetonius, *Augustus* 81.

15 **otio et urtica** 'rest and relaxation, and a vegetarian diet of greens'. Celsus prescribes the same: (4, 5, 8): *in gravedine primo die quiescere*; (4, 10, 4): *utilis in omni tussi est . . . cibus interdum mollis, ut malva et urtica*.

16 f. **grates ago** archaic. A formal solemnity with humorous effect.

17 **es ulta** direct address to the villa.

18 f. **nec deprecor ... quin** 'I offer no plea (or argument) to prevent. . . .'

19 **recepso** archaic future, ending in *-so* (Greek borrowing), but equated with the future perfect.

20 **frigus** 'icy stuff'.

21 **tunc** emphatic, 'who only invites me to dinner when I have read his nasty (dreadful, villainous) book'.

For details on *Antius petitor* consult Ronald Syme, 'Ten Tribunes', in *JRS* 53 (1963) 59, note 2.

83 (CATULLUS 45) *Acmen Septimius suos amores*

Metre: Hendecasyllabic (Phalaecean)
A love idyll, in 'ballad' form. The refrain and the form generally are probably Alexandrian in inspiration but popular verse forms may also have contributed to the idyll. The concern with structure and form is undoubtedly Alexandrian, but the realistic portrayal of

the lovers, the gaiety, the use of alliteration and assonance, are unquestionably Italian.

1 **Acmen Septimius** the verbal juxtaposition of the two lovers suggests the physical nearness and the note of reciprocity which sounds throughout the poem.

Acme, probably a Greek freedwoman, shares a couch with Septimius and rests in his embrace.

3 **perdite** 'desperately'.

5 **quantum qui pote,** sc. *est amare.*
perire 'to love to distraction, or desperation'.

6 **Libya** the home of lions (cf *Odes* I 22, (41), line 15; Plin. *N.H.* 6, 195), frequent imports from Africa for the Roman amphitheatres and *ludi.*

7 **caesio** 'green-eyed'. Cf Homer, *Iliad* 20, line 172.

8 f. Amor favours each protestation (8–9; 17–18); the double sneeze, on either side, underlines the approval and averts all evil omens. H. J. Rose (*HSCP* 47 (1936) 1–2) argued that omens on the right and left favour both Greek and Italian; for Greeks, a sneeze on the right was propitious, for Romans, the left was the luckier side.

10 **at** the attention transfers abruptly to the other party.

11 **ebrios** love's intoxication. Cf Vergil, *Aen.* 1, line 749: *longumque bibebat amorem* (Dido).

12 **purpureo ore** 'rosy lips'.

13 **Septimille** an endearing, familiar diminutive.

20 **amant, amantur** asyndeton (no connective).

D. S. Ross, 'Style and Content in Catullus 45', in *CP* 60 (1965) 256–69.

The structure of the love idyll is formal and symmetrical:

1–7   Septimius to Acme.
8–9   Refrain.
10–16 Acme to Septimius.
17–18 Refrain.
19–20 Mutual love.
21–24 Septimius *misellus, fidelis* Acme.
25–26 The happy couple.

Observe throughout the use of alliteration, assonance, juxtaposition and reciprocity, and striking metaphors.

COMMENTARY

84 (CATULLUS 49). *Disertissime Romuli nepotum*

Metre: Hendecasyllabic (Phalaecean)
Catullus addresses Cicero and discharges a debt of gratitude, perhaps for Cicero's defence of the poet in an unspecified lawsuit. But it is also amusing to conjecture that Catullus may be thanking Cicero for the use of his house to accommodate the clandestine meetings of Catullus and Lesbia. On the other hand, the poem may be suggesting that as a poet Cicero is a very good lawyer.

1 **Romuli nepotum** a quasi-heroic phrase (cf Cat. 58, line 5). Both Cicero and Catullus had provincial backgrounds.

2-3 **quot sunt... annis.** Cf Catullus 21, lines 2-3; and 24, lines 2-3. The expression is formulaic and somewhat extravagant.
Marce Tulli Catullus uses the formal address appropriate to the Senate (Cicero, *Att.* 7, 3, 5) and official documents.

J. H. Collins, 'Cicero and Catullus', in *CJ* 48 (1952-3) 11-17.

85 (CATULLUS 53) *Risi nescio quem modo e corona*

Metre: Hendecasyllabic (Phalaecean)

1 **corona** 'the circle, ring' of bystanders which gathered around the proceedings in the Basilicas (law courts) on the ground floor and in the galleries. Interests often ran high, and applause and interruptions were frequent.

2, 3 **mirifice explicasset** 'neatly unfolded'.
crimina Vatiniana 'the charges against Vatinius'. Cf Cat. 14 (31), line 3 and 44, (82), line 10.

4 **manus tollens** a sign of amazement or admiration.

5 **di magni** cf Cat. 14 (31), line 12.
salaputium Seneca (*Controversiae* 7, 4, 7) portrays Calvus as short (*parvolus statura*); so also Ovid, *Tristia*, 2, line 431: (*exigui Calvi*), and animated and lively (*violentus actor et concitatus*). Catullus uses a slang word with vulgar associations in his compliment, 'what an eloquent little squirt'.

86 (CATULLUS 84) *Chommoda dicebat, si quando commoda vellet*

Metre: Elegiac couplet

Arrius' uncertain aspiration (lines 1-4) affords Catullus and his circle of friends an opportunity to satirize the man at fault and perhaps too their own interest in matters of language and grammar. Arrius probably gave rise to scornful laughter as much for his rustic or plebeian origins as for his inept affectation. Certainly, during the last century of the Republic, there was widespread aspiration of *c* (cf Cicero, *Orat.*, 160; *Q.Frat.* I 5, 19-21); in some words it was obligatory for the purists, and in others permissible. But Arrius used *consonantal* aspiration indiscriminately, and his *initial* aspiration arose either because of his dilemma in the face of an unfamiliar or difficult sound, or because he placed false emphasis on the first syllable. The humour of the poem is found particularly in the last line where the jest is double-edged: on the formal side, because terms applicable to wind and weather conditions were used in current grammatical study for phenomena including aspiration (e.g. *lenis, levis, adspiro, spiritus, asper*) and, more uproariously, because Arrius' aspiration added to the storminess of the Adriatic crossing. A number of alternatives suggest themselves for translation of the aspiration into English: e.g. *chommoda* – hadvantages; *hinsidias* – hambush; *Hionios* – Hionian.

1 **si quando . . . vellet** the subjunctive occurs instead of the normal indicative used in a frequentative clause.

3 **sperabat** 'used to flatter himself'.

4 **quantum poterat** 'as loud as he could'.

5 **credo sic mater** Catullus suggests that Arrius derives his peculiarities from his mother's side.

liber is probably an innuendo, not a proper name (*Liber*); it suggests that Arrius' maternal side of the family was slave-born, but that his maternal uncle claimed free birth.

7 **misso** perhaps a reference to an official journey.

8 **leniter et leviter** 'smoothly and softly', or perhaps 'trippingly on the tongue, without mouthing it'.

10 **horribilis** 'chilling news'.

11 **Ionios fluctus** Arrius would cross the Ionian Sea *en route* from Brundisium to Greece and the Near East.

D. N. Jones, 'Catulli Nobile Epigramma', in *PCA* 53 (1956) 25-6.

COMMENTARY

87 (CATULLUS 93) *Nil nimium studeo, Caesar, tibi velle placere*

Metre: Elegiac couplet

Suetonius (*Divus Julius*, 73) relates that Caesar demanded an apology from Catullus for some lampoons aimed at himself and Mamurra. Thereafter Caesar invited Catullus to dinner and resumed friendly relations with the poet's father.

1 **nil nimium** 'not overanxious'.
velle placere 'to make an effort to please'.

2 **scire utrum sis albus an ater** Cicero (*Philippics* 2, 41) implies that the phrase was proverbial for not knowing the very first thing about somebody.

There is no evidence to indicate when the incident took place which inspired this Catullian retort to Julius Caesar.

88 (HORACE, *Odes* I 16) *O matre pulchra filia pulchrior*

Metre: Alcaic

Horace composes a lyrical palinode or recantation which recalls Stesichorus' Palinode to Helen for his invective against her. Stesichorus was blinded by the gods for his rash rebuke and only recovered his sight when he published his verse apology. So here Horace may be parodying Stesichorus when he appeals for a reconciliation and a mutual agreement to forgo poems of invective for the future. Cf Catullus 36.

2 **quem... cumque** tmesis.
modum ambiguous usage, either 'end' or 'moderation'. Both meanings are clearly allied to the notion of restriction required of both parties.

3 **pones** future indicative, but with force of a jussive (or permissive) imperative. Cf *Odes* I 7 (67), line 1: *laudabunt* 'some may praise'.
iambis a scurrilous form of verse, first adopted by Archilochus, for invective. Horace's iambi (*Epodes*) were his counterpart to Archilochus' poems of personal abuse.

5 **quatit** 'shakes'. For a detailed description of the Cumaean Sibyl, priestess of Apollo and Diana, consult Vergil, *Aen.* 6, lines 77 ff.

8 The Cybele worship was performed with barbaric music and dancing.
geminant 'strike together'.

9 **tristes** 'scowling'.

13 **fertur** Horace's version is unique.
principi limo 'primeval clay'.

14 **coactus** with *addere*. The animals were fashioned first, so that there was finally insufficient clay left to fashion man.
undique 'from every creature'.

16 **stomacho** 'breast', the seat of anger. Cf *Odes* I 6 (5), line 6.

17 **irae** emphatic by position, and context. Cf *otium* and its results in Catullus 51 (10).
Thyesten Greek accusative. Horace's friend, Varius (*Odes* I 6 (5), 1) had only recently published his tragedy entitled 'Thyestes'. Thyestes' violent end is unknown; elsewhere he is the unjust victim of family outrage [cf Horace *Odes* I 6 (5), line 8: *saeva Pelopis domus*].

18 **urbibus** dative case, with *stetere*, such 'lofty cities' as Thebes.
ultimae causae the primal causes.

19 **stetere** 'have been'.

20 **imprimeret** to drive a plough over the demolished ruins of a city symbolized total and permanent destruction.

22 **pectoris** with *fervor*, 'eager passion'.

23 **temptavit** 'led astray, tempted'.

24 **celeris** 'impetuous, hasty'.
mitibus ablative of association, with *mutare* (cf *Odes* I 17 (39), line 2).

26 **tristia** 'bitter words'.
dum clause of proviso.

28 **opprobriis** 'harsh words, insults', 'slanderous taunts', 'abusive insults'.
animumque reddas 'give me back your heart, favour'.

Examine the palinode for traces of a mock heroic tone and a sense of humour about the situation.

COMMENTARY

89 (HORACE, *Odes* I 30) *O Venus, regina Cnidi Paphique*

Metre: Sapphic
A kletic hymn or invocation to Venus to visit Glycera.

1 **Cnidi** the sanctuary of Aphrodite in Cnidus (Caria) contained the Venus of Praxiteles, the first nude statue of the Goddess of Love. (Pausanias I 1, 3; Lucian, *Erotes* 2, line 397).
   Paphique another sanctuary on Cyprus.

2 **sperne** cf *Odes* I 9 (50), line 16: 'spurn, forsake, neglect'.

3 **te** dependent on *vocantis*, and *transfer*.
   Glycera Gk., 'sweetness'.

4 **aedem** 'shrine, or house'.

5 **fervidus puer** Cupid.
   solutis zonis 'with loosened girdles'. Cf *Odes* IV 7 (57), line 5; I 4 (49), line 6.

7 Youth, without love, lacks charm is the 'message' of the ode.

8 **Mercuriusque** Mercury, god of persuasive eloquence, is often associated with *Peithō* (Gk. Persuasion) and *Suada* (Lat.) in love-affairs; but his association with gain and business may equally well fit him for a place in the hetaera's house or private shrine.

90 (HORACE, *Odes* I 38) *Persicos odi, puer, apparatus*

Metre: Sapphic
Horace's ode in praise of simplicity rejects Eastern luxury and costly flowers in favour of plain myrtle wreaths and simple entertainment.

1 **Persicos ... apparatus** 'Persian, i.e. Parthian elegance', cf *Odes* III 1 (70), line 44: *Achaemenium costum*.
   puer the slave attendant. Cf line 6, *ministrum*.

2 **nexae philyra coronae** garlands, made at home with flowers from the peristyle garden at Licenza, or purchased ready-made from shops. The flowers were sewn on to a strip of the inner bark (bast) of the linden-tree (Ovid, *Fasti*, 5, lines 335–8; Plin. *N.H.* 16, 4; 21, 3. *sutiles*). The closest contemporary equivalent is the Hawaian lei, which is used for comparable occasions.

3 **Mitte sectari**, sc. *omitte*: a polite prohibition.
   rosa ... sera the last rose of summer.

5 **simplici myrto** dative case with *allabores*; 'just myrtle' rather than exotic or imported flowers. The wreath is entirely myrtle.

6 **sedulus** 'fussy' 'officious'.
curo 'I take care, mind'.

7 f. **sub arta vite** 'under the thick-leaved vine', suggesting a pergola or trellised bower, designed to offer shade.

L. J. D. Richardson, 'Horace, *Odes* I 38', *Hermathena* 59 (1942) 129–33. M. Owen Lee, 'Horace *Odes* I 38: Thirst for Life', in *AJP* 86 (1965) 278–81.

Comment on the ode's effect in contrast with the Cleopatra Ode [I 37 (69)]. How does this ode help to introduce the Roman themes in II 1 (6)?

91 (HORACE, *Odes* III 9) *Donec gratus eram tibi*

Metre: Second Asclepiadean

A lyrical dialogue connected with the quarrel and reconciliation of Lydia and her lover (Horace ?). Based on Hellenistic models the repartee is elaborate and amusing, and for all its mathematical precision, the ode has a plot with a surprise ending.

1 **donec** 'as long as'. Cf Horace, *Odes* I 9 (50), line 17.

2 **quisquam** adjectival. Cf *ullus*.
potior 'more favoured'.

3 **dabat** sc. *circumdabat*.

4 **Persarum rege** proverbial for happiness. Cf *Odes* II 2, line 17; II 12, line 21.

5 **alia** abl. of cause, with *arsisti*; 'burned with love for another'.

6 **post Chloen** 'second to Chloe'.

7 **multi nominis** genitive of quality.

8 **Ilia** cf *Odes* I 2 (66), line 17.

9 **me** emphatic.

10 **modos** 'measures'.

12 **animae** 'my life' (Chloe). Cf *Odes* I 3 (35), line 8.
superstiti proleptic use: 'and allow her to live'.

13 **me** emphatic by position. Cf line 9.
torret cf *arsisti*, line 6.

14 **Thurini** contrast with *Thraessa*. Thurii, the Athenian colony in Lucania on the site of ancient Sybaris, has connotations of wealth and luxury. Ornytus (cf Vergil, *Aen.* 11, line 677) is given a formal introduction.

15 **patiar mori** poetic construction, 'be willing to die'. Cf *Odes* I 2 (66), line 43: *patiens vocari/Caesaris ultor.*

17, 18 **redit ... cogit,** etc. Vivid present, instead of future tense.
diductos 'estranged, separated'.

19 **flava** cf *Odes* I 5 (36), line 4 (Pyrrha).
excutitur suggests 'cast off, cast out of' heart and house.

20 **Lydiae** genitive.

22 **improbo** 'wanton, wayward'.

24 **vivere amem** poetic use of infinitive. Cf *Odes* I 2 (66), line 50.
libens adverbial.

J. A. Sparrow, 'A Horatian Ode and its descendants', in *JWI* 17 (1954) 359–65.
Compare Catullus' poetic dialogue between Acme and Septimius, Cat. 45 (83), with Horace's ode.
Examine the ode for use of rhetoric, traces of individualism in terms and imagery used by each party, and balanced antitheses. Examine the role of word echoes in the structure and design of the ode.

SELECTED BIBLIOGRAPHY

Key to Abbreviations

AJP	American Journal of Philology
AUMLA	Journal of the Australasian Universities Language and Literature Association
CJ	Classical Journal
CP	Classical Philology
CQ	Classical Quarterly
CR	Classical Review
CW	Classical World (formerly Classical Weekly)
G&R	Greece and Rome
HSCP	Harvard Studies in Classical Philology
JRS	Journal of Roman Studies
JWI	Journal of the Warburg and Courtauld Institutes
PCA	Proceedings of the Classical Association
RhMus	Rheinisches Museum
TAPA	Transactions of the American Philological Association
WS	Wiener Studien
YCS	Yale Classical Studies

I. Catullus

EDITIONS:

R. A. B. Mynors (Oxford, 1958; reprinted with corrections 1960). Text without commentary.

W. Kroll, 3rd ed. (Leipzig, 1959). Text with commentary.

F. T. Merrill (Boston, 1893; reprinted 1951). Text with commentary.

C. J. Fordyce (corrected re-issue, Oxford, 1968). Text with commentary; omits 32 poems.

INDEX:

M. N. Wetmore; *Index Verborum Catullianus* (New Haven, 1912; reprinted Hildesheim, 1961).

DISCUSSIONS:

Books:

H. Bardon, *L'Art de la composition chez Catulle* (Paris, 1943).

E. A. Havelock, *The Lyric Genius of Catullus* (reissued, New York, 1967).

SELECTED BIBLIOGRAPHY

G. Highet, *Poets in a Landscape* (London, 1957).
C. L. Neudling, *A Prosopography to Catullus* (Iowa Studies in Classical Philology xii: privately printed, 1955).
K. Quinn, *The Catullan Revolution* (Melbourne, 1959).
A. W. Wheeler, *Catullus and the Traditions of Ancient Poetry* (Berkeley, 1934).
G. Williams, *Tradition and Originality in Roman Poetry* (Oxford, 1968).

Articles:

H. Bardon, 'Catulle et ses modèles poétiques de langue latine', in *Latomus* 16 (1957) 614–27.
J. Bayet, 'Catulle', in *L'Influence grecque sur la poésie latine de Catulle à Ovide* (Fondation Hardt, Entretiens 2: Geneva, 1956).
F. O. Copley, 'Emotional Conflict and its significance in the Lesbia-poems of Catullus', in *AJP* 70 (1949) 22–40.
J. P. Elder, 'Notes on some conscious and unconscious elements in Catullus' poetry', in *HSCP* 60 (1951) 101–36.
J. Ferguson, 'Catullus and Horace', in *AJP* 77 (1956) 1–18.
R. M. Henry, '*Pietas* and *Fides* in Catullus', in *Hermathena* 75 (1950) 63–8.
R. G. C. Levens, 'Catullus', in *Fifty Years of Classical Scholarship* (Oxford, 1954) 284–305.
K. Quinn, 'Docte Catulle', in *Critical Essays on Roman Literature: Elegy and Lyric*, ed. J. P. Sullivan (London, 1962).

TRANSLATIONS:

C. Stuttaford (London, 1912).
F. W. Cornish (Loeb Classical Library: London, 1913).
H. Gregory (New York, 1956).
F. O. Copley (Ann Arbor, 1957).
R. A. Swanson (Indianapolis, 1959).
P. Whigham (Penguin Books, 1966).

BIBLIOGRAPHICAL SURVEYS:

W. Kroll, 4th ed. (Stuttgart, 1960) 301–14.
H. Leon, in *CW* 53 (1959) 104–13; 141–8; 173–81; 281–2.
R. G. C. Levens, in *Fifty Years of Classical Scholarship*, 284–305.

II. Horace

EDITIONS:

T. E. Page (London, 1884).
J. Gow (Cambridge, 1896).
E. C. Wickham (Oxford, 1877).
Shorey-Laing (Chicago, 1932; reprinted Pittsburgh, 1960).
A. Y. Campbell (London, 1955).
Kiessling-Heinze-Burck (Berlin, 1960).
O. Tescari (Turin, 1958).

INDEX:

Lane Cooper, *A Concordance to the works of Horace* (Washington, 1916; reprinted New York, 1961).

DISCUSSIONS:

Books:

A. Y. Campbell, *Horace, A New Interpretation* (London, 1924).
N. E. Collinge, *The Structure of Horace's Odes* (Oxford, 1961).
S. Commager, *The Odes of Horace* (New Haven, 1962).
E. Fraenkel, *Horace* (Oxford, 1957).
A. Noyes, *Portrait of Horace* (London, 1947).
C. E. Nybakken, *An Analytical Study of Horace's Odes* (Iowa Studies in Classical Philology v: 1937).
J. Perret, *Horace* (Paris, 1959. English trans., New York, 1964).
K. Quinn, *Latin Explorations: Critical Studies in Roman Literature* (London, 1963).
David West, *Reading Horace* (Edinburgh, 1967).
L. P. Wilkinson, *Horace and his Lyric Poetry*, 2nd ed. (Cambridge, 1951).
L. P. Wilkinson, *Golden Latin Artistry* (Cambridge, 1963).

Articles:

W. H. Alexander, 'Horace's Odes and *Carmen Saeculare*: Observations and Interpretations', in *University of California Publications in Classical Philology* 13: 7 (1947) 173–239.
M. Andrewes, 'Horace's Use of Imagery in the Odes and Epodes', in *G & R* 19 (1950) 106–15.
Janice Benario, 'Book IV of Horace's *Odes*: Augustan Propaganda', *TAPA* 91 (1960) 339–52.

E. M. Blaiklock, 'The dying storm. A study in the Imagery of Horace', in *G & R* 6 (1959) 205–10.

C. M. Bowra, in *Inspiration and Poetry* (London, 1955) 26–44.

Steele Commager, 'The function of wine in Horace's *Odes*', in *TAPA* 88 (1957) 68–80.

Janice M. Cordray, 'The structure of Horace's *Odes*: some typical patterns', in *CJ* 52 (1956–7) 113–6.

Alexander Dalzell, 'Maecenas and the Poets', in *Phoenix* 10 (1956) 151–62.

G. E. Duckworth, '*Animae dimidium meae*: two poets of Rome', in *TAPA* 87 (1956) 281–316.

J. Ferguson, 'Catullus and Horace', in *AJP* 77 (1956) 1–18.

W. L. Grant, 'Elegiac themes in Horace's *Odes*', in *Studies in Honour of Gilbert Norwood* (Toronto, 1952) 194–202.

E. L. Highbarger, 'The Pindaric style of Horace', in *TAPA* 66 (1935) 222–55.

W. S. Maguinness, 'Friends and the philosophy of friendship in Horace', in *Hermathena* 51 (1938) 29–48.

R. G. M. Nisbet, '*Romanae fidicen lyrae*: the *Odes* of Horace', in *Critical Essays in Roman Literature*: *Elegy and Lyric*, ed. by J. P. Sullivan (London, 1962) 181–218.

G. Nussbaum, 'Some notes on symbolism in Horace's lyric poetry', in *Latomus* 24 (1965) 133–43.

W. J. Oates, 'Horace and the Doctrine of the Mean', in *Capps Studies* (Princeton, 1936). 260 ff.

B. Otis, 'Horace and the Elegists', in *TAPA* 76 (1945) 177–90.

K. Quinn, 'The Crises in Horace's Poetical Career', in *AUMLA* 5 (1956) 34–43.

K. Quinn, 'Syntactical Ambiguity in Horace', in *AUMLA* 14 (1960) 36–46.

K. J. Reckford, 'Some Studies in Horace's Odes on Love', in *CJ* 55 (1959) 25–33.

K. J. Reckford, 'Horace and Maecenas', in *TAPA* 90 (1959) 195–208.

N. Rudd, 'Patterns in Horatian Lyric', in *AJP* 81 (1960) 373–90.

E. T. Salmon, 'The Political Views of Horace', in *Phoenix* 1: 2 (1946–7) 7–14.

L. R. Taylor, 'Horace's Equestrian Career', in *AJP* 46 (1925) 161–9.

Margaret E. Taylor, 'Horace: *laudator temporis acti?*' in *AJP* 83 (1962) 23–43.

H. Toll, 'Unity in the Odes of Horace', in *Phoenix* 9 (1955) 153–69.

H. L. Tracy, 'Thought-sequence in the Odes', in *Phoenix* 5 (1951) 108–18.

C. W. Whitaker, 'A note on Horace and Pindar', in *CQ* 49 (1956) 221–4.

L. P. Wilkinson, 'The language of Vergil and Horace', in *CQ* 52 (1959) 181–92.

G. Williams, 'Poetry in the moral climate of Augustan Rome', in *JRS* 52 (1962) 28–46.

TRANSLATIONS AND THE ART OF TRANSLATION:

C. E. Bennett (Loeb Classical Library: London, 1914).
J. P. Clancy (Chicago, 1960).
J. Michie (London, 1964).
J. B. Leishman, *On Translating Horace* (London, 1956).
R. Storrs (ed.), *Ad Pyrrham: A Polyglot Collection of Translations of Horace's Ode to Pyrrha* (Oxford, 1959).

BIBLIOGRAPHICAL SURVEYS:

Kiessling-Heinze-Burck, *Oden und Epoden* (Berlin, 1960) 569–620.
R. J. Getty, 'Recent Work on Horace (1945–1957)', in *CW* 52 (1958–9) 167–88; 246–7.

SELECTED BIBLIOGRAPHY: SUPPLEMENTUM (1973)

I. Catullus

EDITIONS:

H. Bardon (Brussels, 1970). Text with commentary.
K. Quinn (London, 1970). Text with commentary.

DISCUSSIONS:

Books:

H. Bardon, *Propositions sur Catulle* (Brussels, 1970).
J. Higginbotham (ed.), *Greek and Latin Literature: A Comparative Study* (London, 1969).
Julia W. Loomis, *Studies in Catullan Verse. An analysis of word types and patterns in the polymetra* (Leiden, 1972).
Kenneth Quinn, *Catullus: An Interpretation* (London, 1972).
Kenneth Quinn, *The Catullan Revolution* (revised impression, Cambridge, 1969).
David O. Ross, Jr., *Style and Tradition in Catullus* (Cambridge, Mass., 1969).
Gordon Williams, *Tradition and Originality in Roman Poetry* (Oxford 1968).
T. P. Wiseman, *Catullan Questions* (Leicester, 1969).
Charles Witke, *Enarratio Catulliana. Carmina 50. 30. 65. 68* (Leiden, 1968).

Articles:

W. Clausen, 'Catullus and Callimachus', in *Harvard Studies in Classical Philology* 74 (1970) 85–94.
N. B. Crowther, 'Catullus and the traditions of Latin poetry', in *CP* 66 (1971) 246–9.
J. Ferguson, 'A note on Catullus' hendecasyllabics' *CP* 65 (1970) 173–5.
G. Luck, 'Uber einige Typen des Gedichtanfangs bei Catull', *Euphrosyne* 1 (1967) 169–72.
Charles Segal, 'The order of Catullus, poems 2–11', in *Latomus* 27 (1968) 305–21.
O. Skutsch, 'Metrical variations and some textual problems in Catullus', in *Bulletin of the Institute of Classical Studies* (London) 16 (1969) 38–43.

Individual poems:

1 J. P. Elder, 'Catullus 1: His Poetic Creed, and Nepos', in *HSCP* 71 (1967) 143–9.
  F. Cairns, 'Catullus 1', *Mnemosyne* 22 (1969) 153–8.
  P. Levine, 'Catullus c. 1. A prayerful dedication', *California Studies in Classical Antiquity* 2 (1969) 209–16.
  D. Singleton, 'A note on Catullus' first poem', *CP* 67 (1972) 192–6.
3 G. P. Goold, 'Catullus, 3, 16', *Phoenix* 23 (1969) 23–9.
4 L. Richardson, Jr., 'Catullus 4 and Catalepton 10 again', *AJP* 93 (1972) 215–22.
5 Charles Segal, 'Catullus 5 and 7: a study in complementaries', *AJP* 89 (1968) 284–301.
  E. A. Fredricksmeyer, 'Observations on Catullus 5', *AJP* 91 (1970) 431–45.
8 M. Dyson, 'Catullus 8 and 76', *CQ* 23 (1973) 127–43.
17 H. A. Khan, 'Image and symbol in Catullus 17', *CP* 64 (1969) 88–97.
31 C. Witke, 'Verbal art in Catullus 31', *AJP* 93 (1972) 239–51.
44 E. S. de Angeli, 'A literary chill. Catullus 44', *CW* 62 (1969) 354–6.
45 H. Dietz, 'Zu Catullus Gedicht von Acme und Septimius', *Symbolae Osloenses* 44 (1969) 42–7.
49 E. Laughton, 'Disertissime Romuli nepotum', *CP* 65 (1970) 1–7.
  E. Laughton, 'Catullus 49, an acknowledgment', *CP* 66 (1971) 36–7.
50 W. S. Scott, 'Catullus and Calvus (Cat. 50)', *CP* 64 (1969) 169–73.
51 R. I. Frank, 'Catullus 51: Otium versus Virtus', *TAPA* 99 (1968) 233–9.
76 J. D. Bishop, 'Catullus 76: elegy or epigram?', *CP* 67 (1972) 293–4.
  H. A. Khan, 'Catullus 76: the summing up', *Athenaeum* 46 (1968) 54–71.

BIBLIOGRAPHICAL SURVEY:
D. F. S. Thomson, 'Recent scholarship on Catullus (1960–69)', *CW* 65 (1971–2) 116–26.

II. Horace

EDITIONS:
R. G. M. Nisbet and M. Hubbard, *A Commentry on Horace, Odes Book 1* (Oxford 1970).

Gordon Williams, *The Third Book of Horace's Odes* (edition, translation, and commentary, Oxford, 1969).

INDEX:

D. Bo, *Lexicon Horatianum* (Hildeheim, 1965-6).

DISCUSSIONS:

Books:

N. A. Bonavia-Hunt, *Horace the Minstrel. A practical and aesthetic study of his Aeolic verse.* (Kineton-Roundwood Press, 1969).
C. D. Costa, *Horace* (Greek and Latin Studies. Classical Literature and its influence) (London, 1973).
F. Cupaiuolo, *Lettura di Orazio lirico. Struttura dell'ode oraziana* (Naples, 1967).
Thomas Halter, *Vergil und Horaz. Zur eine Antinomie der Erlebensform* (Bern/Munich, 1970).
John Higginbotham (ed.), *Greek and Latin Literature: A comparative study* (London, 1969).
Gerhard Huber, *Wortwiederholungen in den Oden des Horaz* (Zurich, 1970).
M. O. Lee, *Word, sound and image in the Odes of Horace* (Ann Arbor, Mich., 1969).
Hans Oppermann (ed.), *Wege zu Horaz* (Darmstadt, 1972).
Viktor Pöschl, *Horazische Lyrik: Interpretationen* (Heidelberg, 1970).
Kenneth Reckford, *Horace* (New York, 1969).
H. P. Syndikus, *Die Lyrik des Horaz. Eine Interpretation der Oden. Bd. I: Erstes und zweites Buch* (Darmstadt, 1972).
Gordon Williams, *Tradition and Originality in Roman Poetry* (Oxford, 1968).

Articles:

F. Cairns, 'Five "religious" odes of Horace (I, 10; I, 21 and IV,.6; I, 30; I, 15)', *AJP* 92 (1971) 433-52.
C. Fuqua, 'Horace, Carm. I, 23-25', *CP* 63 (1968) 44-6.
G. Giardena, 'Sulla struttura delle Odi Orazio', *Lingua e stile* 5 (1970) 45-55.
W. J. Henderson, 'Political and legal imagery in Horace's Odes', in *Pro munere grates. Studies presented to H. L. Gonin* (ed. D. M. Kriel) (Praetoria, 1971) 73-90.
D. N. Levin, 'Horace's preoccupation with death', *CJ* 63 (1968) 315-20.
L. A. Moritz, 'Some central thoughts on Horace's Odes', *CQ* 18 (1968) 116-31.

G. B. Nussbaum, 'A study of Odes I, 37 and 38. The psychology of conflict and Horace's humanitas', *Arethusa* 4 (1971) 91–7.

Viktor Pöschl, 'Poetry and philosophy in Horace', in *The Poetic Tradition: Essays on Greek, Latin and English Poetry* (ed. D. C. Allen, H. T. Rowell) (Baltimore, 1968) 47–61.

P. Salat, 'La composition du livre I des Odes d'Horace', *Latomus* 28 (1969) 554–74.

C. G. Starr, 'Horace and Augustus', *AJP* 90 (1969) 58–64.

R. A. Swanson, 'Latin lyric: craft and subject', in *Classical Studies presented to Ben Edwin Perry by his students and colleagues at the University of Illinois, 1924–1960* (Urbana, 1969) 165–74.

Individual poems:

I, 1 H. J. Shey, 'The poet's progress. Horace, Odes I, 1', *Arethusa* 4 (1971) 185–96.

K. Vretska, 'Horatius, carm. I, 1' *Hermes* 99 (1971) 323–35.

I, 2 F. Cairns, 'Horace, Odes I, 2', *Eranos* 69 (1971) 68–88.

H. Womble, 'Horace, Carmina I, 2', *AJP* 91 (1970) 1–30.

I, 3 L. Amundsen, 'Horace. Carm. I, 3', *Arctos* 5 (1967) 7–22.

T. V. Buttrey, 'Halved coins. The Augustan reform, and Horace, Odes I, 3', *American Journal of Archaeology* 76 (1972) 31–48.

C. W. Lockyer, Jr., 'Horace's propempticon and Vergil's voyage', *CW* 61 (1967) 42–5.

I, 5 M. C. J. Putnam, 'Aes triplex (Horace, Odes I.3.9)', *CQ* 21 (1971) 454.

I, 5 M. C. J. Putnam, 'Horace, Carm 1, 5. Love and death', *CP* 65 (1970) 251–4.

I, 7 A. E. Wilson, 'The path of indirection. Horace Odes 3.27 and I.7', *CW* 63 (1969) 44–6.

I, 9 P. Connor, 'Soracte encore', *Ramus* 1 (1972) 102–12.

C. C. Esler, 'Horace's Soracte Ode. Imagery and perspective', *CW* 62 (1969) 300–5.

W. J. Henderson, 'Horace, Carm. I. 9. An analysis', *Acta Classica* 10 (1967) 11–8.

C. W. Lockyer, Jr., 'Horace, Odes I, 9', *CJ* 63 (1968) 304–8.

I, 10 R. Freis, 'A note on Horace's Hymn to Mercury (Odes I, 10)', *CP* 66 (1971) 182–3.

I, 14 O. Seel, 'Zur Ode I, 14 des Horaz. Zweifel an einer communis opinio', in *Festschrift Karl Vretska zum 70.*

SELECTED BIBLIOGRAPHY : SUPPLEMENTUM 243

Geburtstag überreicht von seinem Freunden und Schülern (ed. D. Ableitinger, H. Gugel) (Heidelberg, 1970) 204-49.
I, 16 M. Dyson, 'Horace, Odes I, 16', *AUMLA* 30 (1968) 169-79.
I, 17 H. G. Edinger, 'Horace, Carmina I, 17', *CJ* 66 (1971) 306-11.
A. W. J. Holleman, 'Horace (Odes I, 17) and the "Music of Love"', *Latomus* 29 (1970) 750-5.
I, 20 M. C. J. Putnam, 'Horace c. I. 20', *CJ 64* (1969) 153-7.
I, 23 R. J. Baker, 'The rustle of spring in Horace (Carm., I, 23)', *AJP* 92 (1971) 71-5.
I, 29 H. Dietz, 'Horaz, Carm. I. 29', *Symbolae Osloenses* 48 (1973) 89-96.
I, 37 A. T. Davis, 'Cleopatra rediviva', *G&R* 16 (1969) 91-4.
F. C. Mench, Jr., 'The ambiguity of the similes and of fatale monstrum in Horace, Ode I, 37', *AJP* 93 (1972) 314-23.
Brooks Otis, 'A reading of the Cleopatra ode', *Arethusa* 1 (1968) 48-61.
R. Verdière, 'Fatale monstrum (carm. 1, 37, 21)', *Maia* 20 (1968) 7-9.
II, 3 A. J. Woodman, 'Horace, Odes II, 3', *AJP* 91 (1970) 165-80.
II, 6 Charles Segal, 'Horace. Odes II, 6 (Septimi, Gadis aditure pecum). Poetic landscape and poetic imagination', *Philologus* 113 (1969) 235-53.
II, 10 C. J. Reagan, 'Horace, Carm. 2. 10; the use of oxymoron as a thematic statement', *Rivista di Studi Classici* 18 (1970) 177-85.
II, 14 W. S. Anderson, 'Two odes of Horace's Book Two (II, 9; II, 14)', in *California Studies in Classical Antiquity* 1 (1968) 35-61.
P. J. Connor, 'The dramatic monologue. A study of Horace Odes II, 14 and II, 3', *Latomus* 29 (1970) 756-64.
II, 16 W. L. Liebermann, 'Die Otium-Ode des Horaz (c. II, 16)', *Latomus* 30 (1971) 294-316.
H. Womble, 'Horace, Carmina II, 16', *AJP* 88 (1967) 385-409.
II, 20 D. A. Kidd, 'The metamorphosis of Horace', *AUMLA* 35 (1971) 5-16.

III, 2 P. J. Connor, 'The balance sheet. Consideration of the second Roman Ode', *Hermes* 100 (1972) 241-8.
   H. Hommel, 'Dulce et decorum', *RhMus* 111 (1968) 219-52.
   L. I. Lindo, 'Tyrtaeus and Horace Odes 3, 2', *CP* 66 (1971) 258-60.
III, 3 A. Bradshaw, 'Some stylistic oddities in Horace, Odes III, 3', *Philologus* 114 (1970) 145-50.
III, 4 A. J. Dunston, 'Horace Odes III, 4 and the virtutes of Augustus', *AUMLA* 31 (1969) 9-19.
III, 13 W. J. Henderson, 'An interpretation of Horace, Carm. 3. 13. O fons Bandusiae', *Nuusbrief* 12 (1967) 7-13, 16-21.
   G. B. Nussbaum, '*Cras donaberis haedo*' (Horace Carm. III, 13)', *Phoenix* 25 (1971) 151-9.
   J. R. Wilson, 'O fons Bandusiae', *CJ* 63 (1968) 289-96.
III, 14 U. W. Scholz, 'Herculis ritu, Augustus, consule Planco', *WS* 5 (1971) 123-7.
III, 30 D. Korzeniewski, 'Exegi monumentum. Hor. carm. 3.30 und die Topik der Grabgedichte', *Gymnasium* 79 (1972) 380-8.
   F. Maróti, 'Aere perennius', *Beiträge zur Alten Geschichte und deren Nachleben. Festschrift für Franz Altheim zum 6.10.1968* (ed. R. Stiehl, H. E. Stier) I (Berlin, 1969) 452-8.
   Viktor Pöschl, 'Die Horazode Exegi monumentum (C. 3,30)', *Giornale Italiano di Filologia* 20 (1967) 261-72.
   M. C. J. Putnam, 'Horace c. 3, 30: the lyricist as hero', *Ramus* 2 (1973) 1-19.
IV, 12 L. A. Moritz, 'Horace's Virgil', *G&R* 16 (1969) 174-93.

A GLOSSARY OF TECHNICAL AND RHETORICAL TERMS

Allegory: a narrative in which the agents and, occasionally, the setting represent general concepts, moral qualities or other abstractions cf Horace, *Odes* I 14 (68), the Ship of State.

Alliteration: the repetition of the same sound, usually a consonant at the beginning of adjacent words or syllables to give life and character to the passage; e.g. Cat. 45 (83), 3–5.

Ambiguity: 'multiple meaning', a poetic device whereby two or more meanings of a word or phrase are relevant.

Anaphora: the repetition of a word in the same or similar form at the beginning of a series of clauses; e.g. Cat. 46 (34), 1–2, 7–8; 51 (10), 13–15.

Anastrophe: the placing of a preposition after its object; e.g. *te circum* (= inversion).

Antistrophe: see Strophe.

Antithesis: a balance or parallelism of grammatical or metrical pattern, but with a strong contrast or opposition in meaning.

Archaism: the use of antique phrasing to arouse memories of the past, to add solemnity and grandeur to the verse.

Assonance: the repetition of identical or related vowel sounds.

Asyndeton: the omission of conjunctions.

Ballad: a song that tells a story.

Brachylogy: a brevity of expression; e.g. Horace, *Odes* I 24 (43), 17: *fata* for *portas fatorum*.

Chiasmus: a criss-cross (i.e. Chiastic) arrangement resulting from the transposition of two corresponding phrases; e.g.

integer vitae scelerisque purus
    a   b   b   a
annorum series et fuga temporum
    a   b   b   a

Didactic: a work which is designed to demonstrate or present in a persuasive fashion a moral, religious, or other thesis or doctrine.

Ellipsis: the omission of words that are necessary for the grammatical structure of a sentence or clause, in order to gain brevity, compactness or force.

Enjambment: (1) a 'run-on line', occurs when the end of a line (or couplet) does not coincide with a normal speech pause of any kind (e.g. Horace, *Odes* I 8 (37), lines 2–3, 6–7; (2) where a word is divided between the end of one line and the beginning of the next (e.g. Horace, *Odes* I 2 (66), lines 19–20: *u-xorius amnis*; Cat. 11 (27), lines 11–12: *ulti-mosque Britannos*.

Epigram: originally an inscription (cf epigraphy, the study of Greek and Latin inscriptions), but extended to include any very short poems, amorous, elegiac, meditative, complimentary, or satirical, always polished, terse, and pointed. The epigram often ends with a surprising or witty expression.

Epithalamium: a poem written to celebrate a marriage; lit. sung 'at the bridal chamber'.

Epode: originally applied to the shorter verse, or iambic dimeter, which served as refrain to the longer iambic trimeter. Grammarians applied the term to Horace's *iambi*.

Genre: a literary form, e.g. epic, pastoral, lyric.

Gnomic perfect: used of a general truth, often with negatives.

Hendiadys: the expression of a single idea by means of two words joined by the connectives *et* or *-que*; e.g. Horace, *Odes* II 7 (45), line 9: *Philippos et celerem fugam*.

Hypallage: an exchange of construction; e.g. Horace, *Odes* I 1 (4), line 36: *sublimi feriam sidera vertice*, also called 'transferred epithet'.

Hyperbole: extravagant exaggeration of fact for serious or comic effect; cf Horace, *Odes* III 1 (70), lines 33–4.

Imagery: a word used to signify descriptive passages in poetry, particularly those which are vivid and particularized, but still more commonly, to signify figurative language, especially similes or metaphors, which provide the clue to poetic intent, structure, and effect.

Irony: a mode of speech, rhetorical and verbal, wherein the implied attitudes or evaluations are opposed to those literally expressed. On most occasions ostensible praise or approval implies the opposite. Irony includes understatement, hyperbole, oxymoron, and paradox.

Litotes: the opposite of *Hyperbole*, intentional understatement, usually in negative form, implying a simple, sincere assertion; e.g. *non bene*, 'ingloriously'; *non sine vano . . . metu*, 'filled with needless fear'.

Lyric: the Greeks equated lyric with a song sung to the accompaniment of the lyre. Modern usage implies a short poem, usually involving a single speaker, who expresses a state of mind involving thought and feeling. The term 'lyric' includes dramatic monologue, elegy, ode, vers de société, and the modern sonnet.

A GLOSSARY OF TECHNICAL AND RHETORICAL TERMS

Metaphor: a concentrated comparison which enables the poet to use two ideas at once; he applies the qualities of one, which is familiar, to give form and substance to the other; e.g. *fumum bibere*, 'to drink the smoke'.

Metonymy: a figure which involves substitution rather than comparison, the application of the name of one thing to another with which it is closely associated; e.g. *Iove*, 'sky'; *cruento Marte*, 'bloody war'.

Ode: a Greek word (=song) usually applied to a long lyric poem, serious in subject, elevated in style, and elaborate in stanzaic structure (strophe, antistrophe and epode). Catullus and Horace used the word *carmina* (=songs) for their lyric poems.

Onomatopoeia: the use of a word or phrase whose sound echoes the meaning e.g. Horace, *Odes* III 13 (62), 15: *unde loquaces/lymphae desiliunt tuae*; *Odes* II 14 (55), 13–14: *frustra cruento Marte carebimus/fractisque rauci fluctibus Hadriae*.

Oxymoron: a combination of words which appear to be contradictory, to indicate a sharp contrast; e.g. *arida nutrix*, 'parched nurse'; *simplex munditiis*, 'plain in your elegance', *festina lente*.

Parody: a term which implies the ridiculing of a particular work or style by imitation of its peculiar features and by applying them to a trivial or discordant subject; e.g. *Catalepton* 10, in Appendix to Cat. 4 (77).

Personification: the simplest form of imagery which endows inanimate things or abstract ideas with human characteristics; e.g. Fama; Curae; Pudor et Iustitiae soror ... Fides ... Veritas, etc.

Prolepsis: ('anticipation') the use of a word in the clause preceding the one where it would naturally occur.

Simile: a comparison between two essentially different items expressly indicated by a term such as 'like' or 'as' in English.

Strophe: the Greek Odes of Pindar, modelled on choric songs in Greek drama, used stanzas patterned in sets of three: moving to the left the chorus chanted the strophe (lit. a turn or turning), then the antistrophe (lit. a counter-turn) and finally, stationary, the epode.

Syncope: the loss of a syllable within a word, usually for metrical convenience; e.g. *formasti* for *formavisti*.

Tmesis: ('cutting') the separation of two parts of a compound word by other words: e.g. *quam rem cumque*.

Tone: a term implying the attitude taken by the poet to his subject matter and to his audience implied in the literary piece. The tone may be characterized, for example, as formal or intimate, solemn or playful, serious or ironic, etc.

Transferred epithet: poetic usage whereby the qualifying word, usually apt, picturesque or impressive, is applied to a word other than the one to which, strictly speaking, it belongs; e.g. *civium . . . tergo libero*, 'the free backs of citizens'; *regalique situ pyramidum*, 'than the princely structure of the pyramids'.

Vers de Société: 'society verse', brief, epigrammatic or lyrical, dealing with the events of polite society, usually in the form of an elegant, witty compliment, rarely serious. The tone is usually conversational, light-hearted.

Zeugma: the use of one word in grammatical relation to two others (a verb with two objects, an adjective with two nouns) although strictly it is appropriate to only one of them; e.g. Horace, *Odes* III 4 (71), 7–8: *amoenae/quos et aquae subeunt et aurae.*

THE METRES OF LYRIC POETRY

Sapphic: there are two components to the stanza –

1, 2, 3   — ∪ | — ⏓ | — // ∪ ∪ | — ∪ | — ⏓   Lesser Sapphic
4   — ∪ ∪ | — ⏓   Adonic

The metre is used extensively by Horace (25 odes) and twice by Catullus 51 (10), 11 (27). The Horatian stanza requires that the fourth syllable of the first three lines be long; and that the caesura should appear either after the fifth or the sixth syllable. *Caesura* or 'cutting' marks above the lines of verse indicate the points at which a reader or reciter would pause because of the sense, and a singer would take a new breath. The caesura rarely coincides with the end of a measure, and is to be compared to the end of a musical phrase.

Example

O Ve-nus, re-gi-na Cni-di Pa-phi-que
sper-ne di-lec-tam Cy-pro- n-et vo-can-tis
tu-re te mul-to Gly-ce-rae de-co-ram
trans-fe-ri-n ae-dem.

Horace, *Odes* I 30 (89)

The Sapphic stanza is used in *Odes*: I 2 (66), 10 (60), 20 (40), 22 (41), 30 (89); II 10 (54), 16 (56); III 14 (74); IV 6 (65).

Greater Sapphic: there are two components to the stanza –

1, 3   — ∪ ∪ | — ∪ | — ⏓   Aristophanic
2, 4   — ∪ | — — | — // ∪ ∪ — | — ∪ ∪ | — ∪ | — ⏓   Greater Sapphic

The first line is a normal Sapphic line minus the opening four syllables; the second line of the stanza is a regular Sapphic with an additional choriamb — ∪ ∪ — inserted. Horace uses the metre only once [*Odes* I 8 (37)].

Alcaic: the component lines are as follows –

1, 2   ⏓ | — ∪ | — — || — ∪ ∪ | — ∪ | ⏓   Greater Alcaic
3.   ⏓ | — ∪ | — — | — ∪ | — ⏓   Trochaic Dimeter
4.   — ∪ ∪ | — ∪ ∪ | — ∪ | — ⏓   Lesser Alcaic

Horace greatly favoured this measure (37 odes). The first two lines resemble the Sapphic, with *anacrusis* (the 'up-beat' syllable) and with one syllable dropped at the end (*catalectic*). The stanza normally requires that the opening syllables in lines 1 and 2 and 3 should take the long form. The caesura in lines 1 and 2 almost always appears at the fifth syllable; line 3 centres on a weighty polysyllabic word (or word-group) running from the third or fourth syllable to the sixth or seventh. Diaeresis (||) usually occurs in the first two verses.

Example

$$\stackrel{\smile}{-}|-\stackrel{\smile}{-}|-\;-\;||-\;\smile\;\smile|-\;\smile|\;\smile$$
E-heu fu-ga-ces, Pos-tu-me, Pos-tu-me,

$$\stackrel{\smile}{-}|-\;\smile|-\;-\;||-\;\smile\smile|-\;\smile|\;\smile$$
la-bun-tur an-ni, nec pi-e-tas mo-ram

$$-\stackrel{|}{-}\;\smile|-\;-|-\;\smile|-\;-$$
ru-gis et in-stan-ti se-nec-tae

$$-\;\smile\smile|-\;\smile\;\smile|-\;\smile|-\;-$$
ad-fer-et in-do-mi-tae-que mor-ti

Horace, *Odes* II 14 (55)

The Alcaic stanza is used in *Odes* I 9 (50), 16 (88), 17 (39), 29 (44), 34 (52), 37 (69); II 1 (6), 3 (53), 7 (45), 14 (55); III 1 (70), 4 (71), 5 (72), 6 (73), 21 (63), 23 (64); IV 15 (76).

Asclepiads: Editors number the varieties differently, but the characteristic rhythm appears throughout in 34 odes:

(i)   — — | — ⌣ ⌣ — | ⌣̄   Pherecratic

(ii) — ⌣̄ | — ⌣ ⌣ — | ⌣ ⌣̄   Glyconic

(iii) — — | — ⌣ ⌣ — | — ⌣ ⌣ — | ⌣ ⌣̄   Lesser Asclepiad

(iv) — — | — ⌣ ⌣ — | — ⌣ ⌣ — — ⌣ ⌣ — | ⌣ ⌣̄ Greater Asclepiad.

The 'First' Asclepiadean stanza consists of lesser asclepiads only, *Odes* I 1 (4); III 30 (8). The 'Second' Asclepiadean stanza consists of glyconics alternating with lesser asclepiads, *Odes* I 3 (35), 13 (38); III 9 (91); IV 3 (9). The 'Third' Asclepiadean stanza consists of three lesser asclepiads and one glyconic in each stanza, *Odes* I 6 (5), 24 (43); IV 5 (75), 12 (46). The 'Fourth' Asclepiadean stanza consists of two lesser asclepiads, one pherecratic, and one glyconic in each stanza, *Odes* I 5 (36), 14 (68), 21 (61), 23 (42); III 13 (62). The 'Fifth' Asclepiadean stanza consists of greater asclepiads only, *Odes* I 11 (51).

Glyconic Stanza: Use of this stanza is confined to two poems;
(i) Catullus 34 (58), a four line stanza containing three Glyconics:

$$- \smile\ |\ -\smile\smile-\ |\ \smile\ \smile$$, and a shortened or 'catalectic' form of the stanza called Pherecratic $$-\ -\ |\ -\smile\smile-\ |\ \smile$$

(ii) Catullus 17 (79), a two-line stanza containing a glyconic, followed by a pherecratic. The stanza is sometimes called 'Priapean':

$$-\ \smile\ |\ -\smile\smile-\ |\ \smile-\ /\ -\ \smile\ |\ -\smile\smile-\ |\ \smile$$

Hendecasyllabic or **Phalaecean Stanza:** a favourite metre of Catullus, never used by Horace: $$\smile\ \smile\ |\ -\smile\smile\ |\ -\ \smile\ |\ -\ \smile\ |\ -\ \smile$$

The spondaic ending is most common, and the caesura appears regularly at the fifth or sixth syllable in the eleven-syllable (hendecasyllabic) line.

Iambic Trimeter: contains six feet in each line, all iambics, Catullus 4 (77):

$$\smile-\ |\ \smile\ -\ |\ \smile\ -\ |\ \smile\ -\ |\ \smile\ -\ |\ \smile\ -$$

Choliambic ('limping iambic') or **scazon** ('limping') **stanza**: a variation of the iambic trimeter in which the last foot is reversed into a trochee. The effect is that of a dragged or limping close: Catullus 8 (19), 31 (32), 39 (81), 44 (82):

$$\cup - | \cup - | \overset{\cup}{-} \, /\!/ - | \cup - | \cup - | - \overset{\cup}{-}$$

Example

$$\overset{\cup}{\text{Mi-ser}} - | \overset{}{\text{Ca-tul-le,}} - | \overset{\cup}{-} /\!/ - | \overset{}{\text{de-si-na-s}} - | \overset{\cup}{\text{i-nep-ti-re}} - | - \overset{\cup}{}$$

$$- - | \overset{\cup}{\text{et quod vi-des}} - | \overset{}{\text{pe-ris-se}} \| \overset{\cup}{\text{per-di-tum}} - | \overset{}{\text{du-cas}} - | - -$$

Catullus 8 (19)

Dactylic Combinations

(i) *Elegiac couplet:* combines a dactylic hexameter with a pentameter line which is identical with the hexameter line save that it omits the last half of the dactyl in the third and sixth feet. In the second verse line the first two feet may have substitutions of spondees, but the fourth and fifth feet do not permit such substitutions. The pentameter line has no regular caesura but a diaeresis (||) where a word's ending, the end of a metrical foot, and a sense-pause may occur simultaneously:

$$- \overset{\cup\cup}{\underline{}} \; | - \overset{\cup\cup}{\underline{}} | - \overset{\cup\cup}{} | - \overset{\cup\cup}{\underline{}} | - \overset{\cup\cup}{} | - \overset{\cup}{}$$

$$- \overset{\cup\cup}{} \; | - \overset{\cup\cup}{} | - \; \| - \overset{\cup\cup}{} | - \overset{\cup\cup}{} | \overset{}{\underset{\cup}{-}}$$

Example

$$\overline{\text{O-}} \overset{\cup}{\text{di}} \overset{\cup}{\text{e-t}} \overset{}{\text{a-mo.}} / \!/ \overline{\text{Qua-re}} \overset{}{\text{jd}} | \overline{\text{fa-ci-am}} \overset{\cup\cup}{} | - \overline{\text{for-tas-se}} | \overset{\cup}{\text{re-qui-ris}} - -$$

$$- \overset{\cup\cup}{\text{Nes-ci-o,}} | \overline{\text{sed fi-e-ri}} \overset{\cup\cup}{} \| \overline{\text{sen-ti-}} \overset{\cup}{\text{o}} \overset{\cup}{\text{e-}} | \overline{\text{t ex- cru-ci-or}} \overset{\cup}{} -$$

Catullus 85 (25).

$$— \;\overline{-}|— \;\;—|\;—|\overline{-\!/\!/}|— \;\;\cup\cup|— \;\;\cup\;\cup|— \;\cup$$
Mul-tas per gen-tes et mul-ta per ae-quo-ra vec-tus

$$— \;\;\cup\;\cup|\;—\;\;\cup\cup|— \;\;—\;\cup\;\cup|— \cup\cup|—$$
ad-ve-ni̯ o has mi-ser-as fra-ter ad in-fer-i-as

Catullus 96 (47)

Catullus 65 (3), 70 (18), 72 (23), 73 (22), 75 (24), 76 (26), 84 (86), 85 (25), 86 (15), 87 (20), 92 (17), 93 (87), 96 (47), 101 (48), 109 (21).

(ii) *Alcmanic Strophe:* a combination of a dactylic hexameter and a dactylic tetrameter, *Odes* I 7 (67).

$$— \;\overline{\cup\cup}|— \;\overline{\cup\cup}|—\!/\!/\overline{\cup\cup}|— \;\overline{\cup\cup}|— \;\cup\cup|— \;\underline{\cup}$$

$$— \;\overline{\cup\cup}|— \;\overline{\cup\cup}|—\!/\!/\overline{\cup\cup}|— \;\underline{\cup\cup}$$

(iii) *First Archilochian Stanza:* a combination of a dactylic hexameter and a dactylic trimeter catalectic, *Odes* IV 7 (57).

$$— \;\overline{\cup\cup}|— \;\overline{\cup\cup}|—\!/\!/\overline{\cup\cup}|— \;\overline{\cup\cup}|— \;\cup\cup|— \;\underline{\cup}$$

$$— \;\cup\cup|— \;\cup\cup|—$$

(iv) *Fourth Archilochian Stanza:* couplets involving the 'greater archlochian', i.e., a dactylic tetrameter followed by three trochees, and an iambic trimeter catalectic, *Odes* I 4 (49).

$$— \;\overline{\cup\cup}|— \;\overline{\cup\cup}|—\!/\!/\overline{\cup\cup}|— \cup\cup|— \;\cup\;|— \;\cup\;|— \;\cup$$

$$\cup\;—\;|\;\cup\;—|\cup/\!/—|\;\cup\;—|\;\cup\;—|\;\cup$$

For detailed information on caesura (masculine and feminine), diaeresis-pause, elision, enjambment, hiatus, hypermetric line, ictus, elision, prodelision, quantitative verse, stress accent, etc., consult:

  L. P. Wilkinson, *Golden Latin Artistry* (Cambridge, 1963). Rosenmeyer, Ostwald, Halporn, *The Meters of Greek and Latin Poetry* (Indianapolis, 1963). D. S. Raven, *Latin Metre: An Introduction* (London, 1965). M. Zicàri (transl. by D. F. S. Thomson), 'Metrical and Prosodical Features of Catullus' Poetry', in *Phoenix*, 17 (1964) 193–205. R. A. Hornsby, *Reading Latin Poetry* (Norman, Oklahoma, 1967) pp. 24–48.

INDEX NOMINUM

ACHAEMENIUS, *adj.*, Persian, from Achaemenes, founder of the old Persian royal house.

ACHAICUS, *adj.*, Achaean, Greek. In 27 B.C. most of central and southern Greece was organized as a province by Augustus, with the name Achaea.

ACHERŌN, -ONTIS, 3 *m.*, a river in Epirus; one of the rivers of the Underworld; *hence* the Underworld.

ACHERONTIA, 1 *f.*, a small town in Apulia (*mod.* Acerenza), near the border of Lucania (71, line 14).

ACHILLĒS, -IS *or* -EI, *m.*, the hero, son of Peleus and the sea-nymph Thetis. When the Achaeans were preparing for the expedition against Troy, they were warned that the city could not be taken without the aid of A.; they sent Odysseus and others to persuade him to join the army, but his mother hid him away, against his will, among the girls at a neighbouring court. However, Odysseus discovered him by displaying, among a collection of rich cloths and jewels which would appeal to girls, a spear and a shield, which A. immediately seized upon. A. was the foremost warrior on the Achaean side until, near the beginning of the tenth year of the siege, he withdrew from battle, over a dispute with his commander-in-chief about his captive, the maiden Briseis. However, he returned to the battle after his dear friend Patroclus was slain by the Trojan Hector; in the ensuing fighting Hector was killed by A., and his body shamefully mistreated. These events are recounted in Homer's *Iliad*. A. met his death soon after, struck by an arrow shot by Paris the Trojan prince whose rape of Helen was the cause of the war; the arrow struck A. in the heel, the only part of his body which had not been made immortal when his mother dipped him, still an infant, in the river Styx.

ACHĪVUS, *adj.*, Achaean, Greek; ACHIVI, 2 *m.pl.*, The Achaeans, Greeks.

ACMĒ, -ĒS, 3 *f.*, an unidentified woman, whose name suggests a Greek freedwoman (83).

ACROCERAUNIA, 1 *f.*, *or* 2 *n.pl.*, a rocky promontory running out into the Ionian Sea from the coast of Epirus (35, line 20).

ĂDRIĀTICUM, 2 *n.*, the Adriatic Sea.

AEGAEUM, 2 *n.* (*sc.* mare), the Aegean Sea.

AENĒĀS, -AE, 1 *m.*, son of Venus and the Trojan prince Anchises (q.v.); after the fall of Troy, A. fled with his father and son, and after many wanderings finally arrived in Italy, where he became the founder of the Roman people; was the hero of Vergil's epic, *Aeneid.*

AEOLIDĒS, -AE, 1 *m.*, son of Aeolus, king of Thessaly, i.e. Sisyphus (q.v.).

AEOLIUS, *adj.*, Aeolian, from Aeolis, the coastal region of Asia Minor between the Troad and Ionia, to which Sappho and Alcaeus belonged.

AETHIOPS, -OPIS, 3 *m.*, Ethiopian, negro; in 73, line 14, Horace is thinking of the fleet of the Egyptian queen Cleopatra.

AETNA, 1 *f.* (*also* AETN-Ē, -ĒS), a volcano in north-east Sicily, beneath which Enceladus, one of the Giants (*s.v.* Gigantes) was imprisoned by Jupiter.

ĀFER, -RA, -RUM, *adj.*, African; ĀFRI, 2 *m.pl.*, the Africans.

ĀFRICUS, 2 *m.*, the African or south-west wind.

AGRIPPA, *s.v.* Vipsanius Agrippa, M.

AGYĪEUS, -EI *or* -EOS (trisyllabic), epithet of Apollo as guardian of streets.

ALBĀNUS, *adj.*, from Alba Longa, the ancient city south-east of Rome (*mod.* Castel Gandolfo, summer residence of the Popes), traditionally founded by Ascanius, son of Aeneas.

ALBUNEA, 1 *f.*, (1) a spring and stream of a sulphurous nature at Tibur (q.v.), near Horace's farm; (2) the nymph who dwelt in the spring; (3) a sibyl worshipped in a grove at Tibur.

ALGIDUS, 2 *m.*, high mountain south-east of Rome (*mod.* Mt. Compatri) (61, line 6; 64, line 9).

ALPĒS, -IUM, 3 *m.pl.*, the Alps.

AMASTRIS, 3 *f.*, port on the south-coast of Black Sea, capital of Paphlagonia (77, line 13).

ANCHĪSES, -AE, *m.*, father of Aeneas (q.v.) by the goddess Venus (76, line 31).

ANCUS (Marcius), 2 *m.*, the third king in line of succession to Romulus among the early kings of Rome; traditionally a good man, and founder of the port of Ostia (57, line 15).

ANIO, -ĒNIS, 3 *m.*, a river which, rising in the Apennines, flows through the country of the southern Sabines, passes over impressive cascades at Tibur (*mod.* Tivoli) before joining the Tiber.

ANTIOCHUS, 2 *m.* (241–187 B.C.), called 'The Great'; ruler of the Seleucid Empire (Persia, Asia Minor, Syria, etc.), whose ambition to expand in the eastern Mediterranean met strong resistance from Rome. Gave sanctuary to Hannibal after latter's defeat at Zama in 202 B.C.; was himself defeated by Romans at Magnesia in 190 B.C. (73, line 36).

ANTIUS, 2 *m.*, a contemporary of Catullus, tentatively identified with C. Antius Restio, tr. pl. in 71 B.C. (or 68?), and author of a sumptuary law (82, line 11).

APHĒLIŌTES, -AE, 1 *m.*, the East wind (80, line 3).

APOLLO, -INIS, 3 *m.*, son of Jupiter by Latona, twin-brother of Diana, born on the island of Delos. Depicted as a youth of great beauty, with flowing hair, usually carrying either a bow or a lyre; god of music and archery, and, more particularly, of prophecy, at his great shrine at Delphi; other cult-centres were at Delos, Patara (in Asia Minor). Taken by Augustus as kind of patron saint; temples to him were built at Actium, to celebrate the victory of 31 B.C., and a particularly splendid one on the Palatine in Rome, which had Greek and Latin libraries associated with it.

ĀPŪLIA, 1 *f.*, region of Italy, on the Adriatic coast, north of Calabria; hence Apulus, *adj.*, Apulian.

AQUILO, -ŌNIS, 3 *m.*, the North Wind.

AQUĪNUS, 2 *m.* (31, line 18), a 'poet', contemporary of Catullus. It has been suggested that he, together with Caesius (*ibid.*), belonged to a group of poetasters who looked for models to the older Roman poets, and would therefore be natural butts for Catullus' scorn.

ĂRABS, -IS, 3 *m.*, an Arabian.

ARCADIA, 1 *f.*, the mountainous central region of the Peloponnese, traditional haunt of Pan, and of the shepherds and goatherds, who paid him reverence.

ARCTŪRUS, 2 *m.*, the brightest star in the constellation Bootes, whose rising and setting were supposed to coincide with stormy weather (70, line 27).

ARGĪVUS, *adj.*, of Argos (q.v.) Argive; Greek; hence ARGĪVĪ, the Argives, Greeks.

ARGOS, *n.*, ancient city in Argolis, north-east Peloponnese, one of chief foundations of the Mycenaeans (67, line 9).

ARRIUS, 2 *m.*, perhaps to be identified with Q. Arrius, praetor in 73 B.C., mentioned by Cicero (*Brut.* 242 f.) as an orator who achieved some success. See Neudling, *A Prosopography to Catullus*, pp. 7–11.

ĂSIA, 1 *f.*, to a Roman meant Asia Minor, and particularly the province so named.

ASINIUS MARRŪCĪNUS, 2 *m.*, almost certainly the brother of C. Asinius Pollio (29).

ASINIUS POLLIO, C., orator and historian, deeply involved in the politics of Rome as a partisan of Caesar in the civil war with Pompey, and later of Antony in the war with Octavian; associated with the circle of Catullus, and later with Vergil and Horace.

Consul in 40 B.C., and recipient of Vergil's Fourth and Eighth *Eclogues* (6; 29, line 6).

ASSYRIUS, *adj.*, Assyrian, from Assyria, region about the Tigris river; 71, line 32, Syrian; *in general*, eastern.

ĀTLANTĒUS, *adj.*, related to Mt. Atlas (q.v.) in north-west Libya; 52, line 11, *Atlanteus finis*, at the world's end.

ĀTLĀS, -ANTIS, 3 *m.*, one of the Giants (*s.v.* Gigantes) who joined Cronus (Saturnus) in the battle with Jupiter; was condemned to support weight of heavens on his shoulders. Chain of mountains in north-west Libya, into which Atlas had been changed, and which supported, according to fable, the heavens. On occasion, three Atlases are distinguished, African, Italian, Arcadian; the latter, father of Maia, was grandfather of Mercury (60, line 1).

ĀTRĪDES, -AE, 1 *m.*, i.e. son of Atreus (Agamemnon or Menelaus); 60, line 13, *pl.*, both Agamemnon and Menelaus.

ATTALICUS, *adj.*, related to Attalus (q.v.), such as Attalus might offer. The Attalids were rulers in the third and second centuries B.C. of Pergamum, a small but wealthy kingdom in Asia Minor, which was bequeathed to Rome and was organized as the province of Asia in 121 B.C.

ATTICUS, *adj.*, Attic, Athenian.

AUFIDUS, 2 *m.*, river in Apulia, Horace's homeland.

AURĒLIUS, 2 *m.*, unidentified contemporary of Catullus, usually associated with Furius (27, line 1); the tone in which Catullus addresses the pair is usually abusive.

AUSTER, -RI, 2 *m.*, the South wind.

BABYLŌNIUS, *adj.*, Babylonian; Babylonios ... numeros (51, line 2), the astrological calculations of the Babylonians.

BACCHUS, 2 *m.*, son of Jupiter and Theban mortal Semele; god of wine, of nature and fertility, patron of the arts and music, especially of drama. Was attended by band of Satyrs and Sileni, compounds of human and animal natures, in constant state of sexual excitement, and by nymphs and maenads. His worship at first met with fierce resistance. Bacchus fell in love with Ariadne, after she had been abandoned by Theseus on the island of Naxos, married her and carried her off to Olympus; her golden crown, a gift of the god, became a constellation.

BAIAE, 1 *f.pl.*, a popular resort of wealthy Romans on coast of Campania north of Naples; in a splendid setting, with vast thermal establishments, gambling casinos, colonnades, wrestling areas, etc., the Palm Springs of its day.

BANDUSIA, 1 *f.*, has been identified with a spring near Horace's birth-place, Venusia, though Horace (62) may have transferred the name to a spring on his Sabine farm.

BANTĪNUS, *adj.*, of Bantia, town in Apulia near Venusia, Horace's birthplace (71, line 15).

BATTIADĒS, -AE, 1 *m.*, son or descendant of Battus (q.v.); an inhabitant of Cyrene; 3, line 16, refers to the poet Callimachus (*c.* 305–c. 240 B.C.), the most distinguished poet of the Alexandrian group, and a sort of high-priest of the new movement in poetry. Catullus 66 is a translation of Callimachus' *Lock of Berenice*.

BATTUS, 2 *m.*, name and title assumed by founder of Cyrene (q.v.).

BĪTHȲNIA, 1 *f.*, Roman province in Asia Minor, on south shore of the Black Sea, where Catullus served on the staff of the governor, C. Memmius, about 57–56 B.C.

BĪTHȲNUS (BĪTHŪNUS), *adj.*, Bithynian.

BOREĀS, -AE, 1 *m.*, the North wind.

BOSP(H)ORUS, 2 *m.*, the strait separating Thrace from Asia Minor.

BRITANNIA, 1 *f.*, Britain, against which C. Julius Caesar made two inconclusive expeditions in 55–54 B.C.

BRITANNI, 2 *m.pl.*, the inhabitants of Britain.

BRŪTUS, *s.v.* Iunius.

CAECILIUS METELLUS CELER, Q., member of a distinguished Roman *gens* with Optimate sympathies, consul in 60 B.C. (6, line 1); married Clodia (probably the Lesbia of Catullus); died, under mysterious circumstances according to rumour, in 59 B.C.

CAECUBUM, 2 *n.*, (*sc.* vinum), Caecuban wine from southern Latium.

CAESAR, -ARIS, 3 *m.*, the cognomen of C. Julius Caesar; assumed by his heir Octavian, who is so addressed by Horace frequently, particularly before 27 B.C., when he took his more familiar title, Augustus.

CAESIUS, 2 *m.* (31, line 18), presumably a bad poet (from Catullus' point of view); it has been suggested that both Caesius and Aquinus (q.v.) may have belonged to a group of poets who found their models in the archaic poets of the past.

CALAIS, -IS, 3 *m.*, the name of a youth, called by Horace (91, line 14) son of Ornytus of Thurii.

CALĒNUM, 2 *n.* (*sc.* vinum), Calenian wine, from Cales, in southern Campania, a centre of the wine industry.

CALLIOPĒ, -ĒS, *f.*, *s.v.* Musae.

CALVUS, *s.v.* Licinius Calvus Macer, Gaius.

CAMĒNAE, 1 *f.pl.*, group of Italian goddesses identified with the Musae (q.v.).

CAMPUS, 2 *m.*, the Campus Martius, the original flood-plain of the Tiber, bounded by the Pincian, Quirinal and Capitoline hills, was the mustering-ground for the army, and assembly area for the centuriate comitia.

CANICULA, 1 *f.*, the Dogstar, which rises late in July and brings the so-called 'dog days'. (Gk. Sirius).

CAPITOLIUM, 2 *n.*, one of the hills of Rome which, because it was the site of the Temple of Jupiter Optimus Maximus, came to be regarded as a symbol of the empire and of Rome's eternity (9, line 9; 69, line 6).

CARPATHIUS, *adj.*, Carpathian, from Carpathus, an island in the Aegean between Crete and Rhodes. Mare Carpathium (75, line 10), the sea off the south-west coast of Asia Minor.

CARTHAGO, -INIS, 3 *f.*, the great Phoenician foundation in North Africa, which challenged Rome for mastery of the western Mediterranean. The two states met in three great wars (264–241, 218–201, and 149–146 B.C.); in the last conflict the city was destroyed and the site cursed, but during the late Republic and the Principate it was colonized and became one of the leading cities of Africa under the Empire (72, line 39).

CASTALIA, 1 *f.*, spring near Delphi, on Mt. Parnassus, sacred to Apollo (71, line 61).

CASTOR, -ORIS, 3 *m.*, with his twin Pollux, called the Dioscuri. Legend described the twins as sons of Leda, one fathered by Jupiter (Pollux), the other by Leda's husband Tyndareus; thus they were brothers of Helen and Clytemnestra. Castor was a noted warrior, Pollux a mighty boxer. In a quarrel over two girls Castor was slain by the girls' brothers, Pollux died of a wound; as son of Jupiter, Pollux was immortal, but Castor was not; rather than be separated, Pollux shared his immortality with Castor, and they alternated between heaven and the underworld. As stars, the Gemini, they served as guides to sailors (75, line 35; 77, line 27).

CATO, -ONIS, 3 *m.*, (1) (63, line 11) M. Porcius Cato (234–149 B.C.), called the censor; type of traditional virtues which, Horace professed to believe, had made Rome great. (2) (6, line 24; M. Porcius Cato, called Uticensis, conservative politician of the last century of the Republic (95–46 B.C.); leader of Senatorial faction, fought with Pompey at Pharsalus in 48 B.C. and led last-ditch stand against C. Julius Caesar in North Africa. His suicide at Utica became a byword among later philosophers and poets, and he achieved the status of a Stoic 'saint'.

CATULLUS, C. VALERIUS, see Introduction.

CAUCASUS, 2 *m.*, a chain of mountains in Asia, between the Black Sea and the Caspian.

CELTIBĒR, -RA, -RUM, *adj.*, Celtiberian (from Central Spain).
CELTIBĒRIA, -AE *f.*, the land of the Celtiberians (81, line 17).
CERĒS, -ERIS, 3 *f.*, identified with the Greek Demeter, sister of Jupiter, mother of Proserpina, goddess of grain. She was worshipped particularly at Eleusis, outside Athens, where her rites were closely restricted and reserved for initiates.
CĒUS, *adj.*, i.e. of Ceos, an island of the Cyclades in the Aegean off Attica. Horace (6, line 38) uses it of Simonides (*c.* 556–468 B.C.) a lyric and elegiac poet known for his epitaphs on those who fell at Marathon and at Thermopylae.
CHLOĒ, -ĒS, 1 *f.*, Greek female name, from Greek meaning 'the first green shoot of plants in spring'; used by Horace (42, line 1; 91, line 6, etc.).
CINNA, Gaius Helvius, a poet of the neoteric 'school', probably to be identified with 'Cinna the poet' murdered by the mob after Caesar's assassination (78, line 30).
CIRCĒ, -ĒS, 1 *f.*, daughter of the Sun; a famous enchantress who turned Ulysses and his men into swine (39, line 20).
CNIDUS, 2 *f.*, a city in Caria, Asia Minor, celebrated for its image of Venus, the work of the famous sculptor Praxiteles (89, line 1).
CŌCȲTUS *or* -OS, 2 *m.*, a river of the Underworld (from Greek, meaning 'river of lamentation').
COLCHUS, *adj.*, Colchian, from Colchis, a land east of the Black Sea, celebrated as the home of the Golden Fleece and the witch Medea.
COLŌNIA, 1 *f.* (79, line 1), perhaps Catullus' home town of Verona, or some other town nearby.
CONCANI, 2 *m.pl.*, a tribe in Cantabria, in north-west Spain.
CORINTHOS *or* -US, 2 *f.*, ancient commercial city in the Isthmus; destroyed by the Romans in 146 B.C., and rebuilt by Julius Caesar in 44 B.C.; became again a flourishing centre of commerce and capital of the province of Achaea.
CORNĒLIUS NEPOS (*c.* 99–*c.* 24 B.C.) historian and biographer; like Catullus, a native of Cisalpine Gaul, who followed a literary and bookish career in Rome. Catullus dedicated the first collection of his poems to him (1).
CORNIFICIUS, QUINTUS (died 42 or 41 B.C.), a poet and orator, friend of Catullus, member of the 'circle' of *poetae novi* (33, line 1).
CORVĪNUS, 2 *m.*, M. Valerius Messala, (64 B.C.–A.D. 8) cos. 31 B.C., distinguished member of Augustan circle, he was also a patron of letters (Tibullus was his best-known protégé).
CORYBANTES, -UM, 3 *m.pl.*, the priests of the goddess Cybele (*s.v.* Dindymene).

CRAGUS, 2 *m.*, chain of mountains in Lycia, in Asia Minor.

CRASSUS, M. LICINIUS (*c.* 112–53 B.C.), cos. 70, 55 B.C., member of the political cabal organized by Julius Caesar and Pompey in 60 known as First Triumvirate; was killed and his army disastrously defeated by the Parthians at Carrhae in 53 B.C.

CUPĪDO, -INIS, 3 *m.*, son of Venus, usually god of Love. Cupidines, the Desires.

CŪRA, 1 *f.*, personification of Care, Anxiety, etc.

CYCLADES, -UM, 3 *f.*, the circle of islands in the Aegean lying about Delos.

CY̆CLOPS, -ŌPIS, 3 *m.*, (1) the three sons of Uranus and Ge (Heaven and Earth), one-eyed creatures who fashioned Jupiter's thunderbolts under the guidance of Volcanus (*q.v.*); (2) a savage race of giants dwelling in Sicily, living a pastoral life, who appeared in Homer's *Odyssey*, Bk. 9.

CYNTHIUS, *adj.*, epithet of Apollo, who was born on Cynthus, a mountain on Delos (61, line 2).

CY̆PRIUS, *adj.*, Cyprian.

CY̆PROS or -US, 2 *f.*, the island off the south coast of Asia Minor, especially associated with the worship of Venus.

CY̆RĒNĒ, -ĒS, and Cyrenae, 1 *f.pl.*, a district and city, founded by Greek colonists about 630 B.C. on north coast of Africa, west of Egypt, in what is now called Libya.

CY̆RUS, 2 *m.*, name of a young man (39, line 25).

CYTHERĒUS, *adj.*, of Cythera; an island in the Aegean south of the Peloponnese, celebrated centre of the worship of Venus.

CYTŌRUS, 2 *m.*, a mountain, covered with boxwood, and a town, in Paphlagonia, Asia Minor; CYTORIUS, *adj.*

DĀCUS, 2 *m.*, a Dacian, member of a tribe dwelling north of the Danube in the area occupied, roughly, by Romania and Hungary today.

DAEDALUS, 2 *m.*, artist and craftsman of legend, father of Icarus (*q.v.*), was imprisoned by Minos, king of Crete, and escaped by fashioning artificial wings for himself and his son; many inventions of antiquity were ascribed to him. Hence DAEDALEUS, *adj.*, of Daedalus.

DANAUS, 2 *m.*, a descendant of Jupiter, who dwelt in Egypt; after a quarrel with his brother Aegyptus, Danaus and his fifty daughters fled to Argos; but his brother and his fifty sons pursued them, determined on a mass marriage. Danaus pretended to agree, but secretly ordered his daughters to kill their husbands on their wedding night. All but one of the daughters obeyed, and were punished in their afterlife by having forever after to carry water in leaky jars (55, lines 18 f.).

DANUVIUS, 2 *m.*, the Danube River.

DARDANUS, *adj.*, Trojan, from Dardanus, founder of the royal house of Troy.

DAULIAS, -ADIS, 3*f.*, the Daulian (*sc.* avis) bird, i.e. the nightingale, Procne; *s.v.* Itys.

DAUNIAS, -ADIS, 3 *f.*, a poetic name for Horace's home region, Apulia, after Daunus, 2 *m.*, a legendary ruler of Apulia. Daunius, *adj.*, Apulian (6, line 34), for Roman.

DELLIUS, QUINTUS, was, like L. Munatius Plancus (q.v.), a political trimmer; first a follower of Antony, he deserted to Octavian, and became a prominent member of his court; was mocked by Messala as 'desultor bellorum civilium'; wrote a history of Antony's eastern campaigns (53, line 4).

DELMATICUS, *adj.*, Dalmatian, from Dalmatae, a tribe dwelling on the east shore of the Adriatic. Delmatico... triumpho (6, line 16). Pollio defeated a branch of the Dalmatians in 39 B.C., and celebrated a triumph.

DĒLOS, -I, 2 *m.*, an island of the Cyclades, birth-place of Apollo and Diana, centre of the Apolline cult. Delius, *adj.*, Delian.

DELPHI, 2 *m.pl.*, the oracular shrine of Apollo, in central Greece. DELPHICUS, *adj.*, Delphic.

DIĀNA, 1 *f.*, an Italian deity, identified with the Greek Artemis; daughter of Jupiter and Latona, twin-sister of Apollo; goddess of chastity and the chase. In Italy her best-known centre of worship was at Aricia, on Lake Nemi, south-east of Rome.

DIESPITER, -RIS, 3 *m.*, *s.v.* Iuppiter.

DINDYMĒNĒ, -ĒS, 1 *f.*, the goddess Cybele, Mother-goddess of Asia Minor, who was worshipped at Dindymus, a mountain in Mysia. Officially introduced into Rome in 205 B.C., her rites were orgiastic in character, attended with the wild music of drums, flutes and cymbals (88, line 5).

DIŌNAEUS, *adj.*, from Dione, mother of Venus.

ĒDŌNI, 2 *m.pl.*, tribe of Thrace, devotees of Bacchus.

EGNĀTIUS, 2 *m.*, a Spanish dandy, rival for Lesbia's affections (81).

ENCELADUS, 2 *m.*, one of the Giants (*s.v.* Gigantes), who was thrust beneath Sicily by Minerva.

EPHESOS *or* -US, 2 *f.*, ancient Greek city in Ionia, most important city of the province of Asia; famous as site of shrine of Diana.

ERYCĪNA, 1 *f.*, a cult-name of Venus, after Eryx, a city in north-west Sicily, site of a famous shrine of that goddess.

ERYMANTHUS, 2 *m.*, a chain of mountains in Arcadia, in the Peloponnese.

ĔTRUSCUS, *adj.*, Etruscan. Mare Etruscum, the Tyrrhenian Sea, portion of the Mediterranean off north-west coast of Italy.

EURUS, 2 *m.*, the East wind.

EUTERPĒ, -ĒS, *f.*, *s.v.* Musae.

FABULLUS, 2 *m.*, a friend of Catullus, not otherwise known (29; 30).

FALERNUS, *adj.*, Falernian, *from* Ager Falernus, a district in Campania, at foot of Mt. Massicus. FALERNUM (*sc.* vinum), Falernian wine.

FĀTUM, 2 *n.*, Fate, Destiny, the Will of the gods. In *pl.*, the Fates (*s.v.* Parcae).

FAUNUS, 2 *m.*, god of shepherds and agriculture, identified with Greek Pan, and represented with horns and goat's feet.

FAUSTITĀS, -ĀTIS, 3 *f.*, personification of Fertility.

FAVŌNIUS, 2 *m.*, the West wind.

FIDĒS, Faith, Loyalty, personified as a goddess.

FORENTUM, 2 *n.*, small town in Apulia (71, line 16).

FORMIĀNUS, *adj.*, from Formiae, a town in southern Latium.

FORS, -TIS, 3 *f.*, the Goddess of Chance.

FORTŪNA, 1 *f.*, the goddess of Fortune, Luck or Ill-luck, with shrines at Antium and Praeneste.

FŪRIUS, 2 *m.*, a contemporary of Catullus, possibly to be identified with M. Furius Bibaculus, a poet of the neoteric group (27, line 1; 80, line 1).

FUSCUS, ARISTIUS, poet and grammarian, friend of Horace; he was the 'friend' who unfeelingly refused to rescue Horace from the bore in *Sat.* I 9, lines 60 ff., and in *Epist.* I 10, is addressed as a true lover of Rome (41).

GAETŪLUS, *adj.*, Gaetulian, from Gaetuli, a people of north-west Africa.

GALLICUS, *adj.*, Gallic.

GELŌNI, 2 *m.pl.*, a Scythian tribe dwelling in what is today the Ukraine.

GERMĀNIA, 1 *f.*, Augustus followed Caesar's policy of containing the German tribes beyond the Rhine until 16 B.C., when an incursion into Gaul gave him an excuse to reverse his policy, and undertake counter-measures. His stepsons, Tiberius and Drusus, secured the passes over the Alps in the years immediately preceding the publication of *Odes* IV.

GĒRYON, -ŌNIS, 3 *m.*, legendary king of Spain, with triple body, whose cattle were stolen by Hercules (55, line 8).

GETAE, 1 *m.pl.*, a Thracian tribe dwelling along the lower Danube; the name is used by Horace, like Scythae, in general for northern peoples who lived on the borders of the empire.

GIGANTES, -UM, 3 *m.pl.*, the Giants, monstrous creatures (often represented with snake-legs), born of the blood of the Sky (Uranus or Caelus) when his son Saturn castrated him; when Jupiter in turn overthrew his father, Saturn, the Giants assaulted Olympus, but the Olympian gods defeated them, and the Giants were imprisoned beneath the earth. See also TITANI. GIGANTĒUS, *adj.*, of the Giants.

GLYCERA, 1 *f.*, name of a female, perhaps imaginary (89, line 3).

GRAECIA, 1 *f.*, Greece. GRAECUS, *adj.*, Greek.

GRĀIUS, *adj.*, Greek.

GRĀTIAE, 1 *f.pl.*, the Graces, three in number, daughters of Jupiter, who personified favour, loveliness, graciousness, etc.

GROSPHUS, 2 *m.*, a friend of Horace, apparently a man of wealth, with estates in Sicily (56, line 7); see also *Epist.* I 12, lines 22 ff.

GYAS, -AE, 1 *m.*, one of the Giants (*s.v.* Gigantes).

HĂDRIA, 1 *f.*, the Adriatic Sea. HADRIANUS, HADRIATICUS, *adj.*, Adriatic.

HAEDUS, 2 *m.*, or HAEDI, 2 *m.pl.*, a double star appearing in the hand of the Auriga or Waggoner.

HAEMONIA, 1 *f.*, a poetical name for Thessaly.

HAEMONIUS, *adj.*, Thessalian.

HANNIBAL, -ALIS, 3 *m.* (*c.* 247–*c.* 182 B.C.) famous Carthaginian general, who invaded Italy in 218 B.C. and led several successful campaigns against Rome (the Second Punic War) until he was recalled to Carthage in 203; defeated by P. Scipio Africanus at Zama in 202, he went into exile at the court of Antiochus (q.v.). His implacable hatred of Rome was notorious, and was typified by the tale of the oath administered to him when still a child by his father. He committed suicide to escape falling into Roman hands.

HECTOREUS, *adj.*, of Hector; son of Priam, foremost champion of the Trojans against the Achaeans.

HELENĒ *or* HELENA, 1 *f.*, daughter of Jupiter and Leda; wife of Menelaus, king of Sparta, was carried off by Paris to Troy and became the occasion for the Trojan War. Fratres Helenae (35, line 2), Castor and Pollux (q.v.).

HERCULĔUS, *adj.*, from HERCUL-ĒS, -IS, 3 *m.*, son of Jupiter and Alcmena, wife of Amphitryon, this hero spent his life performing extraordinary Labours, imposed upon him, in part, by Eurystheus, King of Argos. The Twelve Labours were: (1) the slaying of the Nemean Lion; (2) the killing of the Hydra of Lerna; (3) the Boar of Erymanthus; (4) the Hind of Ceryneia; (5) the Stymphalian Birds; (6) the cleansing of the stables of Augeas; (7) the capture of the Cretan Bull; (8) the capture of the man-eating

Mares of Diomedes; (9) the theft of the Girdle of the Amazonian Queen, Hippolyta; (10) the slaying of the triple-bodied Geryon; (11) the theft of the Golden Apples of the Hesperides; (12) the descent to Hades to bring back the three-headed dog Cerberus. Various other marvellous deeds are also assigned to him. He was slain by his jealous wife Deianira, and became an immortal. He is represented regularly with a lion skin and a great club.

HESPERIA, 1 *f.*, the land of the west; used for Spain or Italy.

HESPERIUS, *adj.*, western, i.e. Spanish or Italian.

HESPERUS, 2 *m.*, the evening star.

HIBĒR, -ĒRIS, 3 *m.*, Iberian, Spaniard. HIBERIA, 1 *f.*, Spain. HIBERUS, *adj.*, Spanish.

HIPPOLYTUS, 2 *m.*, son of Theseus (q.v.) and the Amazon Hippolyta. His stepmother, Phaedra, fell in love with him; when he rejected her advances because of his loyalty to his father and his excessive chastity, she charged him with attempted rape, and his father called upon Neptune to destroy his son. He was torn to pieces when his horses were startled by a monster sent up from the sea. Euripides' *Hippolytus* gives the classic account of the myth.

HISPĀNUS, *adj.*, Spanish.

HYADĒS, -UM, 3 *f.pl.*, the Hyades, a group of seven stars, said to be the daughters of Atlas and sisters of the Pleiades, which portended rain and storm (from Greek ὕω, to rain).

HYDASPĒS, -IS, 3 *m.*, a tributary of the Indus (41, line 8).

HYMEN, -ENIS, 3 *m.*, HYMENAEUS, 2 *m.*, god of marriage, Hymen.

HYPERBOREUS, *adj.*, of the Hyperboreans, a legendary people dwelling in the far north; northern.

HYRCANI, 2 *m.pl.*, the Hyrcanians, dwelling about the Caspian Sea.

IAPETUS, 2 *m.*, one of the Titans (q.v.), father of Prometheus, Epimetheus and Atlas.

IAPYX, -YGIS, 3 *m.*, a wind which blows from the southeastern extremity of Italy, (35, line 4) a favourable wind for travellers to Greece.

ICARIUS, *adj.*, of Icarus, Icarian; mare Icarium, the south part of the Aegean, into which Icarus reportedly fell. From ICARUS, 2 *m.*, son of Daedalus (q.v.), who, with his father, escaped from Crete on wings fashioned by his father; carried away by youthful enthusiasm, he flew too near the sun, the wax which held the wings to his body melted, and he fell into the sea and was drowned.

ICCIUS, 2 *m.*, friend of Horace, known only from the latter's poems; in poem 48, he is preparing to go with Aelius Gallus on an expedition into Arabia Felix (25–24 B.C.), while in *Epist.* I 12 (about 21 B.C.) we find him steward of the Sicilian estates of M. Agrippa.

ĪDAEUS, *adj.*, Trojan, from Ida, a mountain near Troy.

ĪLIA, 1 *f.*, also called Rhea Silvia; daughter of Numitor, King of Alba Longa, mother, by Mars, of Romulus and Remus. She was punished for this violation of her vows of virginity (she was a Vestal) by being thrown into the Tiber (66, lines 17-20).

ĪLION, ĪLIUM, 2 *n.*, Troy

ĪNACHUS, 2 *m.*, the first mythical king of Argos (53, line 21).

INDIA, 1 *f.*, India, generally of the Far East, between the Indus and China. INDI, 2 *m.pl.*, the inhabitants of India. INDICUS, *adj.*, Indian.

IŌNIUS, *adj.*, Ionian. IŌNICUS, *adj.*, Ionian; from Iōnia, 1 *f.*, the region on the Aegean coast of Asia Minor between Aeolis and Caria.

ISTHMIUS, *adj.*, of the Isthmus (of Corinth); site of the Isthmian Games (9, line 3), celebrated every four years.

ĪTALIA, 1 *f.*, Italy. ITALUS, *adj.*, Italian.

ITYLUS, 2 *m.*, confused with Itys (q.v.) (3, line 14).

ITYS, -OS, *m.*, son of Tereus, a king of Thrace, and Procne, an Athenian princess, daughter of King Pandion. Tereus, pretending Procne was dead, ravished her sister Philomela. When the wronged Procne discovered this, she killed her son *Itys* and served him up to her husband for dinner. The two sisters fled and were saved from Tereus' vengeance by being transformed into birds, Procne into a nightingale (or swallow), Philomela into a swallow (or nightingale); Tereus became a hoopoe (46, line 5).

IĀNUS, 2 *m.*, an old Italian deity, represented with one face in front and one behind. He had a temple in the Forum, with two facing doors. In time of war, the gates stood open, but were ceremonially closed in time of peace. Augustus closed them three times during his reign, in 29, 25, and on a third occasion not clearly fixed, perhaps 9 or 1 B.C. Cf *RG* 13: Ianum Quirinum, quem clausum esse maiores nostri voluerunt cum per totum imperium populi Romani terra marique esset parta victoriis pax . . . ter me principe senatus claudendum censuit.

IOCUS, 2 *m.*, the god of jokes and jests.

IUBA, 1 *m.*, a name borne by two of the kings of Mauretania, in North Africa.

IUGURTHA, 1 *m.*, the ruthless but attractive King of Numidia who, by bribery and intrigue, thwarted Roman efforts to unseat him until Gaius Marius took charge of operations. Jugurtha was murdered in 104 B.C. in Rome, after being displayed in Marius' triumph. Sallust wrote an account of the war in his *Bellum Iugurthinum*.

IŪLIUS, *adj.*, Julian; name of Roman *gens* to which Caesar and, by adoption, Augustus belonged.

IŪNIUS BRŪTUS, M. (*c.* 85–42 B.C.) one of the leading conspirators who assassinated Caesar in 44 B.C.; fled to Greece and the East, and raised an army to drive M. Antony and Octavian, Caesar's heir, from Italy. The two sides met at Philippi in 42; Brutus was defeated and committed suicide.

IŪNO, -ONIS, 3 *f.*, wife and sister of Jupiter, queen of the gods, foe of the Trojans who founded the Roman race. Iuno Lucina, i.e. Diana (q.v.).

IUPPITER, IŎVIS, 3 *m.*, an Italian sky-deity, to whom were assigned the functions and myths of the Greek Zeus, he was Father of the Gods; as foremost member of the triad, Jupiter, Juno and Minerva, he was the chief protecting deity of Rome. His temple was on the Capitol. Was worshipped under a variety of titles – Optimus Maximus, Feretrius, Latiaris, Stator, Tonans, etc. *Hence*, heaven, sky.

IUSTITIA, 1 *f.*, the goddess of Justice.

IUVENTĀS, -ĀTIS, 3 *f.*, Youth, personified.

LACEDAEMŎN, -ONIS, 3 *f.*, Sparta. In Homer, the kingdom of Menelaus. In historic times, famous for its rigorous way of life. When Horace (67, line 10) calls her 'patiens', he is thinking, among other characteristics, of the stern command of the Spartan mother to her son as he departs for war, 'Come home *with* your shield or *on* it'. LACEDAEMONIUS, *adj.*, Spartan.

LALAGĒ, -ĒS, 1 *f.*, the name of one of Horace's girls (41), from Greek verb meaning 'to chatter, prattle'.

LANUVĪNUS, *adj.*, of Lanuvium, a town in western Latium.

LĀRISSA, 1 *f.*, a city on the Peneus in Thessaly.

LĀRIUS, 2 *m.*, lake in Cisalpine Gaul (*mod.* Lake Como), on which the colony of Novum Comum was situated.

LĀTŌNA, 1 *f.*, mother of Apollo and Diana. LATONIUS, *adj.*, belonging to Latona.

LĀTŌUS, 2 *m.*, son of Latona, i.e. Apollo.

LESBIA, 1 *f.*, Catullus' mistress. See Introduction.

LESBŌUS, *adj.*, Lesbian; Sapphic. LESBIUS, *adj.*, Lesbian. *Lesbium* (*sc. vinum*), Lesbian wine.

LĒTHAEUS, *adj.*, of Lethe, the stream in the Underworld from which the Shades drank to obtain forgetfulness of their past lives.

LEUCONOĒ, -ĒS, 1 *f.*, a female proper name (51, line 2), from a Greek compound meaning 'clear-minded'.

LĪBER, -ERI, 2 *m.*, an Italian fertility deity, afterwards identified with Bacchus (q.v.).

LIBITĪNA, 1 f., the goddess of burial, whose temple on the Esquiline was headquarters of the undertakers' guild; Death.

LIBURNA, 1 f., used (69, line 30) of a light, swift sailing ship, a Liburnian galley, from Liburni, an Illyrian tribe living on the northern coast of the Adriatic, on the Greek side.

LIBYA, 1 f., Libya, west of Egypt in north Africa; often used for Africa; LIBYCUS, adj., Libyan, African.

LIBYSSUS, adj., Libyan.

LICINIUS CALVUS MACER, GAIUS (82–47 B.C.), orator and poet; as orator, followed Attic style, as poet one of the *poetae novi*; close friend of Catullus (2; 31; 85).

LICINIUS MURĒNA, L., friend of Horace, called *augur* in *Odes* III 19, line 11. Perhaps identical with consul of 23 B.C., brother-in-law of Horace's patron Maecenas. Had a reputation for outspokenness. Was involved in a conspiracy during his consular year and was executed (54, line 1).

LIGUR, -URIS, adj., Ligurian; these people lived along the northwest coast of Italy.

LŪCĪNA, 1 f., goddess of childbirth, identified with Diana (q.v.).

LUCRĒTILIS, -IS, 3 m., mountain in Sabine territory, above Horace's farm (*mod.* Mt. Gennaro) (39, line 1).

LŪNA, 1 f., the Moon-goddess, Diana (q.v.).

LYAEUS, 2 m., lit. 'the Loosener', a name for Bacchus (cf Liber, q.v.); transferred to wine.

LYCAEUS, 2 m., mountain in Arcadia where Pan (Latin, Faunus) was worshipped.

LYCIA, 1 f., a region in south-western Asia Minor.

LYCIDĀS, -AE, 1 m., an unknown youth (49, line 19).

LYCIUS, adj., Lycian; in the Trojan War the Lycians were allies of the Trojans.

LȲDIA, 1 f., a girl, perhaps imaginary, frequently mentioned by Horace (37; 38; 91).

LȲDIUS, adj., Lydian, Etruscan.

MAECĒNĀS, -ĀTIS, 3 m. (died 8 B.C.) Horace's patron (*Sat.* I 6 describes how they met) and one of Augustus' most trusted advisers; proud of his Etruscan ancestry (4, line 2). Is believed to have lost his influence with Augustus in later years.

MAEONIUS, adj., Maeonian, Lydian, but in 5, line 2, Homeric, since one tradition said Homer was born in Smyrna when the Lydians held it.

MAIA, 1 f., mother of Mercury by Jupiter.

MĀNES, -IUM, 3 m.pl., the souls of the dead.

MANLIUS TORQUĀTUS, LUCIUS, consul in 65 B.C., year of Horace's birth (63, line 1).
MAREŌTICUS, *adj.*, Mareotic, from Marea, a town and lake in Egypt, near Alexandria. Mareoticum (*sc.* vinum), Mareotic wine.
MARS, -TIS, 3 *m.*, the Italian god of war, father by Ilia (q.v.) of Romulus and Remus. Under Augustus he was given title of Ultor, with the recovery of the standards lost to the Parthians by Crassus (q.v.) in 53 B.C.
MARSUS, *adj.*, Marsian, of the Marsi, a people dwelling in central Italy around Lake Fucinus, roughly east of Rome.
MARTIĀLIS, -E, *adj.*, of or belonging to Mars.
MASSICUS, 2 *m.*, a mountain in Campania, famous for its wine. Massicum (*sc.* vinum), Massic wine.
MAURUS, *adj.*, belonging to the Moors, Mauretanians; Moorish.
MĒDUS, *adj.*, Median, Parthian. **MĒDI**, 2 *m.pl.*, the Medes, Persians; Parthians.
MELPOMENĒ, -ĒS, 1 *f.*, a muse; *s.v.* Musae.
MERCURIUS, 2 *m.*, son of Jupiter and Maia, identified with Greek god Hermes. Horace (60) lists his various powers and provinces: messenger of the gods, patron of eloquence, thieves and rogues, of flocks, guide of travellers and conductor of the dead to the Underworld (Psychopompos). Horace (66, lines 41 ff.) indicates that he held a special place in Augustus' religious ideas.
MĒRIONĒS, -AE (*acc.* -EN *or* -EM), 1 *m.*, the charioteer of Idomeneus, King of Crete, allied with the Greeks against Troy (5, line 15).
METELLUS, *s.v.* Caecilius.
MIMAS, -ANTIS, 3 *m.*, one of the Giants (*s.v.* Gigantes).
MINAE, 1 *f.pl.*, Threats, Menaces, personified.
MINERVA, 1 *f.*, identified by the Romans with Greek Athena; a warrior goddess, she was active on the Greek side in the Trojan War; was widely regarded as protectress of cities (e.g. Athens); she presided over arts and literature; is regularly represented armed, carrying a spear or shield, and wearing a helmet and invulnerable breastplate *(aegis)*. Pallas, epithet of militant goddess.
MINOS, -OIS, 3 *m.*, a son of Jupiter, King and lawgiver of Crete, after death became one of the judges in the Underworld with Rhadamanthus and Aeacus.
MONAESES, -IS, 3 *m.*, a Parthian whose identity is not clear; may have been either a Parthian noble who spurred Mark Antony on to invade Parthia in 36 B.C., or an alternate name for a Parthian commander (73, line 9).
MORS, -TIS, 3 *f.*, Death personified.

MUNĀTIUS PLANCUS, LUCIUS, a supporter of Caesar and later of Antony, he went over to Octavian in 32 B.C.; was consul in 42, censor in 22. Had a reputation among contemporaries as a timeserver (Velleius Paterculus (2. 83. 1) calls him 'morbo proditor'). Tibur may have been his birthplace, or he may have had a villa there (67; 74).

MŪSAE, 1 *f.pl.*, the nine daughters of Jupiter and Memoria, patronesses of literature and the arts; although each was eventually assigned a special art as her province, there was no hard-and-fast distinction, and Horace often uses the name of one to stand for all, or without any special reference to her area of responsibility. The Muses and their areas were: Calliope: epic; Clio: history; Euterpe: lyric; Thalia: comedy; Melpomene: tragedy; Terpsichore: dance; Erato: love poetry; Polyhymnia: sacred music; Urania: astronomy. *Hence,* song, poem.

MYCĒNAE, 1 *f.pl.*, the 'Golden' city of Agamemnon, with its famous Lion Gate and Treasury of Atreus; situated a few miles north of Argos, in northeastern Peloponnese.

MYRTŌUS, *adj.*, used of a part of the Aegean between Crete, the Peloponnese and Euboea.

MYTILĒNĒ, -ĒS, 1 *f.*, capital of the island of Lesbos, birthplace of Sappho and Alcaeus.

NEAERA, 1 *f.*, a female name in Horace (74, line 21).

NECESSITĀS, -ĀTIS, 3 *f.*, the goddess of Necessity, Inevitability.

NEMESIS, -IS, 3 *f.*, the Goddess of Retribution.

NEPTŪNUS, 2 *m.*, god of the sea, identified by the Romans with Poseidon.

NĪCAEA, 1 *f.*, a city in Bithynia.

NIOBĒUS, *adj.*, of Niobe, daughter of Tantalus; she was the mother of seven sons and seven daughters, who, she boasted, were superior even to the children of Latona, Apollo and Diana. Latona punished her for her pride by sending her children to destroy the offspring of Niobe; Diana slew the daughters with her arrows, Apollo the sons. Niobe was transformed into a rock, which was ever wet with tears.

NOCTIFER, -I, 2 *m.*, the Evening Star.

NOCTILŪCA, 1 *f.*, the moon.

NŌRICUS, *adj.*, from Noricum, a region between the Danube and the Alps, famous for its iron.

NOTUS, 2 *m.*, the South Wind.

NYMPHAE, 1 *f.pl.*, minor deities associated with the sea (Oceanids, Nereids) rivers and springs (Naiads), mountains (Oreads), woods and trees (Dryads, Hamadryads), etc.

ōceanus, 2 m., the Ocean which, in ancient cosmology, surrounded the island which was the world. As a god, he was the son of Uranus or Caelus (Sky) and Ge or Tellus (Earth), and father of the rivers and the nymphs.

oetaeus, adj., belonging to Mt. Oeta, a range between Thessaly and Aetolia, where Hercules ascended the funeral pyre.

olympicus, adj., belonging to Olympia, in north-west Peloponnese, scene of the Olympic Games held every four years.

olympus, 2 m., the name of several mountains in Greece; the most famous is on the border of Macedonia and Thessaly, and was regarded as the seat of the Olympian gods; hence, the heavens.

orcus, 2 m., the lower regions, abode of the dead; Pluto, the god of the Underworld; Death.

ōrīon, -ŏnis, 3 m., the constellation whose rising and setting are attended by storms. On earth Orion had been a great hunter, one of the Giants (s.v. Gigantes), who was killed when he offered violence to the goddess Diana (71, lines 70–1).

ornytus, 2 m., called father of Calais, from Thurii (91, line 14).

ōrpheus, -eos (acc.-ea), 3 m., son of the Muse Calliope, and the great singer of myth. Such was his skill that he even moved the Lord of the Underworld, Pluto, to release his wife, Eurydice, from death. He had the power to draw men, animals, even stones and trees by his music and song. He was torn to pieces by Thracian women in a Bacchic frenzy; his head and lyre, hurled into the Hebrus River, floated to the island of Lesbos.

ortalus, 2 m., undoubtedly Q. Hortensius Hortalus, a somewhat older contemporary of Cicero, and his rival in the courts. Hortensius practised the rather elaborate Asianist style; he appears to have had literary interests, and to have written poetry and history. (3, lines 2, 15.) Cf Cat. 95, line 3.

pacorus, 2 m., a Parthian, son of King Orodes, who defeated the Romans in 40 B.C.

palinūrus, 2 m., the pilot of Aeneas' ship, murdered off the coast of Lucania (Vergil, Aen. 5, lines 833–71); hence, a promontory near the spot, south of Velia.

pallas, -adis, 3 f., s.v. Minerva.

panaetius, 2 m. (c. 185–109 B.C.), distinguished Stoic philosopher who visited Rome c. 144 B.C. and joined the circle of P. Cornelius Scipio Aemilianus (44, line 14).

paphos or -us, 2 f., a city on the west coast of Cyprus, sacred to Venus.

PARCAE, 1 *f.pl.*, the three Fates (in Greek, Clotho, Lachesis and Atropos; in Latin Nona, Decuma and Morta) who allotted to each man his destiny, spinning the thread of life, measuring out the allotted length, and snipping it off.

PARTHI, 2 *m.pl.*, the Parthians, a people which succeeded to control of the Persian Empire in Asia after Alexander the Great's conquests. Since the defeat of Crassus (q.v.) in 53 B.C., they constituted one of Rome's most dangerous foreign threats. Julius Caesar was planning an expedition against them when he was assassinated. Mark Antony conducted half-hearted campaigns against them for some years. Augustus, by diplomacy, recovered the standards of Crassus in 20 B.C. The Parthian soldier was feared by the Romans, who tended to regard his tactic of riding away and shooting his arrow backward as unsporting.

PATAREUS, *adj.*, of Patara, a city in Lycia, site of a shrine to Apollo.

PĒLĪDĒS, -AE, 1 *m.*, the son of Peleus, i.e. Achilles (q.v.).

PĒLION, -I, 2*n.*, a lofty mountain in Thessaly, a continuation of Mt. Ossa.

PELOPS, -OPIS, 3 *m.*, son of Tantalus and father of Atreus and Thyestes, founder of the famous family legend through which ran a curse which brought destruction not only on his sons but upon his grandson Agamemnon as well. The latter's son, Orestes, brought the curse to an end. The theme was a favourite one of Greek and Roman tragedy, and is best known in the *Oresteia* trilogy of Aeschylus.

PENĀTES, -IUM, 3 *m.pl.*, the guardian deities of the Roman household; hence, home, household.

PĒNELOPĒ, -ĒS (*acc.* -EN), 1 *f.*, the wife of Ulysses; during the twenty years of her husband's absence she stoutly resisted the urgent wooings of numerous suitors, and became a symbol of chastity and wifely fidelity.

PĒRITHŌUS, more commonly PĪRITHŌUS, 2 *m.*, king of the Lapiths; shared many adventures with Theseus. They descended to the Underworld to kidnap Proserpina, failed and were held prisoner. Theseus was rescued by Hercules, but P. remained there for ever (57, lines 27 f.; 71, lines 79 f.).

PERSAE, 1 *m.pl.*, the Persians; in Horace, usually means the Parthians (q.v.). PERSICUS, *adj.*, Persian, hence, splendid, luxurious.

PHĪDYLĒ, -ĒS, 1 *f.*, a female name (64, line 1), from a Greek word meaning 'Thrifty'.

PHILIPPI, 2 *m.pl.*, in Thrace, scene of the battle in which the forces of Brutus and Cassius were defeated by M. Antony and Octavian (42 B.C.).

PHOEBUS, 2 *m.*, a title for Apollo as god of light (*s.v.* Apollo).
PHTHIUS, *adj.*, of Phthia, a town in Thessaly, birthplace of Achilles (q.v.).
PĪERIS, -IDIS, 3 *f.*, a Muse (*s.v.* Musae). PĪERIUS, *adj.*, Pierian; sacred to the Muses.
PLANCUS, *s.v.* Munātius.
PLŪTO, -ŌNIS, 3 *m.*, lord of the Underworld, brother of Jupiter; carried off Proserpina, and kept her as wife for half the year. PLUTONIUS, *adj.*, belonging to Pluto.
POENUS, *adj., subst.* 2 *m.*, Phoenician, Carthaginian, Punic.
POLLIO, *s.v.*, Asinius Pollio.
POLLUX, -ŪCIS, 3 *m., s.v.* Castor.
POLYHYMNIA, 1 *f., s.v.* Musae.
POMPEIUS, 2 *m.*, friend of Horace who fought with Brutus at Philippi in 42 B.C. and, unlike Horace, continued the struggle against the Caesarians with Sextus Pompey. Poem 45 records his restoration and pardon.
PONTUS, 2 *m.*, the Pontus Euxinus, or Black Sea. PONTICUS, *adj.*, from the Pontus Euxinus.
PORPHYRION, -ŌNIS, 3 *m.*, one of the Giants (*s.v.* Gigantes).
POSTUMUS, 2 *m.*, a friend of Horace, not otherwise identified (55, line 1).
PRAENESTE, -IS, 3 *n.* (*mod.* Palestrina), ancient city of the Latins south-east of Rome; famous for its shrine of Fortuna, and as a resort for wealthy Romans.
PRIAMUS, 2 *m.*, King of Troy at time of the Trojan War, father of Hector and Paris, among many others. Guided by Mercury (60, lines 13–16) he went to the Greek camp to ransom the body of Hector from his slayer, Achilles.
PROMĒTHEUS, -EI *or* -EOS, *m.*, one of the Titans (q.v.), champion of man against Jupiter; gave men the gift of fire, and was punished for betraying this secret of the gods by being nailed to a peak in the Caucasus while an eagle fed upon his liver; was finally freed by Hercules. A later tale attributed to him the act of moulding men from clay. Horace sometimes situates P.'s place of punishment in the Underworld.
PROPONTIS, -IDIS, 3 *f.*, the Propontis (*mod.* Sea of Marmora), between the Hellespont and the Bosporus.
PRŌTEUS, -EI *or* -EOS, 2 *m.*, a herdsman of Neptune, with the flocks of the seas under his care. Had the strange power to turn himself into innumerable shapes.
PŪNICUS, *adj.*, Carthaginian.
PYRRHA, 1 *f.*, wife of Deucalion, the Greek Noah; sole survivors of

the flood which Jupiter inflicted upon earth in anger at the sins of the men of the Bronze Age, these two, after the flood receded, repeopled the earth by throwing stones over their shoulders; those thrown by Deucalion became men, those thrown by Pyrrha women. (2) name of a woman in poem 36, derived from the Greek adjective meaning 'flame-coloured, golden'.

PYRRHUS, 2 *m.* (319–272 B.C.), a king of Epirus who invaded Italy early in the third century, whose victories over Rome were so costly that such successes have ever since been called 'Pyrrhic'.

PȲTHIUS, *adj.*, Pythian, Delphic; a cult-title of Apollo (q.v.).

QUINTIA, 1 *f.*, unidentified girl who has her good points, but is not a match for Lesbia (15).

QUINTILIA, 1 *f.*, wife of Calvus (*s.v.* Licinius Calvus Macer, C.) (47).

QUINTILIUS VARUS, 2 *m.*, friend of Catullus and member of the literary circle of Horace and Vergil; although called a poet by the ancient scholiasts, he was probably better known as a literary critic. He died in 24 B.C. (43).

QUIRĪNUS, 2 *m.*, a title given Romulus (q.v.) after deification.

QUIRĪS, -ĪTIS, 3 *m.*, more common in *pl.*, QUIRĪTES, -IUM, the Quirites, a name anciently assumed by the Roman people in their civil (as distinct from military) capacity.

REGULUS, M. ATILIUS, 2 *m.*, a Roman general of the First Punic War; best known for an incident after his capture by the Carthaginians, which Horace makes the heart of Poem 72. Sent by his captors to arrange an exchange of prisoners, he urged the Senate to refuse terms, and returned to Carthage to certain death.

RHĒNUS, 2 *m.*, the Rhine flowing between Germany and Gaul, a natural and political boundary.

RHODANUS, 2 *m.*, the Rhone, draining southern Gaul.

RHODUS, 2 *f.*, an island in the Aegean off the s.w. coast of Asia Minor settled by Greek colonists, it came under Roman control in the second century B.C.

RHOETĒUS, *adj.*, belonging to the peninsula of Rhotēum, on the Troad; hence, Trojan.

RHOETUS, 2 *m.*, one of the Giants (*s.v.* Gigantes.)

RŌMA, 1 f., the city of Rome; worshipped as a goddess in the provinces in conjunction with Augustus.

RŌMULUS, 2 *m.*, legendary founder of Rome. After ruling for forty years he disappeared in a cloud while reviewing his army, and was worshipped as a god, Quirinus. Rōmulus, *adj.*, Roman.

SABAEA, 1 *f.*, the land of Saba or Sheba, largest town in Arabia Felix.

SABELLUS, *adj.*, Sabine.
SABĪNI, 2 *m.pl.*, an Italic people dwelling next to the Latins on the central course of the Tiber. SABĪNUS, *adj.*, Sabine. SABĪNUM (*sc.* vinum), Sabine wine; (*sc.* praedium), Horace's estate north of Tibur (q.v.).
SACAE, I *m.pl.*, a people of northern Asia, between the Caspian Sea and Bactria.
SAETABUS, *adj.*, from Saetabis, a town in Hispania Tarraconensis famous for its flax.
SALAMIS, -ĪNIS, 3 *f.*, (1) an island off the coast of Attica in the Saronic Gulf; home of Teucer (67); (2) the chief city of Cyprus, of which Teucer was traditionally the founder.
SALIĀRIS, -E, *adj.*, belonging to the Salii, a college (*sodalitas*) of priests of Mars who, on certain festival days, made procession in various Italian towns as well as in Rome, wearing arms; they performed ritual dances, and in the evenings held feasts of considerable splendor.
SALISUBSALUS, 2 *m.*, (79, line 6) refers either to a god or to those worshipping a god; its form has suggested some connection with the Salii, the 'leaping' priests, associated with the worship of Mars (see Fordyce, Catullus, *ad loc.*).
SĀTURNĀLIA, 2 *n.pl.*, the festival of Saturn beginning on December 17 and continuing for several days. During this time, slaves were permitted to behave with extreme freedom, and gifts were exchanged.
SATYRUS, 2 *m.*, a satyr, a wood-deity, with two goat's feet, attendant upon Bacchus (q.v.), and notoriously lascivious.
SEMELĒIUS, *adj.*, of or belonging to Semele, mother of Bacchus (q.v.).
SEPTIMIUS, name of an unidentified contemporary of Catullus (83, line 1).
SERĀPIS, -IS *or* -IDIS, 3 *m.*, an Egyptian deity who enjoyed a cult in Rome in Catullus' time (78, line 26).
SĒRES, -UM, 3 *m.pl.*, a people of Eastern Asia, the Chinese. SERICUS, *adj.*, eastern, Chinese.
SESTIUS, LŪCIUS, consul suffectus (i.e., a consul elected after the regular time) in the second half of 23 B.C. (49, line 14).
SESTIUS, PUBLIUS, quaestor in 68 B.C., tr.pl. in 57; defended by Cicero on charge of *vis* in 56, and of bribery in 52 B.C. (82, lines 19 f.) SESTIĀNUS, *adj.*, of Sestius.
SICULUS, *adj.*, Sicilian.
SIMONIDĒUS, *adj.*, of Simonides; S. was a Greek lyric and elegiac poet, noted especially for his dirges, epitaphs, etc. (*s.v.* Ceus).

SIRMIŌ, -ŌNIS, 3 m., a narrow promontory projecting into Lacus Benacus (mod. Lago di Garda), where Catullus had his villa (see Introduction).

SĪSYPHUS, 2 m., a typical figure from the underworld; his punishment for his sin was to roll a rock to the top of a hill, only to have it always slide back again.

SŌCRATICUS, adj., of or about Socrates; 44, line 14, Socratica domus, the school of Socrates, i.e., the vast literature which grew up around the figure and teachings of Socrates – Plato, Xenophon, etc.; so also 63, line 9 f. Socraticis . . . sermonibus.

SŌRACTE, -IS, 3 n., a high mountain in Southern Etruria, about twenty-five miles north of Rome and on clear days visible from it.

SPARTACUS, 2 m., a Thracian gladiator who led the slaves of Italy in revolt in 73 B.C. The revolt began in Campania, and spread to the north; five Roman forces were defeated before M. Licinius Crassus (q.v.) defeated him in Lucania (74, line 19).

STYX, STYGIS, 3 f., a river in the Underworld. STYGIUS, adj., Stygian.

SUFFĒNUS, 2 m. (31, line 19), a bad poet, contemporary of Catullus; perhaps to be identified with M. Nonius Suffenas, a parvenu and creature of Pompey.

SULLA, 1 m., (31, line 9), tentatively identified as a freedman of the dictator Sulla, Cornelius Epicadius, a client of Calvus (q.v.), described by Suetonius (De Gramm. 12) as a grammaticus.

SULPICIUS, adj., belonging to Sulpicius; 46, line 18, horrea Sulpicia, the warehouses of Sulpicius; originally the property of the Sulpicii Galbae, these warehouses have been located at the foot of the Aventine, separated from the Tiber by the Porticus Aemilia (see E. Nash, Pictorial Dict. of Ancient Rome, 1, 481 ff.).

SYBARIS, -IS, 3 m., the name given by Horace to Lydia's lover (37, line 2); suggests the famous city of Southern Italy, notorious for its luxury and effeminacy.

SYRIA, 1 f., a country in Asia, on the eastern end of the Mediterranean; organized as a Roman province by Pompey in 63 B.C., SYRIUS, adj., Syrian.

SYRTIS, -IS, 3 f., two areas of sandbanks and shallow waters off the north coast of Africa, called Syrtis Maior and Syrtis Minor, proverbially dangerous for sailors.

TAENARUS, 2 m., a promontory in Laconia on which there was a cave, a legendary entrance to the Underworld.

TANAIS, -IS, 3 m., the river Tanais, now the Don.

INDEX NOMINUM 277

TARENTUM, 2 *n.*, a Greek colony on the gulf which forms the instep of the Italian 'boot'; legend attributed its original foundation to Taras, son of Neptune, but history makes it a colony of a band of refugees from Sparta (*c.* 700 B.C.).

TĒIUS, *adj.*, from Teos, a town in Ionia, birthplace of the lyric poet Alcaeus (39, line 18).

TĒLEPHUS, 2 *m.*, (38), name of a youth, unidentified.

TEMPĒ, *n. pl. indecl.*, a famous valley in northern Thessaly.

TEUCER, -RI, 2 *m.*, son of Telamon of Salamis, brother of Ajax the Greater; one of the Greek heroes of the Trojan War; when he returned home without his brother, his father sent him into exile (67, line 21).

TEUCRUS, *adj.*, Trojan.

THALĪA, 1 *f.*, *s.v.* Musae.

THALIARCHUS, 2 *m.*, a name apparently coined by Horace, a Greek equivalent of 'arbiter or magister bibendi'.

THĒBAE, 1 *f. pl.*, chief city of Boeotia; famous in legend as the seat of the Labdacids, the family of Oedipus and Antigone (67, line 3).

THĒSEUS, -EI *or* -EOS, 2 *m.*, legendary king of Athens, son of Aegaeus, husband of Ariadne, then of Phaedra, father of Hippolytus (q.v.); perennial gad-about, always off on hare-brained schemes, e.g., volunteered to join the seven youths and seven maidens who were offered by Athens as annual sacrifice to the Minotaur; slew a great number of brigands; visited the country of the Amazons and begot Hippolytus by their queen; with Pirithous (q.v.) kidnapped Helen and invaded Hades in effort to seize Proserpina; this last adventure was a failure, and Theseus was held prisoner for four years until he was rescued by Hercules.

THESSALUS, *adj.*, Thessalian, from Thessaly, a region of northern Greece which possessed, for Greece, extensive plains and was rich in grain, cattle and horses.

THETIS, -IDIS, 3 *f.*, a sea-nymph, wife of Peleus, mother of Achilles (q.v.).

THRĀCĒ, -ĒS, THRĀCIA, 1 *f.*, Thrace, region north of Aegean Sea; suggested to the Romans almost constant tribal warfare, frenzied worship of Bacchus, wild and unrestrained drunkenness and resultant brawling, and freezing weather. THRĒICIUS, *adj.*, Thracian. THRAESSA, *adj., f.*, Thracian.

THŪRĪNUS, *adj.*, of Thurii, a Greek colony founded on the site of the destroyed Sybaris, on the Gulf of Tarentum.

THYESTĒS, -AE, 1 *m.*, the brother of Atreus, son of Pelops (q.v.). In revenge for a wrong done him by Thyestes, Atreus served up his brother's sons to their father at a banquet (88, line 17); a favourite theme of tragedy.

THȲNIA (THŪNIA), 1 f., Bithynia (q.v.).

THYŌNEUS, 2 m., son of Thyone, i.e., Bacchus (q.v.). THYŌNIĀNUS, adj., of Bacchus, of wine.

TIBERIS, -IS, 3 m., the Tiber River.

TĪBURNUS, 2 m., an Argive who, with his brothers Catillus and Coras, was mythical founder of Tibur (q.v.).

TĪBUR, -URIS, 3 n. (mod. Tivoli), on the Anio, about eighteen miles n.e. of Rome; a fashionable suburb in the times of Catullus and Horace; both men had estates near it (82; 67, etc.). TĪBURS, -TIS, adj., of Tibur, Tiburtine, also TIBURNUS, adj.

TĪTĀNI or -ES, 2 or 3 m.pl. When Earth (Tellus) was fertilized by Sky (Uranus or Caelus), she bore, in various assortments, three giants, each with fifty heads and a hundred arms (Centimani), the Cyclopes, three one-eyed creatures, and the Titans, six males (Oceanus, Hyperion, Coeus, Crius, Iapetus, and most important Saturn, father of Jupiter), and six females (Tethys, Rhea, Themis, Mnemosyne, Phoebe, and Thia). Sky hated his own children and buried them beneath Earth, but at Earth's urgings they rebelled against their father led by Saturn, who then became chief of the gods. When he in turn was challenged by his son Jupiter, the Titans came to his help, and a fierce ten-year's war ensued (the Titanomachy), from which Jupiter emerged victorious, and a new regime was established, that of the Olympians. Jupiter had as allies the Centimani and the Cyclopes, and his brothers and sisters, Juno, Neptune, Vesta, etc. The Titans were punished by being themselves imprisoned beneath the earth.

TITHŌNUS, 2 m., a handsome youth who won the love of Aurora (Dawn); she carried him off to heaven as her consort and gained from Jupiter the gift of immortality for him; but she neglected to ask also for the gift of eternal youth. Tithonus grew older and more shrivelled, until Aurora finally turned him into a cicada.

TITYOS, 2 m., one of the Giants (s.v. Gigantes) who offered violence to Latona, mother of Apollo and Diana; her children avenged their mother with their arrows, and the slain giant was bound to the earth in the Underworld, covering nine acres.

TORQUĀTUS, advocate, friend of Horace, to whom he sent an invitation to dinner (*Epist.* I 5).

TRANSPADĀNUS, adj., Transpadane, one dwelling north of the Po (Padus) in Transpadane (or Cisalpine) Gaul.

TRIVIA, 1 f., Diana (q.v.), so called because her statues were set up often where three roads met.

TRŌIA, 1 *f.*, the city of Troy, in north-west Asia Minor, scene of the great ten years' siege described in Homer's *Iliad*. TRŌIĀNUS, TRŌICUS, *adj.*, Trojan. TRŌS, -IS, 3 *m.*, a Trojan.

TULLIUS CICERO, MARCUS, the distinguished statesman, orator and writer, and contemporary of Catullus (84).

TULLUS HOSTILIUS (57, line 15), third of the kings of Rome, successor to Romulus and Numa Pompilius.

TȲDĪDĒS, -AE, 1 *m.*, son of Tydeus i.e., Diomedes, one of the bravest of the Greeks at Troy, who, with the aid of Pallas Athena (Minerva) wounded Ares (Mars) and Aphrodite (Venus) when they joined battle on the side of the Trojans (5, line 16).

TYNDARIS, -IDIS, 3 *f.*, (1) a female descendant of Tyndareus, king of Sparta, e.g., Helen of Troy; (2) a girl in Horace's poem 39.

TYPHŌEUS, 2 *m.*, one of the Giants (*s.v.* Gigantes) Typhon, a fearsome monster with a hundred heads, breathing fire and hissing.

TYRIUS, *adj.*, from Tyre, Tyrian.

TYRRHĒNUS, *adj.*, Tyrrhenian, Etruscan; mare Tyrrhenum, the area of the Mediterranean enclosed by Sicily, Sardinia and Corsica and the west coast of Italy (also called mare Etruscum).

ULIXĒS, -IS, 3 *m.*, Ulysses (Odysseus), one of the shrewdest and bravest of the Greek warriors at Troy; his return home after the war took ten years to complete and carried him into many dangerous and bizarre adventures before he reached Ithaca and his faithful wife Penelope (q.v.).

UMBER, -RA, -RUM, *adj.*, Umbrian, from Umbria, a region of central Italy.

URBS, -IS, 3 *f.*, the city of Rome.

USTĪCA, 1 *f.*, probably a small hill near Horace's farm (39, line 11).

VARIUS RŪFUS, LŪCIUS, (5. 1), an epic and tragic poet, member of the circle of Maecenas, Vergil and Horace; one of the editors of the *Aeneid* after Vergil's death; Quintilian (*Inst. Orat.* X 1. 98) praises his tragedy *Thyestes*; wrote an epic panegyric on Augustus.

VĀRUS, Quintilius, *s.v.* Quintilius Varus.

VĀTĬCĀNUS, *adj.*, Vatican, of the hill in Rome on the south bank of the Tiber (40, line 7).

VATĪNIĀNUS, *adj.*, involving Vatinius, such as Vatinius arouses (hatred, 31, line 3); the Vatinius was almost certainly P. Vatinius, one of the most notorious of the political hacks of Catullus' day; twice brought to trial by Calvus (q.v.) (85), once by Cicero; an associate of Caesar.

VENĀFRUM, 2 *n.*, a town of the Samnites, south-east of Rome, celebrated for its olive oil. VENĀFRĀNUS, *adj.*, of Venafrum.

VENUS, -ERIS, 3 *f.*, goddess of Love, to whom were assigned the myths belonging to the Greek goddess Aphrodite. Born of the severed genitals of Cronus and the foam of the sea; she loved, among other gods and mortals, Anchises, by whom she got Aeneas. In Horace's time was honoured as Venus Genetrix, founder of the *gens Iulia*, the family of Augustus. No. 45, line 25, the highest throw at dice. Veneres, 3 *f.pl.*, Loves.

VERĀNIUS, 2 *m.*, a dear friend of Catullus, usually associated with Fabullus (q.v.), served at least twice on *cohors* of provincial governors, in Spain and perhaps in Macedonia.

VERGILIUS MARO, PUBLIUS, the great Roman poet, friend of Horace (35, 43).

VESTA, 1 *f.*, a goddess, daughter of Saturn, who presided over the hearths of families and the state; her temple contained, not an image, but a fire which was never allowed to go out.

VIPSĀNIUS AGRIPPA, MARCUS (*c.* 63–12 B.C.), close associate of Augustus, husband of his daughter Julia. He was largely responsible for the victory at Actium in 31 B.C., and was actively engaged in the physical reconstruction of Rome. Augustus regarded him for a time as his heir (5).

VOLCĀNUS, 2 *m.*, an Italian fire-god, assimilated to the Greek Hephaestus, the lame smith-god, son of Jupiter and Juno, husband of Venus.

VULTUR, -URIS, 3 *m.* (*mod.* Monte Vulture), a mountain in Apulia near Venusia, Horace's birthplace.

XANTHUS, 2 *m.*, the name of several rivers, but especially of one in the Troad, which plays a part in the *Iliad*.

ZEPHYRUS, 2 *m.*, a gentle west wind, the zephyr.